The Ards in the Sixties

Written and Compiled by Terence Bowman and Hugh Robinson

BALLYHAY BOOKS

Published by Ballyhay Books,
an imprint of Laurel Cottage Ltd.,
Donaghadee, Northern Ireland.

Printed by Gutenberg Press, Malta.
ISBN 9781900935 94 4

Foreword by Hugh Robinson

The Ards in the Sixties! Ah yes, I remember it well – or imagined I did until I was invited to assist Terence Bowman on this fascinating new book.

As we began to gather the material from which the content of the book would be distilled, a multitude of memories flooded back – people, places and events and everyday happenings from a much-loved period in my own life, and I'm sure the lives of everyone who remembers the Sixties in The Ards.

Hugh Robinson at his alma mater

Born in Newtownards and raised near Donaghadee, much of popular writer Hugh Robinson's work is inspired by the town and the Ballyhay countryside of his childhood.

Author of four books and a regular contributor to radio and the press (including the Christmas Story in the *Newtownards Chronicle* for over 20 years), Hugh is still very active in the local writing scene and, when not indulging his passions for reading, music, the countryside and supporting Ards FC. is working on a new volume of local short stories.

I've always wished I had the time to pore over every edition of the *Newtownards Chronicle* from the 1960s but now, thanks to Terence who has used his keen news editor's eye to select over 1,000 highlights of that decade's news from The Ards – everything as they say, from the sublime to the ridiculous – I can.

As I read through the pages of the book's early drafts I would muse, "Ah yes, I remember that" or "Mmm, I do remember that, but I had forgotten it" but, I must confess somewhat to my own surprise, there were also many instances when I was brought up short with the thought, "Well, I didn't know THAT happened!"

There is one little news item I continually re-read and chuckle over. I quote: "A Newtownards man, who was receiving National Assistance (a financial safety net for those who did not pay National Insurance contributions), was jailed for three months in late February after he refused several jobs he was offered. Accused by the prosecution (representing the National Assistance Board) of being 'just plain lazy' and 'preferring to sponge on the community', he was found guilty of persistently refusing to maintain himself, his wife and five children".

As well as the news items, *The Ards in the Sixties* was to feature the memories of people of the time, folk whose lives were fashioned by being part of the exciting Sixties Ards and gathering these memories was something I've especially enjoyed. Some contributors are household names. Some would describe themselves as an "ordinary" Ards man or woman. There is no distinction. All come together to create a multi-faceted tapestry of 1960s life as they experienced it.

The Ards in the early 1960s had changed little since it had dusted itself down from the effects of the Second World War. Towns and villages and streets looked as they always had, with none of today's urban sprawl. We still travelled by Ulster Transport Authority bus. For me a big Saturday night out in Newtownards was a visit to the pictures with a big (it was always "big") fish supper to round off the evening at Charlotte Heron's or Smiths in East Street. Even the dance halls emptied just before midnight.

However, as the British Prime Minister Harold "Supermac" Macmillan so eloquently put it "we never had it so good". The Ards of the 1960s was blessed with full employment and every town had its factory – in Newtownards practically every street had one. I worked in Cyril Lord's Regent Street factory. The place was a holiday camp, as anyone who "worked" there will testify. Later I was employed in the Debretta factory in East Street, a very professional outfit. It's gone now, but to quote Jean Galloway, in those days "you could walk into a job". Perhaps that's why the town's pawnbroker in Meetinghouse Lane didn't survive, the *Chronicle* quoting staffing problems. Little wonder, with fortunes being paid at the Berkshire Knitting Mill on the Donaghadee Road.

With full employment and money in our pockets, entertainment in the Ards was at an all time high. The cinemas (or picture houses, as they were affectionately known) played to full houses. Many a Saturday night I queued up outside the Ritz (balcony queue up Frances Street, stalls down Meetinghouse Lane), then had to stand inside until a seat became vacant. The Ritz and the Regent ruled in Newtownards. Donaghadee had its Regal, the place which introduced me to the great stars of the silver screen. Comber, Ballywalter, Portaferry, and even Kircubbin each had their showplace.

But television was gaining in popularity – three channels now available, BBC1, BBC2 and UTV, in glorious black and white, and I couldn't afford to purchase a set. Check Rentals, whose advert we've included in the book, came to my rescue, renting me the latest model for only 9/6 per week so I could view James Ellis in *Z Cars* and Dale Robertson in *Tales of Wells Fargo*. However, television killed the old picture palaces I loved so well. A sad little advertisement from the *Chronicle* in 1968 reminds me of the sale details of the grand old Ritz cinema. Happily the building still stands although the photograph we've reproduced leaves me with a pictorial reminder of the time when it was still the famous ABC Ritz.

Ards was swinging in the Sixties, long before The Beatles caught up with us. The showbands filled dance halls everywhere. I remember travelling one winter night to the Locarno in Portaferry with cousins Tom Daye and Billy Carlisle in Tom's father's ancient Ford Prefect. Coming home we hit a stray donkey which was travelling somewhat inconsiderately without lights. It was permanent lights out for the donkey and the Ford 8, although we survived to walk home to Newtownards.

A dance hall in Kircubbin? I didn't know about that until I read Kathleen Dorrian's charming piece about the village's "ballroom of romance" and the happy dancing nights she enjoyed in the tin hut with the corrugated roof. Delightful!

Back in Newtownards I rocked the night away with Bill Haley in the Queen's Hall. I couldn't believe it – only 7/6 (less than forty pence) to see Haley and the original Comets. Strangely, Haley and the Comets came on stage, launched straight into *Rock Around the Clock* and, thirty minutes of great music later, left without saying a word! When country star Hank Locklin, a lovely gentleman then riding high with *Please Help Me I'm Falling*, came, he talked almost as much as he sang! Van Morrison was over in Comber with Them and St. Patrick's Choral and Dramatic Society brought Brendan O'Dowda (he of Percy French fame) to the town for a grand concert. I still don't know how I missed Roy Orbison, supported by The Hilton Showband, just up the road in Dundonald's Royal Ballroom.

However, Ards in the Sixties was producing its own showbiz stars who would enjoy enormous success, many going on to international fame. I recall The Saints Skiffle Group – complete with tea-chest and washboard, and the classy Roy McCord and his Showband. Newtownards girl Muriel Galway (stage name Muriel Day) went all the way from draper's shop in Conway Square to representing Ireland in the Eurovision Song Contest. I have fond personal memories of the Donaghadee group Trevor and the Hep Cats who became Margo and The Marvettes and finally Margo and Trevor. I stood on the harbour wall at Donaghadee to watch Trevor make his debut with the Pierrots on the pier alongside the great lady of Ulster showbiz, Leila Webster. Margo (originally Margaret Harron) won't remember, but she kindly gave a very self-conscious teenager (as I used to be!) the occasional dance in the Dee's Orange Hall before she hit show business heights with Trevor. So nice to read of their showbiz experiences.

Ards Choral and Orchestral Society set an extremely high standard in the 1960s. Their *Messiah* was always a sell-out. Sadly, I didn't see any of those great performances. So, perhaps it's a sign of maturity that many of us who rocked with Bill Haley now queue for the Ards Choral's evenings, regretting not seeing the great artistes who appeared with the Society all those decades ago. Happily, Anne Iveston, long-time Society member and friend, relives them for me in her piece.

What can one say about sport in the Ards in the Sixties, except that we were pretty good at it! I was a football fan and the soccer scene in the Ards was really buzzing. The popular Factory League ran teams from factories which now no longer exist. I recall playing the odd game for the Regent Factory. I wasn't much good, nor was the team, but we had fun. Hard to believe, but I remember on one occasion a player, frustrated by the referee's decisions, sending the official off the field! Alfie Wright, a sportsman I greatly admire, overcame severe childhood handicaps to play football at the highest level in the Irish League and League of Ireland. Alfie was also a top-class table tennis player. I enjoyed his memories of the great days of the Ards and Glenford clubs which are sadly no more. The Devonshire Hotel in Newtownards High Street seems to have been the preferred watering hole for Ards Rugby Club players after a game. David Coffey refers to it as a place "much frequented by Ardsmen of the rougher sort" – referring, I hope, to his mates who chased the oval ball! My old friend, the irrepressible Billy McCully from Carrowdore, was a highly successful showjumper in the Sixties. I love to sit with him over a cup of coffee in Cafolla's (the one we knew as "the wee Cafolla's") and listen to his horsey stories, especially the one about the nag he bought for £25,000 only to discover it wasn't, in his own words, "worth tuppence"!

Returning to football, It was good to relive memories of that great night in Windsor Park in 1969 when football's Irish Cup returned to Ards and Castlereagh Park, with Greyabbey man Billy McAvoy scoring all four goals for Ards. The mercurial Billy Humphries, probably the best player ever to don an Ards shirt, not to mention being their most successful manager, played that night. I also saw Billy score a hat-trick in a 1-9 drubbing of Glentoran at the Oval, a match no Glens fan cares to be reminded about. I was delighted Billy recalled the game in his contribution!

A picture paints a thousand words, or so they say. It's been fascinating browsing through hundreds of photographs depicting every aspect of Ards life during the decade. I scanned thousands of faces, many familiar to me; children now adults, teenagers now pushing seventy, older folk sadly no longer with us. Each one has their own story and place in *The Ards in the Sixties*.

I also enjoy old advertisements from any decade. The book is full of them, including one for Hampshire's newsagency and toy shop where I always bought my magazines and newspapers. A Ford Capri, the car I always dreamed of owning, was available from James Elliot & Co. in Portaferry for £890. My purse couldn't run to the Capri, and not even to the fine range of BSA motorcycles available from A.E. Paden, High Street, Newtownards. My wheels were a Raleigh moped, probably the worst machine on two wheels ever to take to the road, and which I purchased from Geordie Nicholl in Conway Square. Many of the products in the adverts no longer exist, nor do the retailers who sold them. Some of the ads, and the products, now look quaint. However, there is a charm and decency and nostalgia about them which reminds me of a gentler time.

As it came together toward its final form, reading *The Ards in the Sixties* spirited me back to that time which holds so many, mostly kind, memories. As a writer, and more importantly as an Ardsman, it has been a privilege to have been involved, even in a small way compared to Terence's immense achievement, in the production of this book. Even having read over it several times now, I know that in the future, if ever I need a lift, I will open *The Ards in the Sixties* again and again to bask in the fond memories it revives. I can only hope that Ards people near and far will derive as much pleasure from the following pages as I've had from helping in a small way to put them together.

Hugh Robinson

Contents

The View from The Chronicle

For as long as I can remember I've been fascinated by history. It was my favourite subject at school and I followed that by studying Modern History at Queen's University.

Yes, it might all have been about kings and queens, war after war, in those early days of study, but as my love of the subject continued, the studies started to delve deeper into the communities, the workplaces, the ordinary lives of ordinary folk. That's where the real fascination lay.

But history is not a completed story – it's still being made every second – and now, as editor of a local newspaper, I feel a certain responsibility for documenting today's activities to provide a rich source of information to form the history of the future.

It's a little sobering to think that in 50 years' time someone may be mulling over, highlighting and collating the stories we write today for a nostalgic look back at 'The Ards in the 2010s'. But it's not an unlikely scenario as I believe that today, as in the 1960s, the foremost and most encompassing source of information on life in any community is still the local newspaper.

That's exactly why we in *The Newtownards Chronicle* are delighted to have an involvement in this project.

Since 1873 this newspaper has been documenting the news of North Down and the Ards Peninsula and this rich source of material provides a fascinating insight into the lives of our parents, our grandparents and maybe even a generation or two before that.

To pull all those images and stories of years gone by into a book like this is no mean feat and all involved should be thanked for their effort and commitment in producing such a high quality publication. It's fun to look back – memories are precious things and sharing memories can make them even more precious.

And as time moves on, *The Newtownards Chronicle* will continue to publish the weekly goings-on around the district. Yes, the internet has become a valuable tool and has opened up channels of communication our grandparents could never have dreamed of, but a paper in your hand at the end of the week still has a certain value.

It's real and solid and *The Chronicle* will be real and solid for many years to come.

Mark Bain,
Editor, *The Newtownards Chronicle*

Brian McDonald

introduces ... The Ards in the Sixties

At the beginning of the 1960s Newtownards was a market and industrial town, continuing a role it had performed for several decades. Many of its citizens worked in its numerous factories or in the great variety of shops which served both the people of the town and those of the surrounding countryside. Yet changes which would alter the character of the town were already beginning.

As early as January 1960 the local Council was able to announce that the redevelopment of the town would start later that year. Work actually began in Mill Street and over the next few years further streets were rebuilt with modern attractive housing.

In 1964 work began on building the Glen Estate and during the same year work also began on redeveloping East Street, Greenwell Street, Market Street and Movilla Street. In addition, a new development opened at Donard Avenue, linking John Street and the Scrabo Estate.

Increasing traffic led to many roads being improved. The Bangor Road and the Old Movilla Road were widened and straightened. Improvements were made to the North Road, the old railway embankment to the west of the town was removed and a new large car park was opened in the area between High Street and Court Street.

In 1967 the old courthouse in Regent Street was demolished; it would eventually be replaced by a new building more suited to the needs of the modern

Brian McDonald was born in Dublin shortly after the end of the Second World War. His mother was a native of New Ross in Co. Wexford, while his father was from Newtownards. They returned to the latter town while Brian was still an infant and he has lived there ever since.

He was educated at St Finian's Primary School in Newtownards and St Mary's Grammar School in Belfast. He then trained to be a teacher at St Joseph's College, returning to his old primary school where he taught for 19 years.

Brian subsequently worked for the South Eastern

Widening work was under way at North Road, Newtownards, in January 1963. Midway on the right-hand side of the road is 'Patchy's Loney,' a familiar landmark in the town. *53-72-1*

community and the administration of justice in the late 20th Century.

At this time Newtownards had a number of different factories, including Crepe Weavers, Blaxnit, the Ulster Print Works and Walker's Mill. They employed many men and women who worked to produce a range of goods which were exported to Britain and throughout the world.

However, as early as 1963 competition from cheap foreign imports was beginning to have an adverse effect on the industries in the town. In that year the Berkshire nylon factory announced it was making a number of employees redundant and in January 1964 the W. Ferguson (Ulster) Ltd. hemstitching premises in East Street closed down after operating in Newtownards for 48 years. The factory would be taken over by Debretta, which would employ many of Ferguson's former employees – but its closure was a foretaste of more widespread factory closures in the town in later years.

Newtownards has long had an excellent reputation as a shopping area. In the 1960s this reputation was reinforced by the large number and variety of shops to be found in the town. Among them were F. C. Glasgow's department store, W. I. Houston, suppliers of ladies' and gents' clothes, Gayes Shoes, J. Lyons and Son, hardware and electrical suppliers, and Robert Wallace, jeweller. These were all situated in High Street, one of the main shopping areas of the town. Other retail businesses included Thomas Killick's chemists and Scrabo Electrical, both in Regent Street, and Jack Cairnduff, Riley and MG car dealer in Castle Street.

Competition for customers led to the different shops advertising their wares in the local newspapers. Prices would be very competitive. In 1967 you could have bought a man's shirt for £1 10s in Glasgow's, men's trousers for £1 5s in

Education and Library Board before becoming principal of St Comgall's Primary School in Belfast. He was then appointed as principal of St Joseph's in Newcastle and in 1994 took charge at St Mary's in Kircubbin, where he remained until he retired.

Keenly interested in local history, Brian has been a member of Ards Historical Society since it was founded in 1967. He has served as chairman and at the present time is president, press officer and programme organiser.

Brian has been involved in the publication of many leaflets and booklets on local history and is a well known

Blaxnit Hosiery, Donaghadee Road

W. I. Houston's, and if it was a cold winter you could have bought a hot water bottle in John D. Beckett's chemists for 5s.

Competition between the different retailers took on a new direction when the Chamber of Trade decided that shops in Newtownards would close all Thursdays from June 1964. Not all traders supported this move and decided to keep to the existing practice of closing for the half day only on Thursdays. They took out full-page advertisements in local newspapers to make the public aware of their plans.

Robert Wallace's High Street jewellery shop. *Newtownards Chronicle* picture

Towards the end of the decade it was recognised that shopping habits were changing. There were reports of plans to build supermarkets in the town and there was also the first mention of building a shopping centre on the site of Dickson's rose fields on the Circular Road. This was an early reference to what would become the Ards Shopping Centre which stands on the site today.

In the 1960s Newtownards had two cinemas, the ABC Ritz in Frances Street and the Regent in Regent Street. At the beginning of the decade cinema-goers could watch *Broth Of A Boy* with Barry Fitzgerald in the Regent and *Alive And Kicking* with Stanley Holloway in the Ritz.

However, the growing popularity of television led to a decline in cinema attendances. It came as no surprise to Newtownards residents that Solar Cinemas, owner of both theatres, announced in 1967 that the Ritz would close on Saturday 4 November, leaving the Regent as the town's sole cinema. The last films shown in the Ritz were *The Agony And The Ecstasy* with Charlton Heston and *Three Coins In A Fountain* starring Dorothy Maguire.

Other forms of entertainment continued to prosper. Dancing was especially popular and the Queen's Hall attracted many of the top showbands of the era. Among those who played at the venue were The Crickets, The Freshmen, The Dave Glover Showband and The Telstars. On 9 June 1967 a Dawn To Dusk pop festival was held at Castlereagh Park. The lead group were The Tremeloes and the event attracted a huge crowd. Unfortunately the

speaker on various historical subjects. He is also a Justice of the Peace and a Lay Magistrate in the Northern Ireland Family and Youth Courts.

His other interests include travelling. He has been to most of the continents and has visited such exotic locations as Zimbabwe, Uzbekistan, Cambodia and Brazil. He has been a stamp collector for many years. He is also a keen tennis player and serves on the committee of St Patrick's Racquets Club. Brian supports Ards FC, being a regular attender at their matches.

Perhaps his most enduring interests are railways and aviation. He has travelled by train in North and South America, in Asia, Europe and Australia, and has written articles on both aviation and railway history.

Retirement has allowed Brian to continue to pursue his many interests – something he hopes to be able to do for many years to come.

Frances Street in the Sixties. *Newtownards Chronicle* picture

concert was criticised by nine local church ministers who claimed there was an excess of noise, too much drinking and general bad behaviour. Efforts to repeat the event the following year met with only limited support.

Other forms of entertainment were much less controversial and remained popular in Newtownards in the 1960s. These included guest teas, choral singing and amateur dramatics. Band performances were especially popular during the summer months and local outfits such as Newtownards Silver Band and Lord Londonderry's Own CLB Band entertained spectators in Conway Square with concerts which featured many popular tunes from the period.

The lead singer with the Dave Glover Showband was local girl Muriel Glover (née Galway). Singing under the name of Muriel Day she won the right to represent Ireland in the 1969 Eurovision Song Contest. Although she didn't win the event, she was the first of many singers from Northern Ireland to represent the Republic in the competition.

Newtownards has always had a well-deserved reputation as a sporting town. Soccer, rugby, badminton, hockey, cricket, bowls, table tennis, darts and cycling all figured prominently in the town in the 1960s. Ards Football Club played its games at Castlereagh Park on the Portaferry Road. The venue was famous for having what was regarded as the best playing surface in the Irish League.

The team itself didn't always perform as its supporters would hope. They began 1960 by losing four games in a row, one of which was a 4-1 defeat by near neighbours Bangor. Things didn't get any better that season though they managed to reach the final of the Irish Cup, only to lose 5-1 to Linfield.

By the end of the decade the team was playing better and getting some good results. On 23 April 1969 Ards won the Irish Cup for the fourth time when they beat Distillery 4-2 after extra time in a replay. The hero on that occasion was Greyabbey man Billy McAvoy who scored all four goals. The original match had ended in a 2-2 draw.

Some of the Ards players had begun their football careers playing for Ards Boys. Throughout the 1960s this team proved to be one of the top youth teams in Ulster and brought many sporting accolades to the town.

Ards Cycling Club was very active during the decade and their efforts to promote the sport were rewarded when the Tour of the North cycle race started and finished in the town for a number of years.

At about this time there was a thriving darts league in Newtownards. Clubs included Scrabo, Hospital Social Club, Ards Cycling Club, Fire Service, Ards Olympic, Guildhall, Crepe Weavers, North End, Castle Gardens and Old Cross. They were matched by a strong and popular table tennis league. It included teams such as Glenford, Scrabo Golf Club and Movilla Youth Club, as well teams from Donaghadee, Holywood, Dundonald and Millisle.

Other sports clubs in the town included Ards Rugby Club, Ards Ladies Hockey Club, Ards Homing Pigeon Society and Ards Sailing Club, which was officially opened by Lady Mairi Bury on 15 August 1964.

However, one popular event unique to Newtownards was a very special race. In 1963 the 1,400th anniversary of St Columba's voyage to Iona in Scotland was celebrated throughout Ireland. St Mark's Parish Church was one of the main centres for celebrations. Among the events organised in Newtownards was the Columba Cup Scrabo Race over a course from Conway Square to Scrabo Tower. The event was won by 15-year-old James Harris in a time of 17 minutes and 14.4 seconds. A sponsored walk was held at the same time. Both events would continue for many years and would become an important part of the town's sporting calendar.

The 1960s would end on an optimistic note for Newtownards. Late in 1969 the Town Clerk, Wyndham Scott, outlined plans for future growth and development in the area. He referred to proposals to build 5,000 new houses over the next five years and to continue the redevelopment of streets in the town.

Mr Scott mentioned that plans had also been approved for a number of new buildings. These included a police station, a courthouse, a swimming pool and a hotel. All these projects would be completed. The buildings still play an important role in the life of the town today. As such it can perhaps be said that the modern town has its origins in the plans and developments of the 1960s.

1960

in the Chronicle

Mayor Stanley Woods, in his New Year address to the Borough Council, said a special effort would need to be made during 1960 to attract new industries to Newtownards.

He complained that Newtownards firm Black and Co., which was seeking new premises in the town, had been invited by the Ministry of Commerce to inspect potential sites that were actually in other parts of the country.

"Newtownards is only five to seven minutes away from the city boundary and in a direct line to the docks, which should be a great help to any manufacturer desiring to set up a factory here – a town with such good labour sources and a good industrial history," the Mayor added.

Kircubbin man James Boyd resigned for medical reasons from the seat he had held for half a century on North Down Rural District Council. During that time he had the triple distinction of serving as the first and last chairman of the former Newtownards Rural District Council and also as the first chairman of the replacement North Down authority.

Council proposals to demolish 23 houses at Mill Street, Newtownards, and to replace them with 58 new dwellings became the subject of a public inquiry in mid-January. During the hearing it was stated that of the 3,766 permanent houses in the borough, 900 were unfit and 800 families were still seeking accommodation in the town.

Thirteen-year-old Eileen Woods, a student at Movilla Intermediate School, was placed second in a national essay competition organised by the Central Council for War on Want. She was invited to a youth rally at Westminster where the prizes were presented by Chief Scout Sir Charles Maclean.

Portavogie's new single-storey Technical School opened its doors on 27 January, offering classes in woodwork, cookery, dressmaking, navigation and signals with future plans for motor car engineering and metalwork. It fell within the Downpatrick Technical Area and the overall principal, Dan McNeill, welcomed the large numbers of local fishermen who were enrolling for courses at the new school.

An important new chapter in the history of Greenwell Street Presbyterian Church, Newtownards, opened on 30 January with the laying of the foundation stone for a new church hall. The building, when completed, would serve as a memorial to a much loved former minister, the late Rev. Thomas McIlwrath.

A Newtownards man, who was receiving National Assistance (a financial safety net for those who did not pay National Insurance contributions), was jailed for three months in late February after he refused several jobs he was offered.

Accused by the prosecution (representing the National Assistance Board) of being "just plain lazy" and "preferring to sponge on the community", he was found guilty of persistently refusing to maintain himself, his wife and his five children.

Speaking at the annual meeting of the Ards Unionist Association on 7 April, North Down MP George Currie "profoundly deplored" the fact that Newtownards was not to become the location for Northern Ireland's main airport. He said it should have been recognised that the town was ideally located for a heliport – given the advantage such machines offered for city to city and town to town travel.

Concerned that television was undermining faith and morals and "threatening to overthrow all that is held dearest and holiest", the Rev. Reginald (Reggie) Chisholm, rector of St Mark's Parish Church in Newtownards, urged parishioners to exercise careful restraint in their selection of programmes to watch and to "abstain altogether from Sunday evening programmes until such time as those responsible realise our

intelligence is no longer to be degraded and insulted by such filth."
He mentioned just one programme by name when addressing the annual Easter Vestry meeting on 28 April – declaring that "children are being allowed to wallow in the improbable and impractical situations created by Robin Hood and his merry men at the expense of church organisations."
And the rector added: "If we do not face this challenge now, we are going to pay very heavy dividends in the not too distant future."

Nancy Megarry, of Ten Acre Estate, Comber Road, Newtownards, was selected as Comber May Queen at a dance in the Andrews Memorial Hall on 6 May. Five days later she was also chosen as County Down May Queen.

Cllr Georgina Foulis, who had become the first woman member of Newtownards Borough Council, was also its first Deputy Mayor, receiving her chain of office at the end of May. The new Mayor was Cllr Joseph McCullough.

Responding to many calls for the provision of a swimming pool in Newtownards, the Borough Council agreed in early July to consider the matter at a meeting behind closed doors.

Serious flooding occurred in the Mill Street area of Comber during mid-July after sustained rain, with matters being made worse by the large amount of rubbish and tree branches already blocking a stream leading to the local Enler River.
Arising from the episode, North Down Rural District Council wrote to the Ministry of Agriculture requesting the stream be cleaned.
Meanwhile, in nearby Newtownards water restrictions were in force during the summer because of an earlier period of drought. The water supply was cut off between 11pm and 5am each day, with the use of hose pipes to wash cars and water gardens strictly prohibited.
Newtownards, however, had its own dose of

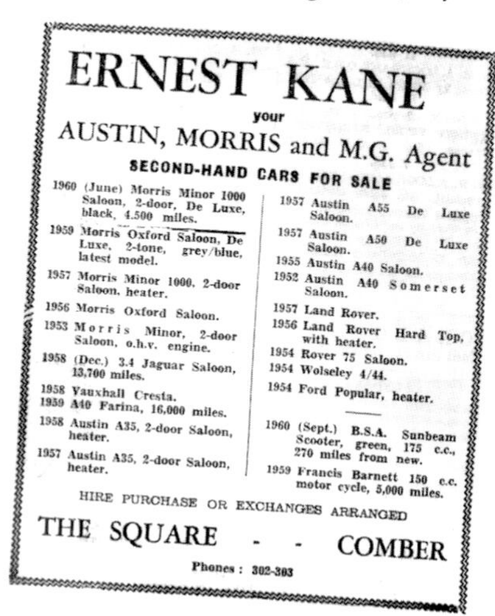

flooding towards the end of August, with the worst-affected partss being in the area of Circular Street, Mill Street and John Street, as well as Manse Road. Nevertheless the restrictions continued well into September.

A quarter of a million pairs of socks were dispatched to the United States and Canada in early August by the Newtownards-based Strangford Knitting Co. Ltd. Orders totalling £300,000 had been placed by the two countries during the previous eight to 10 years.

The death occurred on 4 October of Dora Baxter, from John Street, Newtownards, who was a major figure in the Scouting movement going back more than 40 years. Her earliest role was as Cubmistress of the 1st Newtownards Wolf Cub Pack back in 1918, when Scouting was still in its infancy. By 1931 she was Akela Leader for Northern Ireland and, in 1946, she was appointed Assistant Commissioner for County Down.
In addition to her Scouting role, Miss Baxter was principal of Castle Gardens Primary School, in the town, and an enthusiastic worker for the savings movement.

Some 80 workers employed at the Newtownards (Glen) factory of Short Bros and Harland left their machines and work benches on 27 October to march through the town and then join a larger protest at Stormont over increasing unemployment at the company.
It was pointed out that the factory employed 150-180 workers compared to double that figure in 1955. It was also claimed more staff were being paid off that week.

Employees of Short Bros and Harland on the march through Newtownards in October 1960. *Newtownards Chronicle* picture

The *Newtownards Chronicle* endorsed a growing campaign to have the canal running through the 650-house Scrabo Estate culverted or fenced off. The paper argued that the huge cost of £700,000 cited by the Borough Council was worth paying if it saved lives in the future. There had been a number of drowning tragedies over the years, including young children.

Three hundred and fifty jobs were created in Donaghadee with the opening in November of a £1m. extension to the Cyril Lord carpet factory at High Bangor Road. The new building had an overall floor area of 300,000 sq. ft. Performing the official opening, Prime Minister Lord Brookeborough described Mr Lord as "a man who passionately cares about his country's place among the trading nations of the world."

A plum pudding weighing 20lb was donated by the Australian Dried Fruits Board for the Christmas dinner attended by elderly members of the Newtownards Golden Age Club. It was reckoned the pudding was enjoyed by some 100-120 Ards folk.

Mrs D. H. Caughey congratulates 15-year-old Marlene Heaney, of Balfour Street, Newtownards, on winning the 'Miss Ards' competition organised the North End Ards Supporters Club in September 1960 at the Queen's Hall. Looking on are Messrs. J. Martin, F. McNeilly, J. Morrison, D. H. Caughey, T. Ewing, T. Moffatt and Miss Savage, who presented a bouquet to Mrs Caughey. *Newtownards Chronicle* picture

Prizewinners, judges and officials at the annual horticultural show hosted by Newtownards Young Farmers' Club at the Town Hall in September 1960. Seated: Miss S. Templeton (James Brown Cup), Mrs H. D. Boyd (Warden Cup), TV personality Anne Gregg (who opened the show), Miss M. Milliken (T. Boyle Sen. Cup), Mr D. Gilliland (Lockhart Bros. Cup). At front: Irene Mackey, representing Castle Gardens School, winners of the Newtownards YFC Supporters' Cup). *Newtownards Chronicle* picture

Main prizewinners following the annual Cycling Proficiency Tests gathered for the presentation ceremony at the Town Hall in September 1960. Back (from left): Sgt. R. S. Clements, Cllr Joseph McCullough, Mayor of Newtownards, Winston Jardine, Prof. Lloyd Dodd, Marion Edgar, Cllr Stanley Woods. Front: John McLean, David Thompson, David McKee, Douglas Edmondson, John Thompson, Yvonne Sloan and David Cargo. *Newtownards Chronicle* picture

The platform party at a variety sale held on 24 September 1960 by the drivers and conductors of the Newtownards branch of the Ulster Transport Authority. Back (from left): Messrs. G. E. Dunlop, H. Robson, J. Coffey, T. Galway, D. P. Connolly, R. McCorriston. Front: Mrs Connolly, Mrs Dunlop, Miss M. Cameron (assistant matron at Ards Hospital) and Miss Dorothy Galway (who presented a bouquet to Miss Cameron). *Newtownards Chronicle* picture

Lady Dunleath presents Mr J. A. Boyle with the Anthony Patton Memorial Cup at the Mid-Ards Ulster Farmers' Union branch prize distribution in November 1960. Included are (from left): Lord Dunleath, Mr W. J. Caughey, Mr D. McClements, Mr J. Kennedy, Mr J. Orr and Mr W. Brown. *Newtownards Chronicle* picture

The Ladies Committee of the Field Marshal Montgomery Pipe Band at a guest tea in the Unionist Hall, Carryduff, on 11 November 1960. *Newtownards Chronicle* picture

Office-bearers and guests at the second annual meeting of the North Down County Girl Guides in the Queen's Hall on 12 November 1960. Back (from left): Mrs N. Barker, Miss Ewing Johnston, Senator Mrs Greeves, Miss K. Hogg. Front (from left): Mayor Joseph McCullough, Mrs J. W. Haughton, Mrs J. L. O. Andrews and Miss D. McGuire. *Newtownards Chronicle* picture

Officials and members of Donaghadee Young Farmers' Club at their annual show, held in their Ballyvester clubroom in December 1960. Back (from left): F. Curragh, M. Johnston, H. McKeag, H. Brown, F. Moore, R. Carson, H. Kennedy, F Porter, Front: A. Brown, K Briggs, N. Kennedy, L. Semple, J. Porter, R. Strain *Newtownards Chronicle* picture

Committee and members of Ballywalter Young Farmers' Club at their Christmas social in December 1960. *Newtownards Chronicle* picture

Almost £700 was raised at a sale in St Patrick's Church Hall, Newtownards, over two nights in December 1960. All proceeds went to the Parochial Fund. Deirdre Gilmore was in charge of the bran tub, which attracted these eager young customers. *Spectator* picture

Sister Nixon with children who were spending Christmas 1960 in the McKelvey Ward at Ards Hospital. *Spectator* picture

Sport in 1960

in the Chronicle

Ards hockey players Catherine Brown and Rosalind Armstrong were selected for the Ulster inter pro side in a match against Leinster on 23 January.

Harry O'Prey announced in late January that he was bringing his international table tennis career to a close, 24 years after gaining his first cap against Wales. The Newtownards man's final match, also against Wales, was his 80th for Ireland. He had competed at six world championships and had won 106 major tournaments.

Pollock Anderson was appointed captain of Donaghadee Golf Club at the annual meeting on 9 April. All the more remarkable was the fact he had served as the club's boy captain back in 1921.

IRISH CUP FINAL

Let down for Supporters as Ards are trounced

ARDS supporters had their biggest let down for some time last Saturday at the Oval where Linfield trounced Ards 5-1 in the final of the Irish Cup. With this defeat went Ards' proud record of never having been beaten in a cup final. Who is to blame for this defeat? To me the only culprits are the eleven players who did duty on the field of play. Individually at different times this season they showed the ability to rank with the best of players. On odd occasions they showed the ability of a first class side as a team but on Saturday in the final 45 minutes they had neither the determination, the fighting spirit or showed football capabilities to warrant them winning the Irish Cup.

Hand it out to them they did quite a good job in the opening 20 minutes without getting goals simply because they took the initiative with quick tackling and go-ahead soccer. Then they fell back and the more they fell back the easier was Linfield's prey. This second half was a

Ards were beaten 5-1 by Linfield in the Irish Cup final at the Oval on 30 April. It was the club's third final (the others being in 1926/27 and 1951/52) and the first they had lost. The scorer for Ards was Jimmy Welsh.

In the aftermath of the heavy defeat it was announced that manager Len Graham's contract would not be renewed. His successor was Tommy Ewing.

Harry Cavan, president of the Irish Football Association and secretary of Ards FC, made history in late May by becoming the first

Irish football legislator to be nominated for the vice-presidency of FIFA, controllers of world football. The nomination was ratified the following August.

The newly reconstructed pavilion at North of Ireland Cricket Club's ground in Comber was officially opened on 21 May by the Earl of Clanwilliam. It had been enlarged in memory of members of North Down Cricket Club and North Down Hockey Club who had lost their lives, and in gratitude to those who had served their country, in the two world wars.

Playing for North Down II against Armagh II at Comber on 26 August, S. E. Roberts took the last six Armagh wickets in just two overs – but without a hat-trick being accomplished. For all his efforts, North Down lost the match.

American swimmer Florence Chadwick failed in an attempt to swim the North Channel from Donaghadee to Portpatrick. She had made a similar attempt three years earlier, in 1957, being taken out of the water just over two miles from the Scottish coastline.

Ards FC centre-half Tommy Forde became only the second player in its history to gain international honours when he was selected to play for Northern Ireland against England at Windsor Park in early October and then against West Germany. The other was Andy Bothwell who had gained five caps some 30 years earlier.

Ards resident Robert (Buster) McShane, from Belair Avenue, Bradshaw's Brae, broke the world bench press weight-lifting record live on UTV's *Sportscast* programme on 16 December with a lift of 435lb.

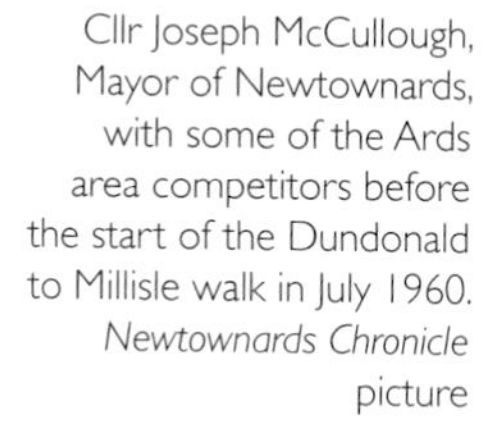

Cllr Joseph McCullough, Mayor of Newtownards, with some of the Ards area competitors before the start of the Dundonald to Millisle walk in July 1960. *Newtownards Chronicle* picture

Mr Robert Masaroon, chairman of the Strangford Lough Wildfowlers Association, presents Mr E. Rodgers with the Nobel Industries Cup for the Single Rise Clay Bird Championship of Ulster in August 1960. *Newtownards Chronicle* picture

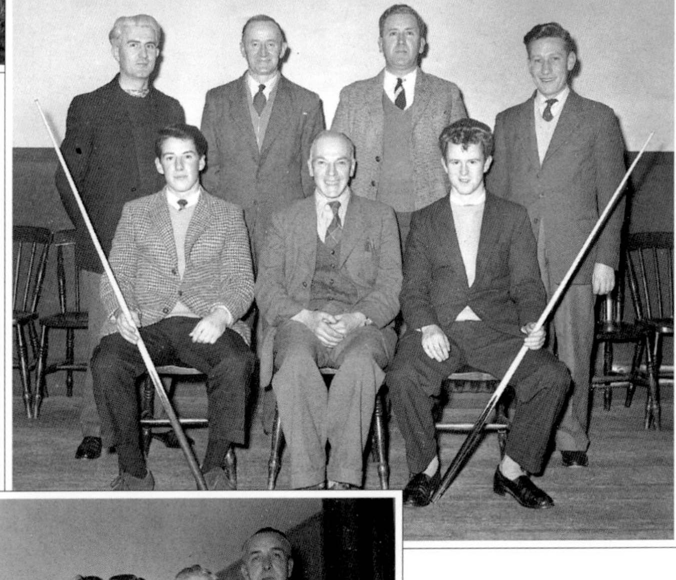

Members of the Comber billiards team, then joint leaders in the Belfast and District Junior League, in November 1960. Back (from left): R. B. Allen, W. Bennett, D. G. R. McKibbin, J. Donaldson. Front: J. A. G. Spence, M. McCutcheon, W. J. McKibbin. *Newtownards Chronicle* picture

Prizewinners at the annual Ards Bowling Club reunion and prize distribution in November 1960. Back (from left): S. Warden, J. Heron, A. Dunlop, W. Smyth, S. Shaw, A. Neill. Front: W. Spratt, R. Keenan, F. McLaughlin, W. Curragh. *Newtownards Chronicle* picture

1961

in the Chronicle

The Queen conferred a knighthood on William Angus Boyd Iliff, a member of a well-known Kircubbin family, in the New Year Honours List. Aged 62 and living in Washington, DC, in the USA, Mr Iliff had been vice-president of the International Bank of Reconstruction and Development since 1956.

Newtownards Borough Council urged the Government to take on full responsibility for the removal of the 'monstrous' abandoned railway embankment that ran through Newtownards, effectively causing an artificial division of the town. It was deemed too expensive a task for the Council to undertake itself. However, it was the property of the Council, having been acquired from the Ulster Transport Authority at the time of the demise of the local railway line – not because it was a valuable piece of land but to ensure any future development would be in the best interests of the Borough.

Councillors believed if the Government undertook to remove the embankment it would create a considerable number of jobs at a time of high unemployment.

THE ROYAL NAVAL ASSOCIATION (Newtownards Branch)

ANNUAL DANCE

QUEEN'S HALL - NEWTOWNARDS

— FRIDAY, 20th JANUARY, 1961 —

9 p.m.—2 a.m.

* Music by ROY McCORD'S SHOWBAND *

Personal appearance of B.B.C. and I.T.V. stars—

DENIS LOTIS and EDNA SAVAGE

(Now appearing in "Cinderella," Empire Theatre)

* Beauty Competition—"Miss Royal Navy."
* Crowning by Denis Lotis.
* Prize Draw—Spot Prizes—Prize to purchaser of lucky ticket.
* Bar facilities.
* Officers and Ratings from H.M.I.S. Vikrant will be attending.

A LIMITED NUMBER OF TICKETS STILL AVAILABLE

Tickets 7/6 ——— Dress Informal

Newtownards Chamber of Trade decided in early January to investigate the possibility of establishing a five-day working week in the town. President Charles

Stewart, acknowledging the idea was "purely tentative", said he did not think it would be possible to introduce the all-day closing of businesses on a Saturday but he could envisage it happening on a Thursday.

Hugh M. Dorrian, a junior porter at Newtownards Railway Station before sailing to the USA in 1925 when aged 18, was invited to the inauguration of Senator John F. Kennedy as President on 20 January. He held a senior government position in Detroit, having previously been an official with the Electrical Engineering Union. He was believed to be the only Ulsterman invited to the inauguration. His mother, Mrs M. J. Dorrian, and other members of his immediate family still lived in Newtownards.

Comber teenager Thomas Wilson (19), of Railway Street, set off for a new life in Australia on 20 February with a party of 15 other young people from all over the United Kingdom. They were travelling there thanks to sponsorship from the 'Big Brother' movement, a voluntary organisation which had been founded in 1925 to assist the settlement of British boys in Australia. Over 2,000 had gone 'down under' after the Second World War.

Royal Humane Society Resuscitation Certificates were presented to three men and a woman, all from Newtownards, who saved the lives of two young Scrabo Estate children who had fallen into the local canal.
The award recipients were James Heaney (31), Samuel Doherty (17), Elizabeth Fuller (25) and John Lowry (40). The rescue had occurred in November 1960 and involved Stephen and Francis McNeilly, aged one and three respectively.

A growing demand among mothers to give birth in hospital rather than at home led to a call in early March from the North Down Hospital Management Committee for the provision of more maternity beds in Ards Hospital which, like its Bangor counterpart, was working at full capacity.

Michael Doherty, a pupil at St Columba's Intermediate School in Portaferry and a member of Kircubbin Young Farmers' Club, was proclaimed Ulster champion in the storytelling class at a Queen's University public speaking competition in March.

Plans for the provision of a new stretch of promenade at Portavogie, running from the harbour to New Street, and costing £8,200, were approved in March by the Playing Fields Committee of North Down Rural Council.

Lt. Col. Edward Brush inspects the parade before officially opening the new Territorial Army Centre at Movilla in April 1961. On the left are Major Morley Hopkins and Sir Douglas Packard. *6-3-7*

The new Territorial Army Centre at Movilla, built at a cost of £49,000, was formally opened on 15 April by Lt. Col. Edward Brush, chairman of the Territorial and Auxiliary Forces Association in County Down.

One of the biggest fires to hit Newtownards in living memory occurred on the morning of 12 April and led to the complete destruction of the coffin factory of W. L. Doggart and Son on the Donaghadee Road. Damage was estimated to be in the region of £15,000 to £20,000. Coffin production was suspended as a result of the fire and it was expected it would not resume until a replacement factory was built.

Firemen examine the charred remains of the coffin factory operated by Messrs. W. L. Doggart and Son. *42-2-7*

The foundation stone for a new £13,000 hall for Second Newtownards Presbyterian Church was officially laid at the end of April by the Very Rev. Dr. T. M. Johnstone, from Nendrum, Mahee Island, who was one of the oldest ministers in Northern Ireland.

The Rev. Albert McElroy, minister of Newtownards Non-Subscribing Presbyterian Church – and president of the Ulster Liberal Association – was prevented from standing for election to Newtownards Borough Council in May. He was barred because of an Act of Parliament dating back to 1840, which prevented any church minister from becoming a member of a local authority.

Mr McElroy's withdrawal also meant that all 12 vacant seats were filled without recourse to an election, there being a total of 12 candidates.

Glen Ward – Cllrs Georgina Foulis, William McGimpsey and J. White; Castle

Ward – Cllrs S. Gracey and William Orr, along with Mr Alexander Bailie (new member); Scrabo Ward – Cllrs A. Edgar, J. McCullough and Stanley Woods; Victoria Ward – Cllrs Mabel Doggart, Norman Francis and J. M. S. Kelly.
The Council also had four Aldermen – Isaac Baxter, Robert Morrow, John Algie and William Spratt – who had all been elected in 1958 to serve six-year terms of office.
At the annual meeting on 25 May Cllr Foulis was elected Mayor, thus becoming the first woman ever to hold the position in Newtownards.

Diane Gillings (20), from Tenacres, Comber Road, Newtownards, was the new County Down Dairy Princess for 1961. She was selected at a YFC dance in the Queen's Hall on 5 May. She worked as a bank clerk in Kircubbin and was assistant Wolf Cub mistress for the 6th Newtownards Pack.

Newtownards firemen moved into their new station on the Portaferry Road (adjoining the former premises) in the middle of May. Displaying a "considerable expanse of glass", there was ample accommodation for three fire tenders. It was formally opened in August by Minister of Home Affairs Brian Faulkner.

Herbert Matier, a member of Newtownards Silver Band for more than 40 years, was presented with an inscribed wristwatch on 16 June as a token of his colleagues' esteem for his valuable services. A dinner was held in his honour at the Devonshire Hotel, Newtownards.

Ritz Cinema manager Campbell Morrison retired on 30 June after holding the position for 25 years. He had commenced his working life in 1917 as manager of the Palace Cinema (which was owned by the Morrison family). It was destroyed by fire in the 1920s and replaced by a new 'Palace.' When those premises were sold to Union Cinemas in 1935 they were renamed the Ritz. Two years later the picture house had another new owner, Associated British Cinemas (ABC).

A new hall for First Comber Presbyterian Church, costing £15,000, was formally opened on 2 September by Mrs Brown, wife of the minister, the Rev. W. R. Brown. The building was dedicated by the Moderator of the General Assembly, the Rev. W. A. A. Park.

Lady Brookeborough, wife of the Prime Minister, laid the foundation stone for a £9,000 recreation hall for the Newtownards Old People's Friendship Association on 14 September. It was on a site at Mill Street where the Borough Council was erecting flats and houses for elderly people.

Fears that a considerable number of jobs in Newtownards would be lost with the closure of the Comber Road factory run by Messrs. Lee Guinness Ltd. were dispelled when it was announced in early October that a new tenant, Messrs. Allen West and Co., had been identified.
The company employed 3,000 people at its headquarters in Brighton and promised to increase the workforce in an expanded Newtownards operation from dozens to hundreds. Both the old tenant and the new one were involved in the manufacture of electrical motor control gear.

A meeting was held in the Blue Peter Café on 9 October to discuss the possibility of forming a Business and Professional Women's Club in Newtownards. At the time there were 21 such clubs in Northern Ireland with over 1,000 members. Donaghadee already had a B&P Club and it sponsored the formation of the new one in Newtownards. The formal launch took place on 15 November.

The first air display promoted by the Ulster Flying Club attracted an estimated crowd of 10,000 to Ards Airport on 7 October. The official opening ceremony was performed by famous World War Two pilot Group Captain Douglas Bader.
Fifteen aircraft, including two helicopters, took part, along with Meteor jets from the RAF Flying College at Manby in Lincolnshire.

Famous Second World War pilot Group Captain Douglas Bader visited Newtownards in October 1961 to declare open the Ulster Flying Club's first air display at the local airfield. Included on the platform are (from left): Mr J. Pullen (secretary), Mr W. Fletcher (chairman), Lady Mairi Bury (president), Miss G. Foulis (Mayor of Newtownards), Mr W. Scott (Town Clerk) and Squadron Leader Cumming.
41-1-20

Almost 100 Civil Defence personnel from around Northern Ireland attended the official opening on 13 October of new premises within the former fire station on the Portaferry Road. Tom Maxwell, senior scientific intelligence officer for East District and local Civil Defence head, said at last they would have room to train and, on the social side, to return the hospitality they had received so often in the past from other CD centres.

Two boys, aged nine and 10 respectively, who robbed a youngster of the 10/- note his mother had given him to do a message, were remanded to the Malone Training School for a fortnight, when they appeared at Newtownards Children's Court. They also admitted stealing a coil of rope worth 19/6 from a store – they had used it to make a swing from a tree.

Angry residents of the Hunt's Park pre-fab estate in Donaghadee, whose homes were badly damaged by a storm on 22 October, said they would refuse to pay their rents if the local Urban Council failed to repair them.
There were several instances of asbestos roofing being blown from one dwelling and causing damage to another. It was claimed Council workmen were being kept away from Hunt's Park because the wind was too strong.

The death occurred on 26 October of war veteran Hugh Clarke, of South Street, Newtownards, almost five years after he had laid the first wreath of remembrance of the South Africa campaign at the Newtownards Cenotaph.
He had joined the Royal Irish Rangers at the age of just 15 in 1895, subsequently serving in South Africa with the Manchester Regiment. His spell of service ended in 1907, but he went on to serve in the First World War as a bugler with the RIR.

Work was nearing completion on the new sewage disposal works near the Strangford Lough shore at Ballyrickard, between Comber and Newtownards. Effluent from Comber and district was already being dealt with but it was expected it would take another nine months before Newtownards could be fully linked to the facility. The project cost around £200,000, with half that sum being met by Government grant-aid.

A major fire in a rear store at the renowned High Street (Newtownards) department store of Messrs. F. C. Glasgow and Co. resulted in the loss of hundreds of children's toys that had been set aside for Christmas. Although the situation was initially described as "hopeless" by a company spokesman, all the toys were quickly replaced thanks to the generosity of the firm's many friends in the wholesale and retail trade.

Enjoying the winter sunshine at the park in Cloughey early in January 1961 are William Palmer, Elizabeth Clint, Anne Cully, Hugh Cully and Elaine Clint.
70-2-1

With friends and colleagues looking on, Mr D. Thompson JP is presented with a clock by Lt. Col. Charles Earle DSO OBE on the occasion of his retirement as honorary secretary of the Cloughey branch of the Royal National Lifeboat Institution in January 1961. The ceremony took place at Cloughey Lifeboat Station.
52-4-3

Kathleen Donnan and Rosemary McAlpine, of Castleavery, Newtownards, with new-born lambs in late January 1961, the first sign of Spring approaching.
47-1-2

Pupils from the Model Primary School in Newtownards received awards at their annual party, held in conjunction with Dr Barnardo's Homes, in February 1961. Included are Mr S. Stevenson (principal), Miss Gilfillan (who presented the awards), Mrs King-Wood (representing Dr Barnardo's Homes) and Miss A. Wright.
29-1-3

Brian McCutcheon, of South Street, Newtownards, helps to clear snow away from the front of his home at the beginning of February 1961.
25-1-3

The new roundabout at the Comber playground proved very popular with local children in February 1961.
32-3-3

Pupils of Movilla Secondary Intermediate School take a break during netball practice in February 1961.
87-3-3

Children from Second Comber Presbyterian Church who took part in a sketch at the Sunday School Social and Prize Distribution, which was held in the Andrews Memorial Hall in March 1961.
95-1-3

Members of the Newtownards Co-Operative Educational Class received awards and certificates at a prize distribution in Zion Hall on 3 March 1961.
62-2-4

Old houses make room for new ones at Main Street, Ballywalter, in March 1961.
92-3-5

Cycling proficiency certificates and badges were presented to 42 boys and girls in the Queen's Hall, Newtownards, on 11 April 1961.
88-2-6

Boys from Regent House School with toys they made for patients in the McKelvey Pavilion (Mental Health Inpatients Unit) at Ards Hospital in 1961. Included is Matron Miss I. M. Percival.
40-3-25

Young cyclists preparing to take part in the proficiency tests, which were being held in Donaghadee for the first time in late April 1961.
27-3-8

A lorry with a load weighing over 30 tons was used to test the new bridge at High Street in Comber before it was opened to traffic in mid-May 1961.
39-1-9

Members of various Comber youth organisations who took part in the annual youth service at St Mary's Parish Church on 21 May 1961.
87-2-15

First Newtownards Wolf Cub Pack members at the County Down Wolf Cub sports in late May 1961. *52-1-10*

Boys from Ballyhalbert Primary School during their lunch break in mid-June 1961. *55-1-11*

Girls from Ballyhalbert Primary School in mid-June 1961. *54-3-11*

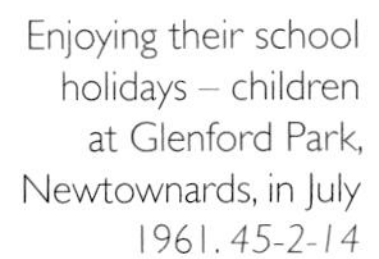

Enjoying their school holidays – children at Glenford Park, Newtownards, in July 1961. *45-2-14*

Glenford Park was certainly a popular place to pass the time during the summer of 1961. *43-2-14*

The original caption, from 21 July 1961, read: 'I'm so hot,' says this little girl (centre). 'I wish we could stop playing ring-a-rosy so I could sit down and rest.' But her playmates seem to be enjoying themselves out on the lawn. No names or location were given – but it hardly makes a difference! *68-2-14*

Sally Hanna and Amy McBride gather potatoes at the farm of John Donnan, Castleavery, Newtownards, in July 1961.
16-1-12

Brothers Robert (8) and Aidan McAllister (7) chose different modes of transport in July 1961.
70-3-15

New pupils who arrived at Comber Primary School in late August 1961.
48-2-17

David Walker, of Gloucester Avenue, Donaghadee, takes his miniature poodle Cindy out for a ride in the town in late September 1961. Also in the picture is friend Billy Jones, of Killaughey Road, also Donaghadee.
74-1-15

Members of the Greyabbey Girls' Auxiliary at a rally in the Village Hall on 29 September 1961, held to celebrate the first 50 years of the Girls' Auxiliary organisation.
97-2-19

Another classic *Chronicle* caption, this time from October 1961: Between scratching, laughing, and generally looking at everything but the photographer, our picture of these young footballers, taken recently at Ballyhalbert playing ground, must surely come into the *Candid Camera* class.
64-1-19

The bran tub was a big attraction at a sale of work held in St Patrick's Hall, Portaferry, over three nights in late October 1961. *49-3-21*

Ex-Head Constable Cowan, on behalf of the Northern Ireland branch of Gideon's International, hands over a copy of the New Testament to a pupil at Scrabo Intermediate School on 29 November 1961. New Testaments were presented to all those attending the school. *93-1-23*

A Christmas party for the children of workers at the local Cyril Lord factory, as well as a group from the Childhaven Centre at Millisle, was held on 16 December. In addition to pianist Bert Fraser, the entertainment was provided by local group Margo and The Marvettes. *23-2-25*

Sport in 1961

in the Chronicle

Ards regained the Belfast and District Senior Table Tennis League title in early February after a 6-3 victory over neighbours Glenford.

Ann Dorrian, from Movilla Road, Newtownards, and Enid Keenan, Main Street, Carrowdore, were selected in February to play for the County Down netball team in a series of inter-county matches. They both attended Movilla Intermediate School. Also selected were Jean Wright, from Greyabbey, who attended Glastry Intermediate, and Vilma Quinn, Killinchy, a pupil at Comber Intermediate.

Alex Stewart, son of Mr and Mrs William Stewart of Crawfordsburn Road, Newtownards, was a member of the Campbell College team which defeated RBAI 16-6 in the Schools Cup final at Ravenhill on St Patrick's Day.

History was made locally when First Division side Wolverhampton Wanderers met Ards at Windsor Park on 8 May in a benefit match for Dessie Hunter and Tommy Forde. Wolves won the match 4-1 with the Ards goal coming from right-half Vince Maguire.

The Ards FC Player of the Year trophy for 1961, awarded by the North End Supporters' Club, went to Sammy Hatton.

Chieftain's Guest, owned by Ballyrainey (Comber) man Eric McCullough and trained by Leslie McNair, Ballyskeagh (Newtownards), won the richest-ever Irish Derby at the Harold's Cross dog track in Dublin on 11 August.

Jack Hoey achieved a hole-in-one at Scrabo Golf Club's 135-yard eighth hole in

October. He was playing with Messrs. H. Stewart, R. Jellie and J. Peden.

With Harry O'Prey as captain and no fewer than three Ards men in the team, Ulster sprang a surprise by winning an inter-provincial table tennis tournament at Cork on 18 November, defeating Leinster and Munster convincingly. In the same week Ards player Carroll McBride was selected to play for Ireland against Scotland on 1 and 2 December.

Ards Boys – winners of the Belfast Summer Youth League – held a victory party and awards night at the Gibson Hall on 23 November. Player of the Year was Rowley Houston and the runner-up was Alfie Wright, while other awards went to top goal scorer Samuel Carron and captain Ronald Murray.

It was estimated that the Ards FC coffers benefited to the tune of £1,100 from three fixtures over the Christmas holidays. That represented their share of the takings from games against Distillery at Grosvenor Park (2-2), Linfield at Windsor Park (3-2 defeat) and Glentoran at Castlereagh Park (4-2 win). It was described as the club's "richest Christmas ever".

The Ards Boys football team were proclaimed the undefeated Belfast Summer Youth League champions in October 1961. Back row (from left): M. Hannon, F. Leonard, J. McKee. Third row: R. Waugh, D. McAleese, S. Carroll, A. Wright, B. Gazzard, R. Houston, R. McCauley. Second row: Mr E. Hawkins (manager), D. Woods, M. McCann, R. Murphy (captain), B. McNally, Cllr. J. M. S. Kelly (president). Front: J. Dinely and K. Woods.
70-1-20

Donaghadee Yacht Club officials at the annual regatta on 22 July 1961. From Left: F.P. Quiery A. Oliver, W. Oliver, T. Pethick E. D. Mitchell, C. Anderson, S. McKee, D. Moore, J. Ferguson
72-2-14

Ray Gilmore, from Kircubbin, won the Flying Fifteen race at Bangor Regatta on 9 August 1961 in his boat *Gooseander* – competing against the Duke of Edinburgh. The awards were presented by the Queen, with Prince Philip looking on. The Royal couple had spent much of the day in Bangor.
58-16-18

The Ards Rugby Club 1st XV which beat CIYMS at their Comber Road grounds in September 1961. Back (from left): J. Dalzell, E. Gourley, W. Whiteside, B. Bishop, W. Clarke, T. West, G. Ferguson, B. Herron. Front: B. Jordan, D. Coffey, B. Shaw, D. Herron, R. Haslett (captain), A. Orr and K. Halliday.
20-1-19

The First Donaghadee Old Boys' darts team, pictured in November 1961, reached the final of the Londonderry Cup during their first season in the Ards Temperance Darts League.
45-2-22

The North Down hockey team drew 3-3 with Montalto in a Qualifying League game at Comber on 11 November 1961.
74-1-22

1962

in the Chronicle

Wing-Commander Robert John ('Mick') Carson, formerly of Ballywalter, received the Queen's Commendation for valuable service in the air in the New Year Honours List. His wife was the former Miss Jean Bailie, of Newtownards.

The Old Priory at the east end of Court Street in Newtownards was targeted by vandals at the end of January. Accused of desecrating the historic church, the culprits had broken into a number of vaults and removed valuable metal fittings. Among items taken were two intricately-wrought copper grilles from the Alexander Stewart vault. A large hole was made in the side of the Londonderry vault, leaving caskets plainly visible.
Two young boys were subsequently prosecuted at Newtownards Children's Court for "damaging, injuring and spoiling" the Old Priory, with fines of £10 each being imposed, while two others were fined £2 each for aiding and abetting.

The new recreation hall, built in Mill Street by the Newtownards Old People's Friendship Association, was officially opened on 1 February by Lady Mairi Bury.

English pop star Eden Kane, who had scored a No 1 hit with *Well I Ask You* the previous year, appeared at the Queen's Hall in Newtownards on 13 February. The show was promoted by namesake Trevor Kane, who would bring The Beatles to the King's Hall in 1964.

Eden Kane was the first fully-fledged Sixties pop star to visit the town, with hundreds of screaming fans giving him an enthusiastic welcome. When he called at record stockist Scrabo Electrical Engineers of Regent Street earlier in the day, the crowd surged around him and it was only with the help of a policeman, promoter Trevor Kane and personal manager Victor Lloyd that he managed to reach the relative safety of the shop. Even the back door had to be locked to stop fans from getting in to the already packed business. Dark-suited and soft-spoken, the singer signed dozens of autographs during the hour-long visit.

Fans gathered round pop star Eden Kane when he visited Scrabo Electrical Engineers on 13 February 1962. *28-58-1*

He brought the house down at the Queen's Hall that night, stepping onto the stage at 11.30pm to even more screams from members of the audience who had paid 6/- for their tickets.

"He went into Elvis Presley-type contortions and this brought more high-pitched appreciation from the hall," reported the *Chronicle*. "He sang his three hit records, as well as some other songs, and at the end of his 25-minute performance the girls at the edge of the stage lifted up the curtain and called for more.

"More came. Eden sang another song and that was all. Back in his improvised dressing room he was surrounded by six or seven girls who were getting his autograph. 'Please come back again, Eden,' said one. They didn't look adoringly at him, but seemed to be quite happy just being beside him and talking to him."

Newtownards Borough Council accepted a tender in early February for work to culvert and divert the canal that wound through the centre of the Scrabo Estate. When completed, members heard, there would be little sign of the canal within the housing estate and parents would no longer have to fear for the safety of their children. It was expected the £100,000 scheme would take two years to complete.

James McBratney retired in February from the office staff of George Walker and

Co. Ltd. (Castle Gardens Mill) in Newtownards after a career that had spanned 51 years.

The Rt. Hon. George Brown, deputy leader of the British Labour Party – and a West Ham United fan – was a welcome spectator at Castlereagh Park on 24 February when Ards met Coleraine in an Irish Cup fixture. He was in Northern Ireland to take part in a series of talks with industrialists, members and officials of the Northern Ireland Labour Party and trade union officials. Ards lost the match 2-1.

The death occurred on 1 March, following a serious illness, of Morris May, Stormont MP for Ards and also the Minister for Education. Aged only 52, he had been re-selected just the previous week by the Ards Unionist Association for the next election. His final function in Newtownards involved his election, early in February, as Worshipful Master of the town's No 4 District LOL.

Nineteen-year-old David Montgomery, son of Major H. E. Montgomery of Rosemount, Greyabbey, commenced a 9,000-mile journey by jeep on 12 March, his ultimate destination being Australia, where a job awaited him on a New South Wales sheep farm. The overland route through Europe and Asia would take David and an English companion as far as Singapore, and then on by ship to Darwin.

On 30 May Shane Fenton and The Fentones became the latest big-name cross-channel act to appear at the Queen's Hall. A decade later Shane would have a second successful career as pop star Alvin Stardust.

In the by-election to fill the vacant Ards seat at Stormont, created by the death of Morris May, Capt. William Long, representing the Unionist Party, defeated Liberal candidate the Rev. Albert McElroy, minister of Newtownards Non-Subscribing Presbyterian Church (who had previously been barred from seeking election to the Borough Council).
Yorkshire-born Capt. Long, who had previously chaired Donaghadee Urban District Council for nine years, enjoyed a 4,493 vote majority – he received 7,501 votes to Mr McElroy's 3,008.

The North Down Hospital Management Committee agreed to ban stiletto heels from Ards Hospital after members heard numerous complaints that women wearing such heels were leaving an expensive "trail of havoc" on floor coverings in the hospital. "Politely phrased notices" appealing to women not to wear stiletto heels had met with a very limited response.

One of Portaferry's best-known tourist attractions, the whale's jaw arch, which stood 15ft high at Ballywhite, was blown down in a gale in late June. It needed extensive repairs but was quickly restored to its familiar location. The jaw was from a whale that had been washed ashore on the Aran Islands some 50 years earlier.

A widening scheme at John Street in Newtownards met with a mixed reaction for it also meant that homes on the canal side of the street would lose half their gardens. It was anticipated the work would be completed by October.

Responding in July to local calls for improved communications along the Ards Peninsula, Commerce Minister John Andrews pointed out that a bridge would be very costly, but added that the Ministry had been considering the merits of an improved ferry service capable of carrying cars across the Lough. The Ministry, he added, would be approaching Down County Council for its views on such a service.

Lady Wakehurst, wife of the Governor of Northern Ireland, opened a new training school, nurses' home, psycho-neurosis unit and day hospital at Ards Hospital on 2 August. The total cost of the different developments was £81,000 and they set Ards ahead of many other hospitals in the Province.

US Consul General Eric M. Hughes was warmly welcomed to Newtownards in late August by new Mayor Stanley Woods and taken on a four-hour tour of six local factories. The visit gave rise to speculation the town could witness the dawning of a new industrial era with help from across the Atlantic.

Regent House School moved from Regent Street to new premises on the Circular Road, built at a cost of £250,000 and immediately becoming among the most modern in Northern Ireland. The first pupils were welcomed to the new school on 5 September. Work had taken two years to complete.

A new hall for Glastry Methodist Church, built at a cost of £3,000, was opened on 1 September by Mrs Cooke, wife of the minister, the Rev. Henry Cooke, and dedicated by the Rev. James Wisheart, president of the Methodist Church in Ireland.

Local Councillors agreed in early September that the 350th anniversary of the granting of a Borough Charter to Newtownards by King James I in 1613 should be celebrated in 1963. A special sub-committee chaired by Mayor Stanley Woods was established.

Newtownards footwear company C. J. Stewart and Son Ltd., of Conway Square, celebrated the 50th anniversary of its opening – which had occurred on 23 September 1912.

Thousands of men and women from Newtownards and the Ards Peninsula travelled to Belfast on 29 September for celebrations to mark the 50th anniversary of the signing of the Solemn League and Covenant in 1912.
More than 40,000 people from all over Northern Ireland marched eight abreast through the city to the Balmoral Showgrounds, setting for an act of remembrance and dedication.

An explosion caused by a home-made metal tube bomb caused damage estimated at £75 to the Regal Cinema in Donaghadee on 6 October. Two young Belfast men subsequently faced charges of causing an explosion of a nature likely to endanger life or cause serious injury to property.
It was accepted by the prosecution that their actions had amounted to little more than a 'boyish prank' and the case was adjourned by the judge for 18 months. Pending the payment of £88 costs (including £13 for damage caused to the Railway Hotel) by the defendants themselves, rather than their parents, he indicated they would hear nothing more about the matter.

Some of the damage caused by an explosion at the Regal Cinema, Donaghadee, on 6 October 1962.
46-63-3

The demolition of rows of houses and other buildings in the East Street area of Newtownards was envisaged in a £500,000 redevelopment scheme proposed in early November by the Borough Council. The aim was to provide new homes, shops, garages, public conveniences, a children's play area and improved thoroughfares.

The Council gave notice of an application for a vesting order for the compulsory acquisition of the land needed for the project, which would involve the loss of 134 dwellings but their replacement by 151 new homes.

Councillors conferred the Freedom of the Borough – for only the third time in its history – on Alderman Isaac Baxter in recognition of his long service, which had commenced in 1929 and included a term as Mayor. Previously accorded the honour were Chevalier Alexander Dickson (of the world-famous Newtownards rose company) and the Dowager Marchioness of Londonderry, both by then deceased. Mr Baxter passed away, in his 80th year, on 28 December 1969.

Sixty employees were laid off during November at the Newtownards firm of Allen West Ltd., leaving the workforce at approximately 100. It was experiencing the knock-on effect of a reduction in orders at the company's headquarters in Brighton.

It was announced that on Sunday 23 December there would be just one general delivery of letters and parcels in all areas, with two collections from the mail box at Newtownards Post Office, namely at 5.30pm and again at 8.15pm.

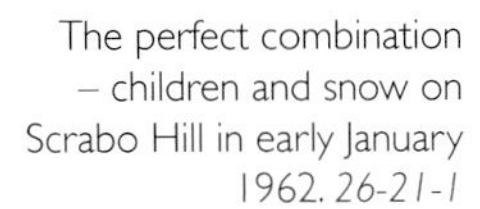

The perfect combination – children and snow on Scrabo Hill in early January 1962. *26-21-1*

Members of Second Comber Youth Guild took part in a pantomime at Newtownards Methodist Church on 19 January 1962. *27-19-2*

The *Newtownards Chronicle* took delivery of the latest Heidelberg cylinder printing machines in early April 1962 (becoming only the second County Down newspaper to introduce such technology). Heidelberg representative Mr S. D. McKeown demonstrates the machine to letterpress machineman Gordon Orr. *31-70-3*

Chronicle reporter Roderick Crilly interviewed 89-year-old Patrick Magee in April 1962 for a series of features he wrote for the paper about local villages and small communities.
31-79-1

Members of Second Comber Scout Troop received new colours in Comber Non-Subscribing Presbyterian Church on 15 April 1962. Included is District Commissioner H. Copeland.
32-60-2

Betty Gardiner (20), of Bowtown, Newtownards, was elected County Down Dairy Princess in May 1962.
33-92-3

It was singles-only as far as those who attended the Bachelors' Ball at Ballygalget on 20 May 1962 were concerned. Many of the men dressed as chefs and waiters to look after the catering.
35-16-1

Mrs Margaret Fowler (73), of North Street, Newtownards, with lamb 'Yogi Bear' and terrier 'Jess' in May 1962. She had tended to the lamb after nephew George Lamb took it to her home following the death of its mother. After a number of weeks on a diet of milk, occasionally laced with a little brandy, 'Yogi' was more of a domestic pet than a farm animal. Mrs Fowler would even take it for walks along the streets of Newtownards on a lead.
33-70-1

Trophy winners at the Comber Primary School sports day, held at the end of June 1962, with the prizes being handed over by Mrs Lockhart (seated), wife of local minister the Rev. R. J. N. Lockhart. Back (from left): Rev. J. E. Jones, Rev. W. R. Brown, W. McClean (boy captain of Ardara House), D. Minnis (best athlete), Rev. Lockhart, Mr N. Nevin (principal). Front: R. Cooke (captain of Ardara House football team), D. Oliver (best sportsman), N. Galway (girl captain, Ardara House), B. Mitchell (who made a presentation to Mrs Lockhart), D. Cromie (player of the year) and L. Jellie (captain of relay team).
38-19-1

The Boyd family held a reunion at the home of Mr and Mrs H. D. Boyd, of 'Edenvale', Ballywitticock, on 20 July 1962. Among the guests were the Venerable Frederick Boyd, Archdeacon of Winnipeg, and Mr George Boyd, an accountant with Eaton Stores in Canada. Back (from left): Mr John Boyd, Mr H. D. Boyd, Miss Jean Boyd, Mr George Boyd, Mr Hugh Boyd, Archdeacon Boyd, Mr W. B. Boyd, Mr Samuel Boyd, Mrs Hugh Boyd. Middle: Mrs M. Alexander, Mrs Lindsay, Miss Hay. Front: Rev. James Boyd, Mr W. Boyd, Mrs W. Boyd, Robin Boyd, Mrs W. B. Smith, Mrs Florence Boyd, Miss Hay, Mrs Marjorie Boyd and Mrs H. D. Boyd. *40-43-1*

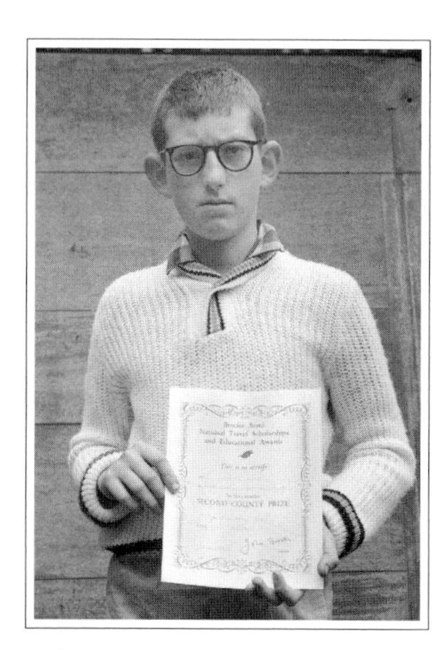

David Caughers (12), of Kilcroney Green, Scrabo Road, Newtownards, holds the certificate he received in August 1962 for gaining second prize in secondary art for County Down in the annual Brooke Bond Tea competition. It had attracted more than 7,000 entries from all over the British Isles. Castle Gardens pupil David also received vouchers worth £3/15/0 for the purchase of National Savings Certificates. *40-69-3*

The Ballygalget Spinsters' Ball proved a great success in early September 1962. Pictured are those who worked behind the scene, dressed appropriately for the occasion. *44-23-3*

Cloughey children pictured in front of the local lifeboat *Constance Calverley* at the beginning of October 1962.
46-21-2

Children take a break from play at the Portaferry shore in late October 1962.
47-19-1

Members of the congregation leave St Patrick's Church, Ballyphilip, in October 1962, after taking part in its bicentenary celebrations.
47-55-3

Recipients of Queen's Scout certificates from Chief Scout Sir Charles Maclean at a reception in Belfast City Hall on 27 October 1962. Back (from left): Raymond Ferris, Thomas Ritchie, Allan Lynch (all First Newtownards), Hugh Ennis (Kircubbin). Front: Jack Brown, Ronald C. Ferris, C. Ritchie and Kenneth J. Magowan (all First Newtownards).
48-2-3

The Meals on Wheels service was introduced in Newtownards in October 1962 as part of the welfare work being carried out by the ladies' committee of the Golden Age Club. For just a shilling (5p), two-course meals were delivered twice a week to seven needy people at the outset. From left: Cllrs Mabel Doggart, Miss A. Neill, Mrs N. Coffey, Mrs M. McKee and Miss M. McCutcheon.
46-12-3

Dawn Bailie, from Talbot Street, Newtownards, was crowned 'Miss Ards' at a dance in the Queen's Hall in October 1962.
47-43-3

Some of the many helpers who ensured the success of a sale of work in Second Newtownards Presbyterian Church Hall, Mary Street, in early November 1962, to raise funds for the 'Debretta Girl Pipers' – a new all-girls pipe band being formed by Debretta employees.
48-58-1

Children from Millisle Primary School at their Christmas party on 18 December 1962.
52-9-1

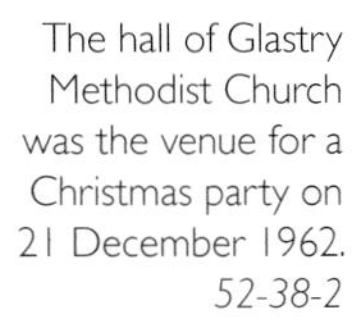

The hall of Glastry Methodist Church was the venue for a Christmas party on 21 December 1962.
52-38-2

Sport in 1962

in the Chronicle

Castle Gardens won the Vinters' Darts League for the first time in the club's history. They finished with 32 points, one ahead of Scrabo, Rosetta and Tyrone, all tying for second place.

Guildhall won the Newtownards Temperance Darts League in early March, having led it for most of the season. They finished just ahead of the "fast finishing" Ards Cycling Club. However, the cyclists had little reason for disappointment as they secured the Knock-Out Cup, the Five-A-Side Cup, the pairs and individual titles, as well as highest score and lowest number of darts.

Newtownards Technical School became the first winners of the Minor Technical Schools Football Cup after defeating Lisburn 2-0 at Solitude on 11 April. Captain Derek McAleese scored both goals, with the team's Bobby McNally missing a penalty. They just failed to achieve a noteworthy double the following week, losing 2-1 to Orangefield in the final of the Belfast and District Cup. McAleese was again on the score sheet for Newtownards Tech.

Ards FC right-winger (and Northern Ireland international) Billy Humphries was transferred to Coventry City – managed by Jimmy Hill – for a fee of £5,500.

Tower United brought the Gibson Cup back to Newtownards on 14 May following a 4-2 victory over Belfast City Hospital at Seaview, while on the same day Comber Rec. defeated the RUC 1-0 in the Clarence Cup final at Cliftonville.

Tom Kennedy, a member of Strangford Lough Yacht Club, was overall winner of the National Flying Fifteen Championships which were held at Whiterock in mid-

July and promoted by Strangford Lough YC.

Pearl Boyd, from Ballywilliam, Donaghadee, was the new Irish Girls Golf Champion, winning the title at Elm Park, Dublin, in August, with a 4&3 victory over Patricia Atkinson (Ballycastle). Pearl was a member of Donaghadee Golf Club.

Lady Bury, president of Ards FC, reaffirmed a previous assurance given by her late father that the club would have the use of Castlereagh Park for a nominal rent for as long as it was in existence.

Ards FC player/manager Tommy Ewing was sacked in mid-October following a series of poor results. He moved over to neighbours Bangor as a player. No replacement had been appointed by the end of the year.

Tower United reached the quarter-final of the Irish Junior Cup in mid-March 1962, only to be beaten 4-1 by Newry United. Back (from left): T. Moore, H. Ritchie, T. Graham, N. Patton, J. Gunning, J. Weir. Front: A. McDowell (manager), Master Dunlop (mascot), J. Ritchie, P. Devaney, J. Murphy, W. Robinson and T. Reid. *30-12-2*

Members of the Guildhall (Newtownards) league championship team who received their awards at the Newtownards Temperance Darts League presentations in the Queen's Hall on 20 March 1962. Included is league president Mr D. Corry. *30-72-3*

The Ards Technical School team became the first winners of the new Minor Technical Football Cup when they defeated Lisburn 2-0 at Solitude on 11 April 1962.
32-29-3

Members of Scrabo Darts Club, winners of the Sportsman's Cup and the McKenna and McGinley Cup, as well as being runners-up in the Newtownards Vintners' Cup, received their trophies during a social evening in the clubrooms on 3 May 1962.
33-88-2

Members of First Donaghadee Old Boys' Association with the trophies they received at the annual dinner on 11 May 1962. Back (from left): William McCaw (chairman), William McNeice (secretary), John Scott, Rev. Glenfield. Front: Rev. Swenarton, Campbell Bell (draughts), John Haisley (all-rounder, darts, billiards), John Bell (footballer of the year) and Larry Kitzler (table tennis).
34-56-1

Cup and medal winners at the Regent House School sports, which were held at the end of May 1962. Back, house medals (from left): W. M. Higginson, Jennifer Brown, C. Moore, Jennifer Beckett, C. Coey. Middle row: Geraldine Kavanagh, Helen Warden, A. W. D. Mitchell, Sally Laverty, S. W. Brown, Arlene Cromie, C. Thompson (cross-country winner). Front, trophy winners: G. F. Gedge (Junior Boys), Noel Wilson (Intermediate Girls), C. G. Kerr (Chronicle Shield), Judy Gamble (Maxwell Trophy), N. Barr (Intermediate Boys), Pauline McMaster (Junior Girls). *35-79-1*

Members of Tower United FC with office-bearers and Mr Dessie Hunter (back, fourth from left) after they received their medals and the Gibson Cup at the end of June 1962. Back (from left): T. Moore, H. Ritchie, T. Graham, D. Hunter, T. Reid, J. Gunning, J. Weir, T. McKibben, A. Dunlop. Front: J. Ritchie, J. Murphy, A. McDowell (manager), N. Patton (captain), W. Robinson, P. Devaney, J. Patton and T. McKee (chairman). *38-22-3*

The Ards cricket team which reached the final of the Minor Cup after defeating the News Letter by eight wickets in late July 1962. Back (from left): T. Savage (umpire), T. C. McBride, R. Dunn, T. West, D. Trolan, R. Braidner (umpire). Middle: W. Montgomery, J. Anderson, N. Lilburn (captain), W. Shaw, J. Clegg. Front: G. Hull and E. McAuley. *40-96-2*

Members of the Ards Olympic football team, winners of the Ards Summer League in August 1962.
42-62-1

Ards Ladies Hockey Club members pictured at a practice game at their Comber Road grounds in September 1962.
44-85-2

Scrabo Golf Club captain Mr T. B. Reid with members who took part in Captain's Day on 15 September 1962.
44-92-2

Donaghadee Ladies who defeated Ards IIs 4-1 at Newtownards at the end of October 1962. Back (from left): S. Crosbie, O. Thompson, M. Ardis, M. Bell, P. Scott, E. McConkey. Front: C. Donnan, J. Kimm, P. Edwards, M. Woods and K. Black. *47-92-3*

The Castle Gardens School team in their new skip in 1962. Back (from left): B. Burns, I. Burns, D. Campbell, D. McAuley, A. Walker, K. Maxwell. Front: W. Hollinger, A. Ballantine (vice-captain), G. Blair (captain), R. Edmonds and F. Crawford. *28-35-2*

Industry and Commerce in The Ards in the Sixties

John Rankin

remembers... Farming

John Rankin is pictured here (second left) with trophy recipients who attended the Millisle Young Farmers' Club parents' night in the Lecture Hall, Carrowdore, in March 1967. From left: Anne Robinson, John Rankin, Elizabeth Brown, Joe Caddoo and Jeanette Finlay. *160-61-3*

I was in my late teens as we entered the Sixties. I'd left Regent House a few years earlier and was working full time on the farm.

In those days it was almost compulsory to join the Young Farmers' Club movement so I became a member of Millisle YFC. There was great competition at that time between the different clubs in the area. Since then, though, Comber, Ballygrainey and indeed Millisle have all disappeared but I'm glad to report that Newtownards, Donaghadee and Ballywalter are still going strong.

John A. Rankin OBE FRAgS has lived on the same farm for over 70 years, from baby to pensioner. It now comprises some 200 cows plus followers and is run by his son Jason.

Keenly involved in farming 'politics', John is a lifelong member of the Ulster Farmers' Union, reaching the position of president in 1995-96. During his term he was instrumental in

In the Sixties the young farmers held dances in places such as the Ashleigh Ballroom in Millisle, the Queen's Hall in Newtownards and the Andrews Memorial Hall in Comber, which were always well attended. They were supposed to start at 9pm and finish at 2am but it was usually around 10.30pm before they got going and then there was a break for supper for everyone at around 11.30pm.

In addition, there were inter-club socials through the week so it's hardly surprising they were often nicknamed

Competitors in a Donaghadee Young Farmers' Club fancy dress parade paused for a picture at the Club Hall, Ballyvester, on 23 January 1962.
27-44-2

'the marriage bureau' as so many members met their future life partner at such events.

Stock judging was another inter-club competitive event which was a definite must for any budding farmer worth his salt although quite often the girls could give the boys a serious challenge for the prizes!

Quiz nights could be great craic and helped us to while away the hours in good company in those days before television held sway. Public speaking and group debating were among pursuits in the Sixties that have actually stood the test of time and definitely helped to develop the confidence of participants.

Members of the cast of Killinchy YFC's production of *Watch It Sailor* in March 1964.
87-63-2

Stooking corn at the Ballyrickard farm of James Donnan in August 1961 are David, John, John (sen.) and Samuel Donnan and Denis Lavery.
54-2-17

Finally, drama and taking part in plays and sketches of various lengths were a regular pursuit and I remember clearly spending many hours rehearsing lines to the seagulls following my tractor and ploughing down the furrows while balancing a book on the steering wheel!

On the farms of the Ards and beyond, new diesel-fuelled tractors were replacing their older petrol and TVO (tractor vaporising oil) predecessors. Back then they still had no cab so on a cold winter's day multiple layers of coats and scarves were necessary protection from the elements as there's never been too much shelter from wind on the Peninsula.

Gordon, Robert and Edwin Gaw, planting new potatoes on the farm of Mr J. McAlpine, Ballyrickard, Comber in 1961.
95-1-3

If a new tractor was bought all the neighbours had to have a look and admire and examine the different models in their gleaming colours. These can still be seen at the many vintage rallies that are held across Northern Ireland at the present time.

Sadly, my father died in 1962 and, as his only son, I had to take control of the farm at a very early age. These were also the years when combine harvesters were being introduced, with the green trailed Activs and the cream and maroon Danias competing with the red self-propelled Massey Fergusons as to which could do the best job under the poor weather conditions that tend to be the norm at harvest time.

This represented a huge change in harvesting technique from the very labour-intensive system of stooking the sheaves that fell behind the binder into neat rows. Then after further ripening they would be built on to carts and then forked into sheds or onto stacks until they would be threshed later, at some time during the autumn or winter.

Prizewinners from the cereal growing competition organised by Donaghadee UFU are pictured at the branch's second annual dinner at the end of January 1967 in the New Mount Royal Hotel. From left: Jack Crawford, Ballyhay (first, oats); Samuel McAuley, Ballyhay (third, barley); Howard Turney, Killaughey (second, oats, and second, barley); Walter Brown, Killaughey (first, barley); David McWha, farm manager, Portavo (third, oats). *157-41-1*

The 'Ards Maltings' was still a major player in the market for high quality barley and exercised a great influence on the crops that were grown. The annual cereal growing competitions, which were organised by the local UFU branches, were always keenly contested. Each branch had its own competition with valuable cups to be presented at the annual social and dance.

The final would see judges arriving from further afield to admire and place in order the winning fields of grain from each of the Newtownards, Donaghadee, Ballygrainey and Six Road Ends, Mid Ards and Upper Ards branches of the UFU. It was not unknown for some of the farmers to drive round the narrow roads of the Peninsula on a Sunday, seeking out the competing fields to check if the judges had got it right.

Potatoes were still being grown on most farms – especially for the early market as in a good year with a good price these could leave enough profit to help purchase a new tractor or motor car.

It was in the winter of early 1963 that we had the last great snowfall on the Peninsula. The lane to our farm was filled right up to the top of the hedges with snowdrifts. I remember how after going through hedges and across a couple of fields I joined a few of our neighbours to fight

setting up the Family Farm Committee (the aim being to involve more women) and was heavily involved in tackling the BSE crisis.

Over the years he has chaired the UFU's Group, County Organisation, Dairy and Animal Health Committees.

Between 1997 and 2005 John was a main Board member of NFU Mutual Insurance.

John was a trustee of ARINI from 1997 to 2006, led the employers' side of the Wages Board from 1998 to 2008, and was an AFBI Board member from 2006 to 2012.

Additionally, he was a Rural Support Board member from 2003 to 2012, including a six-year term as chairman, which commenced in 2006.

John was a member of the Family Farm Development Board, which was set up to assist small farm diversity, from 1996 to 2008, and is a past president of the Ulster Grassland Society. Indeed, he was named the first Grassland Farmer of the Year.

John was the first chairman of LANTRA NI, a skills council for the land-based sector, and he was involved in setting up Agrisearch, which collects voluntary levies for research purposes.

In recognition of his work on these various bodies John was awarded an OBE for services to Agriculture and the Rural Community in the 2000 New Year Honours List.

Outside farming, John was a governor of North Down and Ards FE College from 1998 to 2006 and was a member and past president of Ards Rotary Club.

John Rankin

our way to Newtownards, clearing the road as we went with our tractors.

There were few four-wheel drive tractors in those days. However, we did eventually manage to meet up with the Co-op lorry at Castlereagh Park to get ours and our neighbour's milk away to help feed the folk in Belfast. We were also able to bring back some much-needed groceries to the Ballyblack community.

The mid-Sixties witnessed the acceptance of silage-making as the best way forward for livestock production. This method of preserving grass greatly increased the production of milk and beef during winter time. Cows were also being released from their tied stall byres to roam freely in cubicle sheds, thereby helping to reduce the heavy work needed each day to carry the manure from behind the cows in a wheel barrow.

Milk tankers were starting to replace the traditional can lorries on the roads round the Ards. They were a much smaller version of the very large tankers that travel our roads today.

Sadly, this marked the beginning of the end of mixed farming as it had existed for generations. Farmers started to specialise in either milk, beef or arable crops so the old ways of keeping hens, pigs, cows, beef, sheep and arable crops on the same small farms slowly but surely disappeared.

To sum up the Sixties, it would be fair to say the decade was very much about the increasing speed of change. For generations farmers had managed their farms with crop rotations and multiple enterprises. Those who did not change and adapt would slowly but surely disappear.

It was also a time of opportunity and I know many of my fellow farmers enjoyed a great deal of satisfaction from their endeavours, both then and since. Friendships formed through the YFC all those years ago still continue over 50 years later. The one thing I did learn in those formative years is the more you put into life the more you get out of it.

Derek Harkness

remembers... Newtownards Shops

When asked to put together some thoughts for *The Ards in the Sixties*, it brought quite forcibly to mind the fact I'm now one of the old hands in the local retail sector, having worked in Newtownards for around 52 years. On that basis it should be relatively easy to share a few of my memories going back to the 1960s.

At the beginning of that decade I started work in Drysdale's of Regent Street – now Cafolla's. They were good times in the Sixties; our days seemed to pass at a much more leisurely pace and a big night out for many of us was at the Queen's Hall on Saturdays. Business in the town in the days before the shopping centres was nice and it was friendly.

Derek Harkness with the statue of Blair Mayne in pride of place at Conway Square.

The over-the-counter sales style that existed for so many years prior to the self-service era was something of a therapy for customer and sales assistant alike, and there were plenty of characters on both sides of the counter. I well recall being told how a local shopkeeper once spent all weekend designing a large poster for his window, only to realise the words read: "James Brown's trousers down, come in and see the value."

I could not say for sure if the poster ever went on display,

Born and raised in Carrowdore, Derek was educated at Carrowdore Primary School, Donaghadee High and Newtownards Tech. before commencing employment, aged just 15, at Drysdale's Drapery Store in Regent Street.

After gaining further experience with Johnson and

Phillips, the electrical engineers and cabinet makers on the Comber Road, Derek decided in 1968 to strike out on his own, opening a new business, Derek Harkness Menswear, in Frances Street.

Always taking a keen interest in the life of the local community, Derek soon became involved with the town's Chamber of Trade. Indeed, it was thanks to his enthusiasm and organisational abilities that he was a popular choice for the position of president of the NI Chamber of Trade in 1980.

That same instinctive drive again came to the fore in the late 1990s, when Derek was one of the main instigators and founders of the Blair Mayne Association, which succeeded in getting much overdue public recognition for this locally-born hero.

Today Derek lives in Newtownards with his wife Norma and although both are officially retired, between the demands of family life – they have three children and five grandchildren – and work with various civic bodies, life is busier than ever.

but I've certainly heard the story repeated on more than one occasion!

The camaraderie that existed throughout the business community was excellent, with everyone being on first name terms – from the solicitors to the grocers. I remember looking out of Drysdale's shop door as local dentist Mr Mayne was passing and bidding him a good morning. Bearing in mind he was a professional, and me barely out of my teens, I called him Mr Mayne, but he looked me straight in the eye and said: "Douglas is fine, young man." That was so typical of the Sixties.

As apprentices we particularly looked forward to Christmas for the many and varied Christmas presents we received from the travellers who visited our shops through the year. It was very pleasant to receive a pair of socks or maybe a tie – some might say that's no big deal today but it certainly was to me at a time when my weekly wage was £1.18s. And yet money wasn't everything; it was important but it didn't rule our lives.

Continuing this much cherished walk down memory lane, my thoughts turn to places like the Oak Bar at Regent Street (now Stewarts Solicitors) and a pub called McAlea's (now the Fox and Hounds/Romas), while where B&M Bargains is now located, in the Sixties there were two little shops set back in from the footpath. Between them a photographer, Jim Gray, had a display cabinet showing his work. I believe the *Northern Whig* occasionally published his pictures.

The Arcadia Newsagency. *Newtownards Chronicle* picture

Belvoir Lettings was Tom Killock's Chemists and the Cancer Charity shop was the original Scrabo Electrical before it moved on up Regent Street, where it remains today. Back in the Sixties the management there brought in some big stars such as Dickie Valentine to make guest appearances – no doubt to promote their latest records which were being sold in the shop. Those were certainly big days in Regent Street!

Conway Square was a busy place in the Sixties. Charlotte Heron's (now the Progressive Building Society) sold fish and chips and ice cream and was also a greengrocer – that was some mix of a shop.

The two Cafolla's, the big shop around where Toy Town is now located, and the smaller which is still going strong, attracted customers from far and wide for their ice cream.

Tates Bar and Woolworth's at Conway Square. *Newtownards Chronicle Picture*

Next door to the larger Cafolla's was Cecil Wilson's drapery shop, where Muriel Galway worked. During the decade she became a very famous singer, firstly with the Dave Glover Showband and then she went on to sing for Ireland in the 1969 Eurovision Song Contest.

Anderson's Chemists is still in the same place, while on the lower corner of that side of the Square was McMurray's newsagents, where we got all the bits and pieces we needed for 'Night Tech'. The Tech back then, now known as the Ards Arena, was located in South Street.

High Street back in the Sixties was much envied elsewhere in Northern Ireland since it had both Wardens (which is still there today) and Glasgow's (now Menary's).

My lasting memory of Glasgow's was of pre-Christmas trips there with my mother to visit the upstairs toy department; I suppose she was sounding out my brother and me for

Glasgow's at High Street. *Newtownards Chronicle Picture*

Donaldson's Garage
Newtownards Chronicle Picture

Santa, but our choices rarely changed – either Meccano or Hornby train sets!

Next door to Glasgow's was, I think, the world famous Mairs Tweed House (now Hanna and Browne), where the weaving house to the rear of the big shop was the envy of any town in the British Isles. Next door to it was Bowdens.

This nostalgic journey takes me on to Frances Street, which was a vibrant place in the Sixties with its small communities of houses and businesses. Indeed, very often both the business and the family home were combined.

My thoughts turn to Alex Heron's flat (now Trophies by Design above the Ink Shop and the Kodak Lens Centre), Doggart's Undertakers (now In Sport) and the Doggart family home on the lower side of the *Newtownards Chronicle* offices. Mr Doggart of that same family was its Editor at that time.

On the upper side of the old Electricity Board premises (now a Turkish barbers) was Hugh Thompson's wallpaper shop (now a pizza house) and, as was the case elsewhere, Mr Thompson lived on the premises.

Across the road there was Joseph Cafolla with his son Frank next door. On down the street, on the other side, was the Rice family living on the bar premises still occupied to this day by Brenda Rice. And further down Frances Street was Cherry's Chemists (now the Wool Shop) next to the Ulster Bank.

It has been a wonderful experience casting my thoughts down memory lane; I think I will do it more often.

Paul McAuley

remembers... The Funfair at Millisle

Millisle was booming during the Sixties; it had seven caravan parks and holidaymakers and day trippers alike all flocked to the seaside village. In about 1956 my late father, Benny McAuley, had set up a funfair right on the beach and for the next 18 years or so it became the tourist attraction now so fondly remembered by many people.

Paul, second from right, and friends

Paul, the only child of Benny and Eileen McAuley, was born in Ards Hospital in 1950.

The family lived for a time in Newtownards before moving to his mother's native Belfast. His parents subsequently separated when Paul was 12, with the result that he went to live with his father and grandmother, Lily McAuley, in West Street, Newtownards.

After leaving Movilla High School in Newtownards, Paul began working full-time with his father on the amusements at Millisle Beach, spending the wintertime

As a teenager in the Sixties, I worked with my father and we lived in a wagon on the beach. It was wonderful to wake up every morning to the sound of the lapping waves. We used to stay from Easter until the end of summer – you couldn't stay any longer because of the high tides.

One year we did stay too long. It was September and I was awoken during the night by a banging noise. I went to investigate and found it was the gas bottle floating in the tide and hitting underneath the caravan!

At the beach funfair we had chairplanes, swingboats, darts, hoopla, fish and spinner stalls, a monoplane and car rides, while my granny, Lily McAuley, ran a little canteen.

We used to employ young fellas to work on the stalls – indeed one of my greatest memories from the Sixties is of Gary Moore, who later became a member of Thin Lizzy and one of the greatest rock guitarists in the world.

The beach at Millisle with the funfair in the background

working at markets and collecting scrap.

The former Ashleigh Ballroom has since been demolished and replaced by a housing development.

Paul still lives in Millisle with his wife Margaret. The couple have five children, Mark, Amy, Lewis, Graham and Laura.

Originally from Belfast, Gary was spending the summer with his granny, who lived at Shore Street in Millisle. I'll never forget the first time I saw him. I was 16 or 17. It was a glorious day and we were standing under cover when this young guy walked along the promenade wearing a three-piece check suit. He had long hair and an earring. He came down the steps and asked: "Any chance of getting a job here?" We said there certainly was and gave him a job on the darts stall.

Gary only stayed a few weeks but in that space of time I got to know him well. I loved playing the drums myself and by then we also owned the Ashleigh Ballroom in Millisle. The two of us had a few nights where we went in there and he played guitar and I was on the drums, with me of course never realising what he was going to go on to become. Wow! He was brilliant and so beyond his time.

Gary was a really nice fella and got to know all the lads around Millisle. He was just one of us whenever he came back to visit. The last time I saw him was in 1968 after he'd been in Cork where he joined a band called Skid Row. I remember he came walking up the street wearing a pair of red flares, a blue coat and a Tommy Cooper hat.

I couldn't believe I missed meeting up with him during a later visit. My job on a Sunday night was to take the workers home. That particular time I got back around midnight and my father told me my friend Gary had visited while I was away and "had a wee half-caste guy with him with fluffy hair called Phil Lynott." I was gutted I'd missed them.

I never saw Gary again and was very upset when I heard he'd died suddenly on holiday in Spain in February 2011, aged just 58. I am so proud to say that I knew Gary Moore.

We had some fun times on that beach and we got to meet so many people. Many a time I had to pull cars out with a tractor after the owners drove onto the strand and then got stuck in the soft sand!

Walking on that sand all day used to pull the legs out of you; at night we would take off our boots and shoes and dip our feet in the sea to ease them. I'll have to say there was nothing nicer than closing time when we turned off the ride engines and there was total silence. Then it was time for something to eat; we lived on fish and chips!

I remember one time we were asleep in the wagon when there was a knock on the door at about 7am. My father opened it to find a police sergeant and a USPCA officer who said they had reason to believe he was keeping 30 horses that had been neither fed nor watered. My father, managing to keep a straight face, replied he'd no idea when they were last fed. The USPCA man asked where the horses were being kept and my father explained they were in a tent and offered to show them to him.

He walked over to the carousel and hauled back the canvas we always pulled over it at night. The very embarrassed pair quickly disappeared; someone had obviously phoned for a gag to say the merry-go-round horses were being neglected!

At the end of each season we had to wash everything down to remove the sand and salt, otherwise it would rot. Then we had about a fortnight off before we were back painting and doing repairs in readiness for the next year.

My father was known by everyone and was a colourful character. Originally from Newtownards, both he and his father before him were scrap dealers and they ran an antiques shop attached to their house at West Street.

As a boy, my dad ran away four or five times to join the

circus. On the final occasion that my grandfather went to get him back, the circus owner, Mr Duffy, told him: "If we get him a wee wagon, we'll look after him." So my father stayed, played in the band and did a bit of clowning while touring all over Ireland.

Back home in Newtownards one winter, he was walking 12 donkeys along Regent Street when a pretty shop worker with long ginger hair like Maureen O'Hara's caught his eye as she stood at the front door of Stewart's Cash Stores. They eventually married and I came along.

My mother and I used to join my dad and the circus during the summer; I so loved the sweet smell of the grass inside the tent. I also vaguely remember as a toddler sitting in my feeding chair one day when a baboon, which had escaped from its cage, ran into our wagon. My mother had been cooking dinner but dropped everything and ran out, leaving me behind. Apparently when they returned the baboon was feeding me!

At the time my father drove an ex-Army jeep and lived in a stainless steel caravan. It didn't matter how big a star you were, at the end of a show everyone had to don a boiler suit and help with the 'pull down.'

After packing up, my father was the first to leave and he was always on the road about 4am, heading to the next destination. People back then used to think it was funny to turn signposts the wrong way. It was my dad's job to stop every so often and to drop a grass sod on the road as a sign to the others of the correct direction.

I was about five or six when my father left the circus to become a professional accordionist. He travelled all over the country doing cabaret shows and one year even got a summer season at Newcastle seafront with the famous Pierrots. He was billed as 'Tony Valento, all the way from Italy' and appeared complete with the tan and curls. All went well until his cover was blown when some of his mates from Newtownards happened into the show and as soon as my dad stepped onto the stage started to bawl out: "Ach luk, it's only Benny McAuley fae Newtown!" He had to tell them to be quiet – they knew he was no more Italian than the man down the street!

Eventually, my father had the opportunity to buy a small lot of show equipment. The local Council gave him permission to set them up in Millisle and that's how he got started there, finally leaving the beach in 1974.

It was around 1965 that my father had bought the Ashleigh Ballroom. It was the only big hall in the vicinity and was used for everything – even the Rev. Ian Paisley preached there. Mostly it was used as a dance hall and at weekends the place was literally bunged to the doors – though sometimes, when fights broke out, there could be a bloodbath.

I remember 1967 as the flower power era. It was a golden time with both The Beatles and The Rolling Stones at the height of their fame and, of course, the Troubles hadn't started in Northern Ireland. Millisle was so busy; it was fabulous.

Paul McAuley

However, the dancehalls were becoming less popular and many of the dances ended with the arrival of what we'd see as the modern age and the advance of television. The Ashleigh also closed around that time and we eventually converted the ballroom into an amusement arcade offering bigger rides such as the Waltzers. That's where I met my lovely wife Margaret while she was on holiday in Millisle.

My father died in February 1986, aged just 57. In line with his wishes, his coffin was conveyed for burial to Movilla Cemetery in Newtownards on the back of a four-wheel cart.

I continued to run the amusements until 1989 when I went out on my own. I now have a beautiful little ride, comprising an antique set of hobby horses, which I take to fairs, markets and shows all over the place. I'm also a member of the Showmen's Guild and I do a bit of scrap dealing.

I'm carrying on from where my grandfather and my father left off. It's in my blood and I'm very proud of what I do.

Jim Shannon

remembers... The Family Business in Ballywalter

Jim Shannon

Educated at Ballywalter Primary School and Coleraine Academical Institution, Strangford MP Jim Shannon was first elected to Ards Borough Council in 1985, serving as Mayor in 1991-1992. He remained a member of the Council until 2010 when, after 25 years of service, he stood down after being elected to Parliament.

He was elected as a member of the Northern Ireland Forum for Political Dialogue in 1996, remaining until it completed its work in 1998. He was subsequently elected to the Northern Ireland Assembly, representing Strangford.

I was four years old when we moved to Ballywalter in 1959. My parents had bought the shop, previously owned by the Graceys, at 78 Main Street in the village. The shop was a general merchant's where you could buy anything from a needle to a spade, or from a tin of beans to a bag of coal; if we didn't have it in stock we would get it for you – nothing was a problem.

My parents worked long and arduous hours, my father in the coal lorry and my mother in the shop. I can well recall the bad winter of 1963 with the snow piled up against the windows; at five feet high it seemed to tower over me.

In primary school our principal was Mr Whisker and his punishments for any wrongdoing were highly effective – a swift clip around the ear or rulers rapped on the knuckles. That would never be allowed these days but back then it was just the norm. At school I can recall answering questions in my native tongue, using Ulster-Scots words learnt from my grandmother and mother, and being told it was not proper English. What a change from today when the Ulster-Scots language is coming back and is in everyday use.

The coal business my dad ran involved three merchants in the village, Morrison, Bryce and Shannon, and between them they had a coal boat that arrived at the harbour in Ballywalter. The coal had to be removed manually from the base of the boat into a large container and then conveyed to a lorry on the quay.

My dad employed two of the hardest working men I ever had the privilege of knowing, Alfy Jeffrey and Sandy (Alexander) McCready. To clear a coal boat by hand took a strong back and considerable strength – and those men had it in abundance. At the end of the day it would take as many as three baths to remove all the soot and coal dust from their skin.

I can recall a time of great excitement, back in the 1960s, when the crew of my dad's coal lorry left the handbrake off and the vehicle careered down the Dunover Road and into two houses at the bottom of the hill. Both of the houses are now long since away.

As the years went by one of the merchants dropped out, then another, and my dad was left as the sole local supplier. However, the cost of a full ship-load of coal was simply too much for one person to manage and deliveries to Ballywalter Harbour drew to a halt – it was truly the end of an era for the village.

I have so many fond memories of that period. As a boy growing up in Ballywalter, with two busy working parents, Alice Ramsey was always there to look after us. I knew her as Aunt Alice and her husband was Uncle David, even though they were not actually blood relatives – but as far as we were concerned they were just like real family. He had driven an ambulance during the Second World War and often kept us entertained with his stories of wartime courage and bravery – so much so that more than anything else we all wanted to be soldiers when we were older.

George and Maggie Donnan, both familiar figures in Ballywalter, were fervent Ards supporters and rare was the Saturday night when she didn't call into the shop to eagerly tell us the score from that day's match. She and George travelled everywhere on a Quigley motor bike, with

Within the Assembly Jim served on both the Public Accounts Committee and the Agriculture Committee. He was re-elected in both 2003 and 2007, but stepped down from the Assembly in 2010 after he was elected to Parliament.

Living near Greyabbey with his wife Sandra, Jim has three sons and is now a grandfather to Katie-Leigh.

Coal boat at Ballywalter pier

Newtownards and Kircubbin people enjoy themselves at the Ballywalter 'field' on 12 July 1963. *70-2-1*

Maggie wearing her red and blue Ards scarf – some three times her height and not unlike the one Tom Baker's Doctor Who would wear a decade later – wrapped round and round her neck.

She enjoyed telling us about the time during an Ards v. Glentoran match when two visiting supporters grabbed each end of the scarf and pulled it – with dear old Maggie caught in the middle. Thankfully she survived the experience and something tells me those Glensmen headed for home knowing never to tangle again with our Maggie!

Walter McCready was another local character. In all conditions, rain or shine, he would ride his bicycle with his shirt open from neck to navel. We could never understand why he didn't feel the cold, but then men like Walter were a hardy bunch in those days.

Then there was Bobby Dunn who ran a shoe repair shop where nothing was ever thrown out – it was all patched up or repaired. Come to think of it, my very first bike actually turned out to be the best I ever had. Even though it was assembled from parts of other bikes it was well known as the quickest in the area; I could beat everyone on it.

Then as now I loved the time approaching the Twelfth of July when the Orange Lodges and accompanying bands would parade every night. Ballywalter was certainly a great place to be brought up in; they were simpler times back in the Sixties and even though we may not have had much I would suggest we were much happier then.

Desmond Rainey

remembers... Comber

In 1960 I was a pupil at Comber Primary School doing battle with vulgar fractions and finite verbs, and in the process stretching the patience of my poor teachers, first Sam McGibney and later Davy McRoberts.

Norman Nevin was headmaster, and we lived in dread of becoming a "bloodstain on yonder wall". But Norman really had our interests at heart and gave up his time on Saturday mornings to provide extra coaching for those taking the Qualifying Examination. Like myself, he was interested in history, and from him I learned about our famous general, Sir Robert Rollo Gillespie, perched high above Comber Square. He was fond of reciting the poem *Gillespie* by Sir Henry Newbolt. I remember also that he had a collection of clocks.

On Empire Day we would make our way in an orderly procession to a service in one of the churches, while on other occasions the cinema was the destination. Comber Cinema was one of the great attractions of the Sixties with queues along the street for the big blockbuster movies. In June, Sports Day was held, usually at the ground of North Down Cricket Club, a club with a glorious past although alas in the Sixties it had fallen on hard times. The sports began with the fancy dress parade, followed by the races, including sack, potato and spoon, sprints, and a parents' event.

Desmond Rainey is a retired civil servant, having worked in the Department of Agriculture and Rural Development for over 40 years.

He grew up in and still lives in Comber. He is an elder in Second Presbyterian Church, Comber, and has in the past sung in the church choir, participated in amateur dramatics, and played badminton and tennis.

Desmond has always been fascinated with history and was a founder member of Comber Historical Society in 2000. Since that time he has been kept busy researching Comber's past, presenting talks and giving guided walks round the town.

He is also an avid collector

of old postcards of Northern Ireland (some 15,000 to date), photographs of Comber and music of the 1950s and 1960s. He is the co-author of two books – *A Taste of Old Comber* (with Len Ball) and *A Chronicle of Comber, Town of Thomas Andrews, Shipbuilder* (with Laura Spence).

In 1962 I transferred to the 'big school' – Regent House in Newtownards, which had just moved into new premises. Each morning a convoy of double-decker buses transported crowds of eager youngsters to their destination. We used to vie for the honour of being the first bus to arrive (I don't know why), and there was an unwritten rule that you weren't allowed upstairs until Fourth Form.

I attended Second Comber Presbyterian Church where the Rev. J. E. Jones was minister until he retired in 1969 after 42 years. Woe betide anyone found talking during his sermon, because Mr Jones was known to stop when in full flow and administer a solemn warning to the offenders. I remember Sunday School teachers such as Dave Browne and Harold Cameron, who took the Bible Class. He was also principal of the Intermediate (Secondary) School.

Cast members from the pantomime *The Babes In The Wood*, which was presented by Second Comber Church Guild in December 1967. *175-58-1*

I frequented the fortnightly meetings of the Young People's Guild with its plays, quizzes, debates, etc. A highlight of the year was the pantomime produced by Mary Minnis. The Guild met in the Smyth Hall, and I was intrigued by a tablet to the memory of John Smyth who was praised for his munificence. There's a big word for a young schoolboy. I remember also that when you looked out the windows of the Youth Hall you could see the Distillery Dam down below. This is now the church car park.

The Sunday School social (or soiree) was held in the Andrews Hall. Here you were handed a bag of buns and got your prize for attendance. The Hall itself had great significance. It was a memorial to Thomas Andrews who had designed the *Titanic* and who drowned when it hit an iceberg and sank in 1912. The Andrews family were (and still are) active in Comber, and Willie, Thomas' youngest brother, could be seen being chauffeured around.

Leisure time was spent playing football 'down the bank', as the area in front of our house was known, or in summer time there was tennis at the courts beside the Andrews Hall. Betty McLaughlin coached the juniors on a Friday night. In recent years her son Brian was coach for the Ulster rugby squad.

The newly-installed slide at the Comber playground proved very popular with local children in February 1961. *31-3-3*

Occasionally Duffy's Circus came to town and the big tent was pitched in either Park Way or on the ground known as the Holm in front of Lower Crescent. I can remember the ponies and some more exotic animals such as camels being watered down at the river. The Holm was another football venue, and further attraction was added when a playground was laid out with swings, a roundabout, slide, swingboats and a witch's hat.

Doughty swimmers at Island Hill, Comber, in late September 1961. *6-2-18*

There was a variety of walks. Island Hill was a popular seaside destination in the Sixties, often to be seen buzzing with activity in glorious sunshine. You could have mistaken it for the Costa Del Sol. Contrast this with the heavy snow of 1963, when Comber was completely cut off. No school for over a week! You could also walk round the 40-acre field where the Copeland and Dermot Estates were later built, or down Cherryvalley past the haunted house – or so we liked to pretend. And there were the swans and ducks at the dams in Laureldale.

The bed of the old railway track between Killinchy Street and Newtownards Road was another favourite outing; you could imagine steam trains chugging along here in bygone days. Part of the line (Killinchy Street to Belfast Road) was converted into a bypass in 1962, but for a time some

The Glen Road bridge, which was under construction in April 1961, would carry the new Comber by-pass road, which for most of its route would make use of the defunct railway line. The old Comber railway station is visible in the background. 24-2-7

of the old station buildings remained.

The Sixties was a different world. Some people went off potato picking in the summer. Personally, I preferred just eating them and where better to go than Davy's Chip Shop (in High Street, later Bridge Street), where you always got free samples while you waited. You could see the huntsmen ride down the road past our house with their pack of hounds, and a herd of cows being driven into town was not unknown. Upping the pace slightly, there was the annual Tour of the North bicycle race passing through. In the evenings you might be treated to the skirl of the bagpipes as a 'kiltie' put in a bit of extra practice.

What about industry? The distilleries had closed down by this time, but the buildings still remained as a reminder of the famous Old Comber Whiskey. There was of course the Andrews Flax Spinning Mill on the Ballygowan Road, employing 500 people in its heyday producing linen yarn. And there was the Albion Stitching in Castle Lane; the foundation stone for a new factory was laid in 1960. The Old Grain Store stood near the banks of the Enler. We knew it as 'The Piggery' because in recent years two retired Indian Army colonels had kept pigs there; one of these men was the father of former Lib Dem leader Paddy Ashdown.

Shops included that of Jim Milling in the Square, a business proclaimed on a plaque to date from 1731, while the impressive frontage of Macdonald's shop in Mill Street looked back to Edwardian days. Jim Miskelly sold newspapers and confectionery in Castle Street close to Smyth & McClure's grocery shop, which was part of the old Andrews house of Uraghmore (the place of the big yew trees). McWhinney's butcher's shop, then as now, was at the corner of Castle Street and High Street. Kane of

Comber was well known in the motor trade.

The Post Office was in the Square, and one of its postmen was Willie Brown, at 4ft. 8ins. the smallest postman in Ireland. Tommy Calvert could be seen around the town doing bread deliveries for Inglis, while Barry Millar brought doorstep deliveries on his electric milk float. For a haircut you could choose between Martin Smith, Robbie Wright or Sam Brown. Doctors included Brian Henry (and his wife Muriel Gault), Dr Murphy and Dr Gibson, who owned a mink farm.

Comber postman Willie Brown

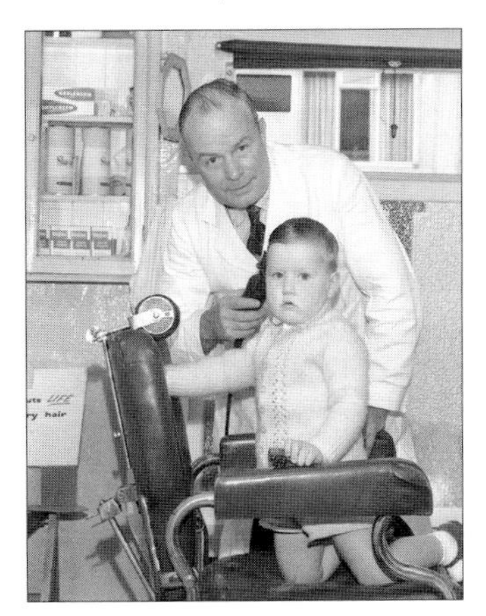

Barber Sam Brown 45-19-3

Some new buildings were erected, such as the new church hall at First Comber in 1960/61 and the Health Centre and Library in 1967. The latter became another source of amusement for me. The Baptist congregation was formed in 1966 and met initially in the Laureldale Hall. But imagine a town without the Enler Car Park and Supervalu, when Bridge Street Link didn't exist and cars parked in the Square. This was also where the buses left from, because there was no depot as yet in Killinchy Street.

Just to mention a couple of buildings now gone. One was the Thompson Hall in Mill Street which became Comber Technical College; the other was the Methodist Church in Bridge Street with its date of 1820 and the message proclaiming 'Glory to God in the Highest'. Also worthy of mention is the cobbled footpath outside the house called *Aureen* in the Square with the figure of a hound chasing a hare, and of course the town's War Memorial which was the scene of services on Remembrance Sunday and on 1 July to commemorate the Battle of the Somme. My memory doesn't stretch back quite that far, but I do remember the Sixties rather fondly.

Margaret Cavan Day

remembers... The Chronicle

Margaret at a fashion show organised by Georgina Foulis in the Town Hall. *Newtownards Chronicle picture*

Margaret Cavan Day was born and raised in Newtownards, the daughter of Harry and Anna Cavan, and younger sister of Clara and Jean.

At the age of 16 she began working as a junior reporter for the *Newtownards Chronicle*, moving on to the *News Letter* in Belfast as a news reporter. After

Newtownards was a happening place at the start of the swinging Sixties. Manufacturing jobs were plentiful, business was booming, Ards Football Club was filling Castlereagh Park for home games, church pews were still reasonably full, and in 1961, Georgina Foulis, a factory worker, became the first woman Mayor in the town's history.

In the 50-plus years since that historic election Newtownards has changed dramatically. The one constant, the eyes and ears of the community, then as now, has been the *Newtownards Chronicle*. Two years prior to Georgina taking office, at the age of 16, I began working at the newspaper. I was quite likely the youngest female reporter in the country.

Living two streets apart, we often walked to work together, the Lady Mayor and the teenage reporter. Little happened in town that we didn't hear about on those early morning walks down Marquis Street and along Mary Street. A stop at Ella McCullough's shop, the hub of the neighbourhood, to pick up a snack for our mid-morning work break, often resulted in an impromptu meeting of sorts with Georgina holding court.

By the time we went our separate ways at Strean Church, Georgina had made promises, handed out her unique pearls of wisdom, listened to unsolicited advice or skilfully evaded questions on any number of burning local issues. In a world without wireless technological wizardry, when the majority still walked to work, she was a true grassroots politician, in touch with the day-to-day issues of her constituents. Walking to work with the Mayor often provided the cub reporter with some promising story leads to be followed up back at the *Chronicle* office.

ANY TIME IS CAMERA TIME . . .
ANDERSON (Chemists) LTD.
11 CONWAY SQUARE - NEWTOWNARDS

THE NEWTOWNARDS Chronicle AND COUNTY DOWN OBSERVER

Newtownards gets first woman Mayor

"Historical treble" for Miss Foulis

AT 12.25 p.m. precisely yesterday, Councillor Georgina Foulis, J.P., won a three-fold achievement by becoming Mayor of Newtownards. She was (1) the first woman to be elected a member of the Borough Council; (2) the first woman to become Deputy Mayor; and (3) the first woman to be appointed Mayor. And, not until yesterday, was there ever a woman Mayor in Northern Ireland.

Nine years a member of the Council, Miss Foulis represented Glen Ward and was top-of-the-poll three years ago. A notable tribute was paid yesterday by the other lady member of the Council, Councillor Mrs. Mabel Doggart who said it was to the credit of the 14 male members of the 16 strong Council that they had confidence in electing a woman to the position.

Undisputed

IN CEREMONIAL ROBES

OUT - GOING MAYOR SAYS THANKS

ARDS MINISTER'S CALL

NEWTOWNARDS FEATU[RE]

ALL REA[...] 'TECH.'

Exhibition

How the election of the Borough's first woman Mayor was reported in 1961

Oddly though, while we talked about everything under the sun on our way to work, I don't recall Georgina and I discussing the burgeoning women's movement or any place we might possibly occupy in it. I'm pretty certain, at that time, we would have rejected the notion that we were actually fighting on the front lines.

Not being taken seriously as a reporter, age jibes and sexual innuendo were just everyday annoyances compared to the constant challenge of having to break through the almost impenetrable crust of the established order of gender, still very much in place in the Sixties. There was the magistrate who ordered me to leave and not return unless "properly attired" for the courtroom by wearing a hat! Another judge had me removed for fear the evidence, about to be heard by the court, would sully my fragile female sensibilities. "What's coming is not the stuff a young girl should hear," he added.

The hat problem was an easy fix. My Aunt Sally, an expert bow maker, who decorated gift boxes of linen handkerchiefs for a living at George Woods' factory (on High Street across from Glasgow's store), made me three or four tiny bows which I sewed onto a small piece of hair-coloured net. I would plop this creation, barely perceptible to the naked eye as it was, on the top of my head only when I passed the door jamb into the courtroom.

Its first appearance drew a quizzical look. I put my head

settling in Canada she was a news reporter for the *Peterborough Examiner*, and then for Canada's smallest daily newspaper in its prettiest town, the *Port Hope Evening Guide*.

Margaret then ran the law office of her husband Wilfred Day in Port Hope, working for 30 years on cases ranging from family law to personal injury claims, so she claims her writing skills have been polluted by legalese!

Their son Adam Day writes on military affairs for *Legion Magazine* in Canada. Their daughter Alexia teaches in Port Hope, while Alexia's daughter Emilia, at the age of 10, is already a talented writer and visited Newtownards not long ago.

down, to make sure the bows were visible, and waited. His Worship made a funny remark about the new fashion in hats but nothing more. It wasn't long before the 'barely-there' hat was not there at all, and no one noticed.

Cllr Georgina Foulis (extreme left)), the Mayor of Ards Borough, and Margaret Cavan Day (extreme right), at a charity ball at Mount Stewart House, the home of the Marquess and Marchioness of Londonderry.

On hearing that a judge had removed me from another courtroom, my Editor was firm: "Go back and tell him you're there to do your job." He left no room for argument. I slunk back into the courtroom, sat down at the press bench beside two hatless male reporters, and started scribbling in my notebook, trying hard, despite the trembling, to look like I belonged there. I knew for absolute certain that I'd be struck dumb if the gavel came down a second time. Fortunately the strategy worked, but His Honour never did address his change of heart.

There would be many other gender-related traps and challenges in the years to follow, as I'm sure there were for the town's first woman Mayor. Unfortunately, any trail Georgina may have blazed for women politicians had gone cold before the next woman Mayor, Gladys McIntyre, was elected almost a quarter of a century later. In the years since, there has been only one more woman Mayor, Margaret Craig, in 2001. Women reporters fared somewhat better but it would be years before they broke free, in any considerable numbers, from the "fashion, food and family" restrictions of the women's pages and into general news reporting, and even longer to climb to the top of the editorial and publishing ladders.

Georgina, the Mayor of the people, worked hard in the political trenches to reach the top job. I, on the other hand, in applying for the junior reporter job, had little more going for me than teenage bravado and minimal experience at two short-term jobs.

The first, my 'Cinderella' summer job, was spent at The

Troccadero, on High Street opposite the Old Cross, famous for its sugar-coated gravy rings and its owner, Wee Sarah, who fluttered over her confections and her customers like a moth in a honey pot. Alas, my summer was spent up to the elbows in dish water, scrubbing the never-ending stream of pots, pans, enormous oven trays and every other greasy, sticky implement required to produce the avalanche of breads and baked goods for the busiest bakery on the Ards Peninsula.

My older sisters, Clara and Jean, had each worked a summer with Wee Sarah. They warned that the job description leaned more to drudgery than bun decoration and they knew, for absolute certain, that little sister was more into bun decoration than drudgery. They placed bets on how long I would last! To their astonishment, I scrubbed and cleaned my way through the entire summer, never getting to decorate a single bun. All bets were lost.

My only other work experience came courtesy of a sweet-talking henchman of 'Carpet King' Cyril Lord, who persuaded half the secretarial class at Newtownards Tech to quit school and jump on Mr Lord's magic carpet to untold success and prosperity. The reality took us through a nondescript gateway on Regent Street (close to the Ulsterbus Station) to a dank, freezing industrial space where a "typing pool" was haphazardly set up.

The massive media advertising blitz Cyril Lord unleashed across the UK and Northern Ireland had everyone clamouring to replace their oil cloth and mats with wall-to-wall plastic carpet. Every advertisement included a "clip me" coupon for a "free carpet sample." These were returned by the thousand and dumped each day, like grey confetti, on the rusty old desks of the typists in Newtownards.

The aim was to get as many carpet samples as possible out the door before the burning desire for wall-to-wall weakened. The stress level was as high as the pay, with a seldom-reached bonus, was low. It soon became clear there was only room on the magic carpet to prosperity for "the Lord" (as the plant workers called him) and a few of his chosen people. So when my brother-in-law Gordon Orr, one of the printers of the *Chronicle*, suggested (half in jest) that I apply for the newly-advertised junior reporter job, I jumped at the chance.

And so it was, a short time later, all dressed up in a new green suit, I sat, for a formal interview, across from the formidable, white-haired Davey Alexander, a co-owner of the *Chronicle*. He cut short the questions and pleasantries, handed me a shorthand jotter and pencil, and proceeded to dictate a section from the front page of the previous week's *Chronicle*. Before I had a chance to transcribe, he reached out, took the jotter, and transcribed it himself. Davey Alexander, it turned out, had a passion for, and an extensive knowledge of, Pitman shorthand. I got the job.

Newtownards Chronicle staff in the early 1960s, with Margaret Cavan Day making a presentation to reporter Carl Anderson prior to his departure for a city newspaper. Up top drinking tea is her brother-in-law Gordon Orr (mentioned in the story). Beside him are Warwick Stewart (left) and Bobby Ballance (right). Also at the back are Jimmy McKay and Jimmy Boal, then (partially hidden) Isobel Murphy and Dick Cunningham. At the front (from left): Wesley McClements, Sheila Regan, Alex Haslett, George Newell, Unknown, Unknown, Carl Anderson, Evelyn Norman, Margaret Cavan Day, Louie McCutcheon and Anne Porter. *Newtownards Chronicle* picture

The following Monday I went through the *Chronicle* office gates on Frances Street to start a career in the newspaper business and to join an amazing cast of characters, who were already acknowledged experts in grooming young journalists. Alumni of the *Chronicle* and its sister paper, the *County Down Spectator*, in Bangor, could be found in newsrooms and editorial departments far and wide. It was generally accepted, in the profession, that there was no substitute for the real world, on-the-job training of a small town weekly.

When I arrived on the scene Norman Boal, 'Big Norman', the news editor/chief reporter/sports editor, was well on his way to legend status. He was always first to arrive at the office in the morning and last to leave at night. The story was that since he had no phone at home, he never left the building at all, sleeping in his chair, at his desk all night, for fear he might miss a good tip from any one of his legion of contacts. Nothing happened in Newtownards, day or night, Norman didn't hear about first. Just sharing an office with him was an education in itself.

In those days the *Chronicle*'s two small editorial offices occupied a partitioned-off section of the commercial printing department where a half dozen or so noisy, continuously operating, printing presses churned out everything from wedding invitations to season tickets for the football club. Photographer Farnham Nixon's darkroom was beyond the presses. All revolved around a smoke-belching, pot-bellied stove. On cold, wet days the aroma emanating from the ring of bodies, jostling for warmth, overpowered the usual potent smell of printer's ink and arid coal fumes combined.

The paper was 'put to bed' on Thursday night, hitting the streets and distribution centres the following morning. In the beginning I lived in dread of Friday, when the true meaning of 'on-the-job' training came into play. An incorrect fact, a figure transposed in the Comber cricket scores, or worse, and the phone would start ringing.

One Friday afternoon the front office receptionist came on the intercom and, in an unusually pinched voice, announced that "the late Mr John Smith" wanted to speak with Margaret and "her boss". The *Chronicle* that day had carried my story about a young local man who had just returned from a stint as a Baptist missionary in some foreign country. Getting all his details for the story, I asked for the full name of his father. His mother, who sat close to her son throughout the interview, looked up to the heavens and quietly replied: "He's gone." Assuming Mr Smith was in a nice, tidy grave at Movilla Cemetery, I described the missionary as the son of Mrs Smith and "the late" Mr Smith.

Editor Bob McNinch, after satisfying Mr Smith with the promise of a published apology, and while trying to hide his obvious amusement, delivered the "check, check, and re-check" your facts and the "never, never assume" lecture.

Divorce and separation were still taboo subjects in Newtownards in the 1960s. I found out later the deeply

Margaret Cavan Day

religious Mrs Smith had a difficult time accepting her husband had left both her and the church, and was living three streets away with a woman a few years younger than his son. Visualising the first Mrs Smith's reaction when she read the apology, on the front page of the *Chronicle*, was a much more effective lesson than any lecture.

There would be more uncomfortable Fridays, more lessons to be learned and more gender-related hurdles to jump, before I moved on to the *News Letter* in Belfast and eventually to newspapers in Canada.

I have always looked back with fondness to my days at the *Chronicle*, and in this age of instant, on-line news, when newspapers everywhere are struggling to stay afloat or are closing down, it's comforting to know the *Newtownards Chronicle* still hits the streets every week.

Will McAvoy

remembers... Strangford Lough and Greyabbey

Strangford Lough has long been recognised around the world for its remarkable wildlife and awe-inspiring landscape and there's not a yard of it I don't know. I was born on Mid Island, about half a mile off the coast at Greyabbey, and have spent much of my life – now into its tenth decade – on or near the Lough.

Will McAvoy out on Strangford Lough

Arthur Irvine, who was warden of the National Trust's Strangford Lough Wildlife Scheme, was looking for someone back in the Sixties to do a bird count and as I knew every bird, every nest, every island and every rock, he reckoned I was the man to ask. Later, he thought enough of me to make me his assistant.

Arthur was one of the few people who ever got into the front parlour of our house in Greyabbey. It was the good room and the door was always kept closed!

As the Sixties arrived my wife Jean and I were renting 40 Main Street, beside the butcher's shop, for 7s 6d a week. It had a large open fire with a crook and we stored the coal in a 'coal hole' under the stairs. We had a jaw tub for a sink and two enamel buckets to fetch water from the cowtail pump in the street.

Nearly every house had a well and we also had a dry

William 'Will' McAvoy was born on 10 May 1923 on Mid Island, off the coast of Ballyurnanellan, the smallest townland in Ireland. One of three sons born to William and Alice McAvoy, he and his family lived in an 18th Century keeper's cottage which had also been his grandparents' home.

As a child Will walked across the sand or, if the tide was in, he paddled to the mainland to attend school some two miles away. Up to 90% of local people at the time were of Scots descent and spoke Ulster-Scots – much to the annoyance of the headmaster!

Around 1930 'Borstal boys' from the Malone Training School, using local stones, constructed a rough roadway beside the causeway to the island to facilitate some wheeled traffic. This happened after landowner Major Montgomery gave them permission to use Mid Isle as a summer camp.

Among Will's most treasured possessions is a shotgun, dating from 1832, retrieved from the cottage's attic, which, he recalls, was "hotching" with mice. It had belonged to his grandfather's cousin and was hidden there after it became illegal to keep a gun without a licence

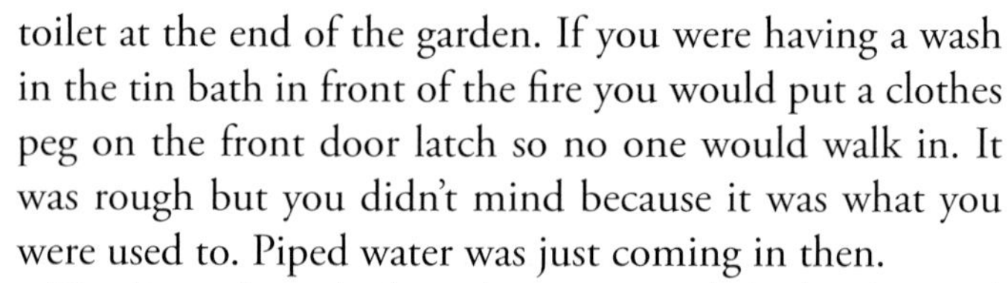

toilet at the end of the garden. If you were having a wash in the tin bath in front of the fire you would put a clothes peg on the front door latch so no one would walk in. It was rough but you didn't mind because it was what you were used to. Piped water was just coming in then.

The front doors had sandstone around the borders and you can still see today where the women used to sharpen their knives on the corners. This was to let their neighbours see they were having meat that day – and sometimes, even if they had no meat, they would sharpen the knives anyway, just to make it look good!

You could have walked up the street in Greyabbey in 1960 and seen a key in every front door. Folk had little need to fear for their safety. There were about 11 shops in the village then. The early Sixties bore witness to the gradual change from scooping and weighing everything. Up till then sugar was supplied to the shop in a hemp hessian bag and tea in a tea chest. Everything was brought to you – the breadman, milkman and butcher all made deliveries.

Will and his cot gun

In my younger days, like my father before me, I was a professional wildfowler. Shooting was a way of making an extra shilling or two. You could sell the birds then but it was a hard, dangerous way of making a living. We shot widgeon, teal, mallard and pigeons, and snared rabbits and hares – whatever was edible. We would sell them to Sawers in Belfast, then a well-known fruit, veg and fowl store and still very much in business as a delicatessen today.

I remember the first time my father let me try a cot gun, a cannon-type apparatus loaded on a boat, but I never got near the birds – my arms weren't strong enough to paddle the cot. I got my first shot the day after the shooting season closed. My father was making up a bag to go to Sawers and let me have a go. I fired off a shot and got the Barnacle, which is the name we gave to the Brent Goose. Because of the date I was actually breaking the law but boy was I pleased!

Of course that all ended when the authorities banned the killing of wildfowl for human consumption.

After that I went to work for James Brain, a meal distribution company in Belfast. Unilever, who made soap, then decided to open a meal firm, also in Belfast. Robert Caughey from Greyabbey got the offer to drive the lorry and asked if I would work as his helper. I was on £5 a week with Brain's but was going to get £7 or £8 so I took the job.

The yellow-coloured lorry we drove was hired from the Ulster Transport Authority and was kept at the bus depot in Newtownards. We first had to go Unilever's head office in Corporation Street to collect the delivery dockets and we then motored all over Northern Ireland.

At that time I owned a Mini I'd bought from car dealer Jack Cairnduff at the Old Cross in Newtownards. That was how Robert and I travelled each morning from Greyabbey to Ards before collecting the lorry and travelling on to Belfast.

Each night I would wedge a big stone behind the back wheel after parking the car in the lane behind our house. One night two Belfast boys stole the Mini and we were left with no transport. Eventually word reached us that the police had located the car at North Street in Belfast and it was ready for collection. However, we found the wires had been tampered with and it wouldn't start. I went to Jack Cairnduff and the following Saturday we headed to Belfast with a mechanic from his garage and got the car going again.

Unilever had little idea about running an animal feed business and after a few years the local business folded. I had seen the signs and decided it was time to move on. It was around 1964/65 and Ards Football Club was looking for a groundsman. I had no wish to sign on the dole so I took the job for a couple of seasons. Renowned

and he refused to pay the fee. The shotgun was literally a mass of rust and Will spent six months restoring it.

He remembers naturalist Sir Peter Scott's visit to Mid Isle on New Year's Eve 1937. He went on to found the UK's Wildfowl and Wetlands Trust in 1946. Castle Espie, outside Comber, is one of nine wetland nature reserves run by the WWT and aims at encouraging the public to care for the natural world.

At the time Sir Peter was an avid wildfowler who wanted to shoot Brent Geese in moonlight on the Lough. Told to contact Will's father, who could show him where to get the best shot, he arrived on 31 December with his punt and gun.

Will's mother was instructed to have a fry ready for the pair's return. She became increasingly anxious when they failed to appear and had the family out searching the shore with lamps. It turned out they had become stuck in mud at the top end of the Lough and had to wait for a tractor to tow them out.

Will McAvoy (third from left) with friends at a social event in the early 1960s.

Sir Peter eventually made it back for the New Year's Eve ball at the Grand Central Hotel in Belfast, albeit in the early hours of the next day, and had to walk across the ballroom to get to his room "covered in gutters." He soon gave up shooting, having missed out on the Brent Geese that night, and started the WWT.

Will met Jean Porter, from Cardy Corner, between Ballyboley and Ballywalter, at the Mountstewart tearooms. The first time Will took her home to meet his mother on the island, poor Jean got stuck in the sand while inspecting some cockles and ended up all wet and filthy.

The couple married in 1950 and later moved from Greyabbey to Newtownards. Sadly, Jean died in May 1998.

Will served as assistant warden on Strangford Lough for 19 years and one month, retiring in 1988.

Englishman George Eastham was enjoying his second spell as manager at the time.

In 1969, with Mr Eastham still in charge, my nephew Billy McAvoy, from Greyabbey, was playing for Ards and scored all four goals in the Irish Cup final. This equalled an Irish League record that stands to this day.

There wasn't much going on in Greyabbey back in the Sixties but Summer League football matches on a Saturday night would always attract spectators by the busload and as many as 300 to 400 supporters would gather along the touchline.

The village also had a Scout Troop and it was through it that I later became involved with the Greyabbey Amateur Dramatic Society, along with people like Bertie Kelly, Ella Taylor, Jessie McKeag, Muriel Bambury and the Reids. We would perform in local village halls with audiences numbering 200-300 people. We must have done about a dozen plays. They were great times and very good fun. We certainly didn't make any money as we had to pay royalties towards staging the play and we also had programmes printed.

I still have some of the scripts and can remember the lines. We did plays like *Mugs and Money, The Pope in Killybuck* and *Johnny Comes Marching Home*. My favourite was *The First Cuckoo* which was about two auld boys making poteen and keeping it hidden. John Davison never learned his lines and always ad-libbed. It was hilarious!

Ernie Hall and I once went to Bangor to be trained by a professional actor. Comedy was the hardest thing to do because it was all about timing. They wanted me to go up to the Group Theatre in Belfast to act but I wouldn't go. I loved poetry and would often recite work by local authors on stage, which went down very well. My friend Eddie Reagan taught me local history.

Returning to my other love, it was in the early Sixties that the National Trust set up the Strangford Lough Wildlife Scheme to regulate wildfowling and habitat management for nesting birds. The Duke of Edinburgh officially opened the scheme in Kircubbin in 1968 and a plaque was placed there to mark the occasion.

Members of Greyabbey Amateur Dramatic Society presented *Johnny Comes Marching Home* at the beginning of the Sixties. Back (from left): Will McAvoy, John Atcheson, Hugh McConnell, John Davidson, Sydney Reid, Tom Brown, Andrew Atcheson, Albert Patton. Front: Margaret Pagan, Jessie McKeag, Iris Patton, Robert Patton and Emma Atcheson.

Warden Arthur Irvine was a retired RUC Head Constable from Enniskillen. He knew his birds and was ideal for the job but as he was a stranger to the area he needed help. He remembered me from the time of the bird count and that I knew the Lough. When the post of assistant warden was advertised I was advised to put in for it; I was interviewed and got the job.

Local landowner Major Montgomery was on the committee and had a big hand in it. His death in 1969 coincided with the arrival of a Black Swan. They are an ornamental bird and don't migrate so it caused quite a stir when one arrived that year and stayed for about a fortnight.

Will McAvoy

By then I had long changed from killing birds to protecting them. My job required me to carry a gun but that was purely to tackle vermin. To shoot on Strangford Lough you had to be a member of a wildfowling club or take out a private permit costing £7 or £8. Otherwise you risked prosecution.

My role was like a policeman, making sure anyone on the shore with a gun had a permit. I also had to visit all the Trust's car parks and lay-bys around the whole Lough to ensure no dumping was going on and to deal with any complaints.

I had to walk every yard of the Lough to carry out a survey of the predator weed Spartina Grass, which came from America. I worked from home and thankfully there were no mobile phones in those days so if you wanted to do a wee message you had plenty of time!

I also became a Grade A ringer of birds. The training on how to catch and handle birds without causing suffering took five years and I was then licensed by the British Trust for Ornithology and the Department of the Environment. The rings helped keep track of the birds so if one was found dead there was always an address to contact. The oldest return we had was a 22-year-old bird that was found in Africa.

Mid Island

At one stage the Trust bought a small fishing boat called the *Cuan Ranger* to patrol the Lough. It wasn't working right so it was sent to Harland and Wolff for an overhaul. Once it was ready I set off with Tony Lord, who was director of the National Trust, Bob Brown, who had replaced Arthur as warden, and a young YTP worker, Jim Galloway from Kircubbin, to bring her down to the Lough.

We launched her with a bottle of beer and began our journey. However, just off Holywood the engine blew and there was smoke billowing out. A tug boat, *The Clandeboye*, pulled up alongside and offered to tow us back to Belfast. To me towing meant pulling behind but they actually towed us side by side after tying ropes to the back and front ends of our boat.

Unfortunately, the front rope came loose and our boat drifted at a right angle to the tug with the result that everything ended up in the water, including me. I was in the water for about five or 10 minutes and going under before, thankfully, I managed to get a hold of the boat.

When the *Cuan Ranger* was finally fixed and ready for the return journey I declared: "No way!" Instead I drove to Ballywalter and watched it sail past! From then on I just preferred to use my own wee boat.

That was my nearest miss. Strangford Lough is a curious place. It gets a name for being dangerous and has to be treated with respect. A wise man once told me the water was like the neighbour's wife – not to be played with!

Over the years there has been a terrible number of tragedies on the Lough. Twice I have found men's bodies on the shore. Usually a body is washed up after about nine days. I worked out the way the tides would go and on each occasion I found the remains on Chapel Island and just 50 yards apart. Something like that stays with you.

There have been many changes on the Lough over the years. I think there is more wind nowadays and the tides are getting bigger. A lot of the islands that previously had grass on them are just stones now and the bigger islands are getting wee'er. There are not the same birds about and even their ways have changed – in the past the wintering birds didn't arrive until Harvest Fair Day on 23 September; now they're here by the end of August. There's less feeding now and more disturbance.

There used to be roughly 30,000 widgeon on Strangford Lough but now it's maybe one or two thousand. I've no idea why. There are more nature reserves and I think the birds from Russia are stopping further east.

It seems strange to me when you think there were more birds in the old days when the cot guns were chasing after them and shooting them. There's a whole lot more protection nowadays but for all that there are still fewer birds.

Of course, it would be a bad job if things didn't change. It doesn't matter what things were like before – we can't bring them back. They tell us we're better off but I don't doubt if my granny could return right now, she would hurry straight back to where she came from!

Willie Lennon

remembers... The Boats in Donaghadee

From left: Muriel Magowan, Margaret Lennon, John Lennon, Alan Gilmore, Willie Lennon, Bob Cooke and John Bunting aboard *The Laura*

William (Willie) Lennon was born and raised in Donaghadee. His lifelong passion for the sea first manifested itself when he helped John Bunting with his pleasure boat business.

In 1950 he commenced a career with the Post Office that lasted 20 years, though he never lost his love for

Back in the 1960s, when cheap air flights were only a dream and foreign travel was still the preserve of the wealthy, most Belfast families took their holidays closer to home. That's why, in the summer months, Donaghadee awoke from its winter slumbers to become a bustling, thriving seaside resort.

From Easter onwards the local hotels and guesthouses began to fill as families made their annual migration to swap the smoke and congestion of the city for the fresh sea breezes of Donaghadee.

Indeed, during the peak time in July and August, when many families would move to the town for a month or more – with the men commuting to their jobs in Belfast and leaving their wives and children during the day – the hotels and guesthouses would be full to overflowing and many of Donaghadee's permanent residents would bolster their annual income by moving into temporary accommodation and renting their homes to holidaying families.

Of course, all these visitors had to be entertained and it was natural that in Donaghadee, with its famous pier, lighthouse and nautical tradition, boating activities would

Donaghadee in its summer heyday with crowds thronging the pier and the harbour filled with pleasure boats large and small ready for business. *Photograph courtesy of Walker Simpson*

be a highlight of any holiday there and, to cater for the need, a fleet of pleasure boats operated from the harbour from Easter Monday on.

Because it was a highly seasonal trade, it was vital for the boat owners to maximise their business in the limited time available. Hence, from the very moment holidaymakers appeared near the harbour they would be approached by local lads, as young as nine or 10, touting for trade for the boats. Trips started at 10.30am with deep sea fishing on the Rigg Bank, a sand bank located three miles east of Donaghadee, where the fishermen whiled away a few hours until they were returned to harbour at about 1pm for lunch.

In the afternoons the boats cruised back and forth to the Copeland Islands (both to the Large Island and Mew Island), although having gone to all the bother of getting the passengers in the first place, it made sense to attempt to hold on to them for a few days by offering a bit of variety. As a result, folk returning from the Copelands would often be asked by the skipper: "Well, where do you want me to take you tomorrow?"

Potential destinations for day trips included Ballywalter and the Skulmartin light vessel to the south, or Bangor

the sea. He bought the *Miss Ruth* in 1964, running deep-sea fishing trips and outings to the Copeland Islands for many years. He combined this with part-time fishing which became full-time after he left the Post Office.

Willie maintained a contract with the Irish Lights and ferried the lighthouse keepers to and from Mew Island until the lighthouse was automated in 1990.

He joined the RNLI as a member of the Donaghadee Lifeboat crew in 1954, being appointed 2nd coxswain in 1981 and coxswain in 1984. He retired in 1991, having been awarded the British Empire Medal for his services to the RNLI.

Willie was married to Margaret and they had two children, John and Ruth – the latter joined the same crew in 1984 as the first female member on an offshore lifeboat anywhere in the UK, serving on the Donaghadee Lifeboat for 20 years.

Willie Lennon and daughter Ruth on the Donaghadee LIfeboat

and around Belfast Lough to the north. Although the area of operation for the boats was tightly regulated and, strictly speaking, Donaghadee boats were not supposed to operate on the north side of the Lough, their skippers' knowledge of the various rules, regulations and associated loopholes meant many an enjoyable afternoon was spent in Carrickfergus or Whitehead!

However, no matter where they'd been, the boats would generally arrive back in Donaghadee at 5.30pm in time for the passengers to get their tea and to allow the crews to prepare for the evening activities, whether deep sea fishing, stream fishing or cruises round the islands.

For deep sea fishing the skippers would position their boats over favourite fishing spots as the anglers sought to catch bottom-feeding fish such as cod and whiting, while the stream-fishing boats would slowly trawl for bloken and lithe near the surface. As for the midnight cruises for courting couples, though many a catch was made, no fish were harmed in the process!

Although there were plenty of good days when the sun shone and the boats were full, it didn't offer a particularly easy living for the boat owners with the relatively short season. Come September, many of us returned to trades or had to take part-time jobs to make ends meet through the long winter months.

Skulmartin light vessel

Such limited incomes were often supplemented by a bit of fishing for scallops, clams and lobsters, which was hard and sometimes dangerous work. I well remember an incident in the mid-Sixties when only the quick-witted actions of colleague Hugh Nelson, who was fishing nearby, saved my life after I became entangled in the heavy metal dredge used to dig up the scallops from the sea bed as it was thrown over the side of the boat, taking me down with it.

Maybe it was due to our awareness of the dangers of the environment we worked in, or maybe it was due to the sense of community that prevailed in Donaghadee, but you could always be sure – despite the intense rivalry and high passions that sometimes led to fallouts and disputes – that your fellow fishermen and neighbours would never see you stuck.

A typical example of this occurred during my first year with the *Miss Ruth*. Coming back into the harbour on the 11th July, I heard an ominous knocking noise coming from the rear of the boat. In order to investigate it further, I ran her onto the beach at Lemon's Wharf.

Willie Lennon's boat, the *Miss Ruth*

Imagine my horror when I discovered the propeller shaft bearing had been damaged, rendering the *Miss Ruth* unusable – right at the peak of the season with no prospect of me being able to get a new one as everywhere was closed for the July holidays! However, only an hour or two later, as I lay under the boat working to remove the bearing, my black mood was interrupted by the sight of a pair of legs on the other side of the boat.

Then I heard the voice of Sammy Martin, who worked in the machine shop in the local carpet factory, declaring: "The wee man Cyril Lord said he'd heard you were in bother an' told me to come down an' see if there was anything I could do."

Somehow the word had got passed through the grapevine that I was in trouble and Cyril Lord, owner of not only the carpet factory but also several private boats (but whom I really didn't know at all), had seen it as his community duty to step in and help. In next to no time Sammy had the bearing whipped out, taken to the machine shop, refurbished and replaced, saving my livelihood for another year.

It's easy to be nostalgic about such things and to gloss over the hard times as passenger numbers started to dwindle and one by one the pleasure boats were laid up until today only a couple remain, but looking down a list of the boats I can recall being around in the Sixties, my memory – while maybe not the most accurate at times – is filled with more good times than bad. I can still picture those young lads weaving through the crowds of happy holidaymakers and calling out: "Trips to the Copelands, Mister? Only two shillins, best boat in the harbour."

Boats operating out of Donaghadee Harbour in the 1960s were as follows:

Boat name	**Owner**
Henrietta	William Campbell
Carpathia	Alex Nelson
Brothers	Nelson Bros
Star of Ulster	Bobbie Simpson
Miss Dorothy	Tom Simpson
White Heather	John Trimble
Sunrise	Hugh Nelson
Seven Sisters	Hugh Nelson
Laura	Jim Davidson
Mercedes	Andrew White
Seagull	William Bunting
Lady Franklin	John Bunting
Miss Ruth	William Lennon
Miss Josephine	George Lindsay
I'm Alone	George Dunwoody

Harry Murray

remembers... the Strangford Ferry

The ticket cost me 6d and was numbered 42 – which meant I was among the first passengers to travel on the brand-new Strangford Lough car ferry on its maiden crossing back in 1969. Only one other person boarded after me and, in addition, there were a couple of cars as we set sail from Portaferry. It was a fairly low-key event but I wanted to be able to say I'd been on board that first crossing.

Once the new ferry reached Strangford the ramp went down and the cars were guided off. Another one or two vehicles drove on for the return journey but then the ramp jammed; the hydraulics had stuck. So the old small sailing boat, which had served as a ferry for many years, had to be brought back into action. I don't think many people ever realised what had happened as the problem was quickly sorted out, that same day I think.

The MV *Strangford* was built at the Verolme Shipyard in Cork and was launched on 6 September 1969. It was the culmination of a decade of debate and lengthy discussions at the highest government level on ways of providing a satisfactory link between Portaferry and

Harry Murray

Harry Murray is an ex-seaman. Born on 10 October 1924, Harry was brought up at The Shore in Portaferry and attended Ballyphilip Boys Public Elementary School.

He joined the Merchant Navy and later spent 14 years employed by the Commissioners of Irish Lights, the body that serves as the General Lighthouse Authority for the island of Ireland and its adjacent seas.

It had 11 lightships dotted along the Irish coastline where lighthouses couldn't be built, including two dangerous reefs off County Down that had been the scene of many shipping disasters in the 19th Century.

Harry spent considerable time on the light vessels at Skulmartin Rock near Ballywalter and South Rock off Cloughey. The vessels were boarded via Portavogie and Harry would spend four weeks on board and four weeks off with food being delivered to the crew fortnightly. The Skulmartin lightvessel was discontinued in 1967, while the South Rock lightship was withdrawn in 1982. Both were replaced by 'super-buoys'.

Harry later joined the Union Castle Shipping Company and worked on a passenger ship taking emigrants to South Africa.

Finally back on dry land, he became a bus driver for the South Eastern Education and Library Board, retiring aged 75 after working for a local motor business.

He still lives in Portaferry with his wife May. The couple have three sons, John, Peter and Declan, and a daughter, Anne.

Strangford.

Historical records show a ferry link had been in existence over The Narrows since 1180, dating back to the time of John De Courcey. To travel from Portaferry to Strangford by road involves a journey of some 45 miles and takes around 90 minutes by car, whereas a ferry can cross the 0.6 nautical miles in about eight minutes, depending on the tide.

Over the centuries small boats had ferried people and livestock across the Lough. However, as cars became increasingly popular it was recognised that the absence of an adequate connection, particularly for motor traffic between Portaferry and Strangford, was causing considerable inconvenience for those living in the area. In addition, it was agreed that tourists, as well as the commercial and agricultural communities on either side of the Lough, would benefit.

So by 1959 three main proposals were on the table – a barrage or dam, a bridge or a car ferry – and studies were carried out. During the early Sixties the barrage idea, estimated to cost around £750,000, was rejected as it would have turned Strangford Lough into a freshwater area instead of a moving seawater one. A bridge was also ruled out due to the high cost – reckoned then to be about £1m – as well as fears that the speed of the current and range of the tide would present considerable engineering problems during construction.

Thomas Keating (right), a key figure in the Strangford Ferry project, is pictured in early September 1969 with Hugh Kelly (centre) and James Savage during final work on the new ferry ramp at Portaferry Quay. *211-36-3*

The only option left was a new and improved ferry service. Under the provisions of a Local Act of Parliament dated 4 December 1967, Down County Council was authorised to acquire the then existing privately-owned ferry service and establish a new passenger/ vehicle service. With the help of a 90% grant from the Ministry of Development, the new purpose-built vessel, MV *Strangford*, was constructed at an approximate cost of £200,000 and went into operation that autumn day in 1969. Portaferry Quay was extended into deep water and a sloping ramp was added to permit the loading and unloading of vehicles in all tides.

The ferry proved an instant success. By the following Easter cars waiting to cross were queued up for about a mile each way out the Kircubbin Road and the Cloughey side of Portaferry.

John Fitzsimmons

The first skipper was John Fitzsimmons, who had worked on the small ferry boats before that. Other ferrymen before him included Joe Trainor and Johnny Blaney, John Murray's grandfather, while Malachy Rogers was a part-time ferryman in the Sixties. From Strangford there were three traditional ferry families; the Quails, the McDonnells and the McDowells. A lot of the ferrymen were retired seamen and among them there were plenty of characters.

Johnny Blaney

They were licensed to carry 12 passengers in 30ft motor boats. In those days there was no timetable or set fare; it was up to the passenger's discretion. You would pass the ferryman half a crown and there was no change given. They all made a living. There were three or four boats on the Portaferry side and the same on the Strangford side.

George McDonnell was always on the go. He had two vessels. If he wanted to catch the attention of the boat on the other side he would set fire to a sheet of newspaper and wave it to get the boat back quickly because he had a passenger.

George McDonnell

Another ferryman, Billy Hinds, used to stop working in the winter. George McDonnell called him 'the cuckoo ferryman' because he only came out in summer! As a boy I was the only one allowed on Billy's boat. I would go up to his house at 6pm and his wife would give me his tea to take down to him at the quay. At the end of the week he would give me sixpence.

As the ferrymen were getting older, they would get lads about the harbour to tie up the boats for them when they pulled up at the slip. It saved them having to get off to do it themselves. George McDonnell was the last

Portaferry breadserver Tommy Ferris, who was in his mid-50s, retired in early September 1969 after almost 27 years with Inglis and Co. to become a ticket collector with the new Strangford Lough car ferry. Although born in Kirkistown, he had lived in Portaferry from the age of 12.
211-37-3

ferryman left on the old boats. His son is now a skipper on the Strangford Lough ferry and maintaining the family tradition.

There always seemed to be a boat waiting and you rarely had to hang around too long to get across. Nor would the boats ever have been off too often. Occasionally the fog might have delayed them. When it came down, the tallest tree on the Strangford side always seemed to sit above the fog and could be used as a guide.

During the war the ferries weren't allowed to run from dusk until daylight; not only was there a curfew during the hours of darkness, but there was also a complete blackout. I remember coming home on the last bus one night and there was a girl sitting there in a distressed state. When I asked her where she was going, she told me she was on her way to catch the ferry to Strangford as the police had informed her that her mother, whose surname was Travers, was seriously ill. I advised her there would be no ferry until the morning because of the blackout.

A conversation followed between officers in Portaferry and Strangford and it was agreed if I could get a boat then I could take her across. It was about midnight but I managed to borrow a punt and some oars and took her across to Strangford. On the way back the flood tide took me past the end of the quay. Next thing I heard a voice shout: "You shouldn't have been out there." It was some customs men who took me up to the police barracks. Jim Boland was the policeman on duty and they told him I'd broken the law by being out on a ferry at night. Boland said he knew nothing about it and I had to give a statement. Thankfully, however, nothing ever came of it. I never saw the girl again or found out what happened.

Over the years livestock was carried across the Lough by horse boat, while passengers were carried in the privately-owned ferries. The horse boat was a heavy craft with a sail and two pairs of oars. When motor ferryboats were introduced, they took on the role of towing the horse boat.

Occasionally, whenever a car needed to cross the Lough, which wasn't very often, planks were positioned across the boat. Skids were put at an angle from the slipway and the car was driven off the slip and onto the planks. I can't ever remember a car being lost.

In June 1946 Chandos Leigh brought two World War Two tank landing craft to use as ferries capable of carrying two cars and 36 passengers. The first crossing was a big occasion and the boat in question was all decorated. However, two days before Christmas 1947 it left Portaferry carrying a cow, a sow and her piglets and a lorry loaded with feed meal. The ferry began to list and on encountering the strong tide it capsized with the unfortunate loss of Bob Drysdale, who had been looking after the livestock. The remaining craft was withdrawn after only 10 months' service and it wasn't until the ferry came into operation in 1969 that vehicles were again carried across the Lough on custom-made ferries.

The MV *Strangford* was eventually replaced by a newer model and these days the service operates each day of the year except for Christmas Day, Boxing Day and New Year's Day. The ferry operates from 7.30am until 10.45pm every weekday and later at weekends, with two boats being required at busy times such as bank holidays.

The ferry carries tens of thousands of vehicles across the Lough each year, as well as an estimated 500,000 passengers. Over 200 local schoolchildren use the ferry to get to and from school each weekday. While the short trip is a novelty and tourist attraction for some, the ferry remains an essential service for many more that we couldn't do without. Looking back to 1969, I'm so glad I can say I was aboard that very first day.

The Horse Boat crosses the Lough

Car ferry in 1920

Some crew members of the newly-introduced Strangford Lough car ferry pictured on the opening day of the service in October 1969. Included are W. Swail, J. Caldwell, P. Curran, J. Fitzsimmons (Master), G. McDonnell (Superintendent) and L. Fitzsimmons. *213-57-1*

Harry Murray

Jean Galloway

(née Boal) remembers... Factory Life

Jean Boal (centre) with friends at Walker's Mill

Jean Boal was born on 26 May 1932. The only daughter of Mary (née Robinson) and James Boal, she also had a brother, James, now sadly deceased. The family lived at Lower Greenwell Street in Newtownards before moving to the Scrabo Estate, but Jean later returned with husband Jim Galloway to live within yards of where she grew up.

A past pupil of Castle Gardens School, Jean vividly recalls the Blitz of April 1941 and hearing the bombs being dropped on Belfast. She,

Like so many other 14-year-olds at the time, back in the mid-Fifties, I finished school on a Friday and started my first job the following Monday morning. You could walk into a job back then, right into the Sixties – and Newtownards was a busy town with plenty of workplaces.

The textile industry was the town's economic mainstay, with over a dozen factories employing literally thousands and you could have your pick of where you wanted to work. There was Debretta (which made ladies' blouses), Crepe Weavers, Walker's Mill (yarns), Black's (socks), Berkshire (nylons), Ulster Print Works (textiles), Webb's (yarns), Anny Lewinters (knitting), David Corry's (ties), George Woods, Freeland and Ferguson, The Regent Factory, Strangford Socks, Ferguson Hemstitching, Swiss Embroidery, Miekles and Blaxnit, as well as the Glen Laundry, Lee Guinness and Shorts.

Whole families used to work in the factories. It was mainly women on the floor while the men looked after the machines. Back then you had no choice but to go out to work to make ends meet.

My first job was at Walker's Mill, which was on the site of the old Telephone Exchange and Clark's Funeral Parlour. It was a large employer and people used to travel from the low country – Greyabbey, Ballywalter, Portaferry, etc. – to work there. It was very hard work and involved long hours, with just two weeks' holiday a year. We worked from 8am until 6pm, with about half an hour for lunch and a tea break in the middle of the morning.

Walker's Mill

I worked in the reeling room. Although my uncle, George Carlisle, was in charge there it didn't make any difference, I was treated just the same as the others. My Aunt Agnes worked there too, while my brother James worked in the bundling room.

I had to put cones onto the big machine, loop the thread round it, pull a handle to start it winding and then watch to make sure it didn't break. If the thread did break, I had to stop and join it again. Every so often the manager would come down and take away a cone to count how many threads were on it. If it was good you got the prize of an extra sixpence a week in your wages but if it wasn't you were fined.

The wages were hopeless – little more than coins when I think of it. I remember coming home with £3 for a week's work and handing it all over to my mother. Then she gave me back what she was able to. You thought nothing of it back then; it was the thing to do.

I had been at Walker's for about a year when I started to feel unwell and was diagnosed with tuberculosis, which was rife at the time. My granny set up a bed for me in the living room of her home at Upper Greenwell Street in Newtownards and I lay there for three months before I got a bed in Musgrave Park Hospital. I was there for a total of 13 months, and for nine of them I wasn't even allowed out of bed.

I was lucky to walk away from it. My mother later told me six people from Ards had gone up to Musgrave with

her brother and their Uncle Jimmy were sheltering under the stairs of her granny's home at Upper Greenwell Street when she heard the noise of a plane overhead. Going to the door, she saw a German war plane overhead with the Nazi swastika clearly visible and watched it fly over the top of the local church.

On another occasion Jean, her brother and some others had climbed up to Scrabo Tower when the air raid sirens sounded. They saw another German plane flying overhead but reckoned it was on a reconnaissance mission taking photographs.

The Germans had already bombed Newtownards airfield, killing 10 members of the Royal Inniskilling Fusiliers on guard duty. Jean remembers townspeople taking blankets and heading to sleep in fields, believing they would be safe there.

Later, Jean recalled how the young folk in the town would congregate around the Square on a Sunday night with the Cafolla's side being the 'posh side'. She loved the dances and learned to dance at The Hut in Comber along with her cousin Margaret Carser, with the Queen's Hall in Newtownards and Milanos in Bangor also being favourites.

She and Jim went everywhere on their motorbike and she recalls one particular night how, after meeting Emile Ford and The Checkmates following a show in Belfast's Grand Opera House, she clung to her crash helmet coming home along Bradshaw's Brae as she was afraid the rain would wash his autograph off the helmet where he had signed it!

When their son Stephen was older, Jean returned to work in the local Wellworths restaurant, retiring when she was 60. She and Jim enjoyed many happy years of retirement before his death in September 2010.

TB – and I was the only one to come back. Unknown to me, at one stage I was given only three months to live. Some of the scenes I witnessed at the hospital haunted me for many years.

We had been living at Greenwell Street but while I was ill my mother put in for a transfer to a flat on the Scrabo Estate. After I was released from the sanatorium, I stayed in and looked after the house.

My mother used to get me to make fries and to bring the food over to her and her friends during their lunch break. Looking after our home didn't really suit me. I wanted out a bit more and to see a bit more of life. After about a year the authorities got quite strict and I had to return to work.

My mother wasn't keen on me going back but she got me a job in the Ulster Print Works, where she already worked in the finishing room, so I could be near her. The factory at Trasnagh Drive was close to where we lived and produced mostly curtain material, table cloths and tea towels.

I worked in the screen shop. Part of my job was to help lay out large rolls of fabric on a table. Tubs of colour were made up in the colour shop, depending on how many colours were to be printed on the material, and it was our job to carry the tubs for the men who did the screen printing. I could have been on blue, for instance, and another girl on yellow. The colour was poured onto the screen, a blade was used to push the colour over the material and then someone came along with the next colour. You had to stay with them until the end of the process and point out any marks on the material. You would go right up one side of the room then turn back and do the other side with the screen. The tables were heated to help the colours dry, which meant it got unbearably hot in there during the summer.

When finished, the screens were put up against the wall, hosed and washed to ensure all the colour was gone. We had to carefully lift the material, hop up onto the

Jean (centre) is pictured with her late husband Jim Galloway and good friend Stella Armstrong

Screen printing at the Ulster Print Works

Screen shop staff at the Ulster Print Works

table and attach it to clips hanging from the ceiling to allow it to dry out properly. Then we cleaned the tables and got ready for the next batch.

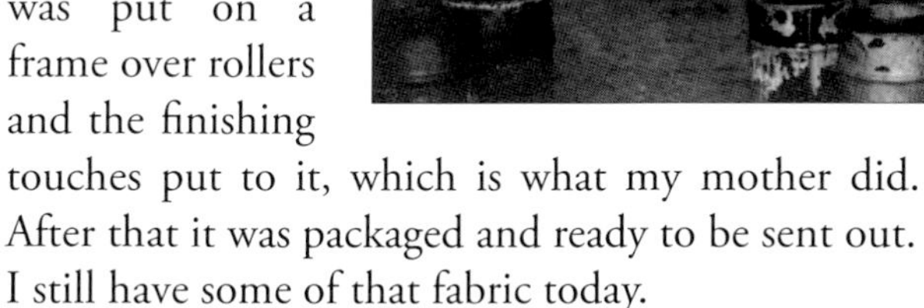

The material was put on a frame over rollers and the finishing touches put to it, which is what my mother did. After that it was packaged and ready to be sent out. I still have some of that fabric today.

It was while I was working in the Ulster Print Works that I met my future husband, Jim Galloway, who came from the Cottown, between Six Road Ends and Donaghadee. He was working in the quarry at North Road in Ards when we married in September 1956, but I got him into the Ulster Print Works where he worked as a handyman.

Checking print at the Ulster Print Works

Eventually we received word the factory was closing down. Jim got a job in Ferguson Cars on the Movilla Road and I went to work at the Black's sock factory in Thomas Street. It was run by two brothers and we worked shifts week about from 6am to 2pm or 2pm until 10pm. The wages were great – £8 a week; I'd never had money like it and thought I was rich!

I worked as a cutter in Black's. There was a knitting room with two rows of machines. I used to cut the socks, separate them and put them into bundles before they were taken to be examined in another department. We made hard-wearing Pathfinder socks, thick socks and fine socks.

Like other factories, sometimes Black's would send a bit of work home. Occasionally, I had to work on a Saturday morning for a couple of hours but getting overtime was very rare. All the same, nobody ever seemed to leave Black's. It was mostly older people who worked there. None of the

Taking a tea break at the Ulster Print Works

factories were easy to work in but that was a likeable enough job.

Eventually, it too closed down and nearly all the workers moved to the Berkshire nylon factory on the Donaghadee Road. I worked there as an examiner checking the nylons. They were stricter to work for and I was once reprimanded for talking to Billy Nixon who had worked with us in Black's. They thought you shouldn't be making yourself so free with the bosses!

I saw out the Sixties at the Berkshire, only giving up work when I discovered I was expecting our son Stephen, who was born in 1970.

In time, the factories closed one by one. We didn't realise how fortunate we were to have been able to get jobs so easily. Things have changed terribly in the intervening years. When you walk up the street now you hardly see a face you know. It's so different from what it used to be like.

Everybody seemed to know everybody back then and there was some great banter amongst the factory staff. I've stayed in contact with a number of the great friends I made over the years, including Marie McMaster, whom I worked with in the reeling room at Walker's, Marie McGreehan, from Portavogie, and Olive McDaid, from Bangor. Good friends from the Ulster Print Works included Maureen Ferguson, from Newtownards, and Margaret Patton, who moved to England.

We were lucky in a way. I have plenty of good memories. I was always a hard worker; it never did me any harm. Having the TB taught me the value of good health. You could have all the money in the world but if you don't have your health, you have nothing.

Joe Mawhinney

remembers... Portavogie

I was 24 when my brother and I bought our first fishing boat together. That was in 1967; I bought a boat and got married in the same year. I had spent much of my childhood around Portavogie Harbour. My uncles were fishermen and during school holidays, when I was about 11 or 12, they would take us herring fishing.

Pictured at Portavogie in October 1961, while preparing for a herring fishing trip to Dunmore East, are (from left): Samuel McVea, Jonnie Warnock (Whitehead), Jonnie McClements and Joe Mawhinney

The first time we went to the Isle of Man, I thought I was on the other side of the world! You would have got a pound or two for helping but just getting to the Isle of Man was reward enough. We returned home every weekend.

The year I was due to finish school they put the leaving age up from 14 to 15 so I had to stay on for another year. I cried! I finally left at 15 and went to the fishing in November 1958. The first vessel I served on was the *Aig Vie*. It had a crew of five and was skippered by Robert Coffey. We fished for whiting, which were very plentiful in those days. Sometimes we were away for weeks on end. The following year I moved to the *May McMaster*, which was skippered by John McMaster.

By 1967 I had learned a lot about the fishing so my

The Mawhinney family has had a long association with the fishing industry in all its forms. Portavogie is the most easterly village in Ireland and local people have shown great initiative and resourcefulness over the years in seeking to make a living from the sea.

Joe's grandfather started local fish merchant business F. B. Mawhinney, based in Portavogie, and in time it became the biggest shellfish exporter in Ireland.

Joe's father Robin served his time as an engineer while his uncle Willie Mawhinney went to sea and another uncle, Joe, took over the family fish merchant business. His uncle Tommy Mawhinney ran the local grocery shop, West End Stores, and as a lad Joe worked as a message boy delivering groceries as far away as Cloughey.

The village sweet shop opened every Friday and Saturday and local people headed there for their weekend confectionery treats and cones, with the ice cream being supplied by the famous Cafolla's in Newtownards. Occasionally, a grateful Joe would receive a sixpence tip from a customer which was quickly spent on a quarter of sweets!

Joe was born at Cloughey Road in Portavogie on 15 November 1943, and had just the one brother, Edwin (also known as Ebby). He attended school in Portavogie and later Ards Technical College, before commencing his 40-year fishing career.

brother Edwin – or Ebby as he was known by everyone – and I became partners when we bought the 20-year-old 65ft *John Chambers* for £7,500 from Edmund McCullough of Annalong. We fished her off Ardglass and the Clyde for prawns and whitefish.

Like about 10 other Portavogie boat owners, we fished out of Ardglass as it took too long to get home. We would leave our home port at about midnight on a Sunday and wouldn't return until Friday evening. We would set off from Ardglass at about 5am each morning and get back at around 5 or 6pm in the wintertime. It was hard work and involved long hours but it was prime fish you were getting. There was no machinery then; everything had to be done by hand. You could have been gutting 100 boxes of fish in a day. There was no rest.

In 1970 we bought the 70ft *Fragrant Rose* from Buckie in Scotland for £19,000. We thought we would never be out of debt! Two years later we went from a 150hp to a 360hp Caterpillar engine, which gave us more power to tow the nets faster, especially for the herring. We had some very good catches.

The best herring fields were around the Isle of Man and the season lasted from June to about November. We would fish for sprats in November, December and January in the Clyde and then from February for whitefish until the herring season started again.

The harder you worked the more you made. You went where you wanted to go. There were no 'days at sea' restrictions, quotas or not being allowed into certain parts of the Irish Sea. It's hard being a fisherman these days – you need a secretary aboard just to keep up with all the paperwork!

Fragrant Rose

Back in the Seventies grants became available to build new boats and in 1976

The Cathzelle and the *Sparkling Wave*

we had the 70ft *Sparkling Wave* built at the Bangor boatyard. She cost £200,000. There is nothing as nice as something you have designed yourself. Everything in that boat was where we wanted it. The last few months before it was ready, I was down in that yard every day!

On one particular occasion we got more of a catch than we bargained for on the *Sparkling Wave* when we picked up a World War Two bomb off the Isle of Man. There was a big hole in the side of the bomb and there was me standing close by looking through it. We brought it back to Portavogie and then the Royal Navy arrived. They found there was still 500lb of explosive inside! They took it away and detonated it off Ballywalter.

Joe's father-in-law George Calvert (right) is pictured at Portavogie Harbour in the 1960s with Sam McMaster (smoking the cigarette) and Sammy Thompson

There were other lucky escapes over the years in bad storms and some memorable gales, especially in the North Channel. It's a cruel bit of sea between Rathlin and Fair Head. Sometimes, if there was an easterly wind, you couldn't get into Portavogie Harbour – it has such a narrow entrance. There were times when we had to turn and go away to the Isle of Man because we just couldn't get into the harbour.

You couldn't have too big a boat or you would have problems. When I started back in '58, Portavogie had a fleet of about 30 fishing boats. That number rose gradually and about 20 years ago there were over 100 boats in the harbour. We'll never see the likes of that again. Now it's down to between 30 and 40. All Portavogie boats are registered in Belfast, which explains the B before the number on the side.

In 1987 Ebby and I stepped up again to buy the 80ft *Wisteria II*. She could pump 50 tons of fish in eight minutes. It was like being on a farm and moving away from working with horses to a tractor – it took all the heavy work out of it. The job definitely got easier over the years but the regulations got stricter! We partnered for many years in the herring fishing, pair-trawling with the *Willing Lad* skippered by James McClements. My pal Samuel McVea, who was best man at my wedding, was also on the crew.

We had the same crew on our boat for years. It was a real family affair and we had good times. There was myself and Ebby, George Calvert (my father-in-law), Robin Mawhinney (my son), David Coffey (who became my son-in-law), Sam McMaster and Billy Adair.

My other passion over the years has been Portavogie Orange Lodge. I was in the Juniors as a lad, which meant we could take part in the service held on the Sunday before the Twelfth. My father wasn't in the Lodge but my mates were joining so I went along too.

I joined the Senior Lodge – Portavogie LOL 552 – in 1961 when I was 17. At that time there would have been up to 100 of us walking on the Twelfth. We were the biggest lodge in our district and would have had 10 or 12 joining every couple of years. These days there would seem to be too many distractions for the young ones.

A young Joe Mawhinney holding the rope (fourth from right, middle row) during the unveiling of a new banner for the Portavogie Juniors in the late 1950s. Also included is the Rev. Henry, Presbyterian minister in Portavogie at the time, the Rev. Smith, minister at Glastry, and the Rev. Cotter (wearing glasses).

Portavogie has hosted the Twelfth twice in my lifetime – in 1972 and 2008. I was privileged to serve as Worshipful Master between 1976 and 1978 and recently received my

50-year medal.

When I was about 13 or 14 I became a drummer in Portavogie Pipe Band. I really enjoyed it but once I started the fishing it meant I couldn't get to band practices which were held on Thursday nights.

Portavogie Orange Lodge members during a Twelfth demonstration in Dundonald in the late 1960s

Later I joined the local accordion band, which was formed in 1967, as its practice night was on a Friday, when I was just home at the end of the week. I was a drummer in that for a good few years and we won the Junior Section of the Irish Bands Association competition in the Ulster Hall in November 1969. The band went from strength to strength; at one stage it had 50 accordions and 10 side drums and enjoyed much success. Eventually, the flute band came along and the accordion band didn't parade any more.

I also enjoyed football. I played for Portavogie Rangers and Comber Rec. During the Sixties the young blues who couldn't get into the big team entered the Summer League and made history by winning it seven years in a row and the Knock-Out Cup five times within those seven years. My team mates included Samuel McVea, Billy McVea, Leslie Young, Jimmy Palmer, Hugh Cully, Bert McMaster, Willie McMaster, Robbie Thompson, George Shaw and Robert Gibson. We were managed by Jim Thompson and Billy Ross. Two decades later I was the assistant manager.

I have been away from the fishing now for 15 years. Ebby died suddenly during a crossing to the Isle of Man at the beginning of September 1997. It was the day after Princess Diana died. He had watched the coverage of her death that Sunday then he died himself the next day. It

Joe's uncle Willie Mawhinney (looking at the camera) aboard *The Glorious* in Portavogie Harbour in the 1960s, along with Ivan Adair and Adam Palmer (with back turned). Pictured in the background are Willie Hugh Ambrose in the second boat (wearing white coat) and Johnny Cully, while James Cully is on the third boat, *Boys' Pride*.

was a terrible shock. After that we decided to sell the boat.

I have some great memories and we met some wonderful people over the years. After being away from home so much I really enjoy spending time now with my wife Gina and our family. She has been a great support to me over the years and I couldn't do without her. I knew Gina Calvert, as she was then, from Sunday School at Glastry Methodist Church and we spent our first Twelfth together in Ballywalter in 1963. We went out together for four years before we married, on 25 March 1967, and had two children, Robin and Julie.

Julie married David Coffey, who had been part of the crew on our boat, and they have two children, Rachel and Joshua. Robin worked with me on the boats for over 10 years and he and his wife Claire also have two children, Nicole and David. They all live nearby.

I still miss the fishing sometimes, especially on a fine summer's evening. During all the years I was fishing, I never ate much fish. Now I could eat it every day of the week!

Stewart Mackay

remembers... The Newtownards Spectator

Well, 'twas getting on past the heat o' the year
When I rode to Newtown fair
I sold as I could – the dealers were near
Only three pounds eight for the Innis steer
And nothing at all for the mare.

Stewart and wife-to-be Renee after their engagement in 1960

Stewart Mackay got his first break into journalism while working in the offices of the *Tyrone Courier* in Dungannon. The editor at that time, Ernie Richardson, asked him to provide a weekly column centred around the Coalisland area and this soon developed into general features writing and some reporting.

When an opportunity arose to move to Newtownards, Stewart jumped at the chance to work for the *Newtownards Spectator*, and after about six months he was transferred to the *Co. Down Spectator* in Bangor.

Those words from the poem *The Man From God Knows Where* by Bangor writer Florence Mary Wilson, who died in 1946, spring readily to mind when I recall being tasked to my first job as a fledging reporter on the *Newtownards Spectator* in September 1956.

It was to cover the annual Harvest Fair in Conway Square in the town – just down the street from the tiny *Spectator* office in Frances Street. And while at the time I had no prior knowledge of the history of the fair, I soon learned from talking with traders, buyers and sightseers, that this was more than just a one-off country market.

I had arrived in Newtownards only a couple of days previously from "Tyrone among the Bushes" where I had worked briefly as a reporter and general dogsbody on the *Tyrone Courier* in Dungannon shortly after leaving school.

My first night was spent at the Devonshire Hotel just off the Square and I remember almost falling over half-a-dozen well-used bicycles propped against the wall of the

The *News Letter* in Belfast soon beckoned and in 1959 Stewart moved to the city where he further developed his writing and reporting skills. First as a general reporter, then features writer, sub-editor and, under the direction of the paper's editor Cowan Watson, took over and expanded the paper's long-standing daily column *Around and About* by 'The Roamer'.

With the onset of the Troubles in 1969, Cowan moved Stewart to the News Desk to strengthen the reporting team and there he assisted the Chief Reporter at the time, David Kirk. Before long he was manning the News Desk – either during the day or at night – getting reporting and photographic staff to the scenes of atrocities throughout the Province.

In 1976 he left main-stream journalism and moved to the Police Press Office where he continued to write – this time for UTV's *Police Six* programme. He wrote the scripts for the programme's

old RUC station just a couple of doors away. One obvious lifestyle change as the 50s gave way to the 60s was that it soon became apparent that most policemen would now be able to afford cars.

To me, a young man just out of his teens, Newtownards was indeed a strange but exciting place. A market town certainly, and about the same size as Dungannon I reckoned. But at least it was flat – unlike the town I'd left behind which was perched on a hill-top. And as I dandered inquisitively round the unfamiliar streets on the evening I arrived, I made a point of locating the *Spectator* office in Frances Street, where I was to report the following morning.

It didn't look at all impressive – just a doorway opening off the street – but I do seem to remember the paper's name, *Newtownards Spectator,* stuck across two first-floor sash windows. I also found that the *Chronicle* offices were almost directly opposite, near Stevenson's photographic studios. The *Chronicle,* I have to say, was much more impressive and I wondered if I'd made the right choice. However, I soon learned that while the *Spectator's* premises were merely a base for a couple of journalists and an office girl who dealt with customers, the *Chronicle* was a complete printing works. The *Newtownards Spectator* was printed at the main printing works in Bangor's Main Street. Although the *Spectator* office in Frances Street has gone, the *Chronicle* is still there. The Devonshire Hotel has long since disappeared as well.

The Harvest Fair at Conway Square, Newtownards, in September 1960. *Newtownards Chronicle* picture

The *Spectator's* Editor then was Jim Irvine, a lovely young man who sadly died shortly before Christmas 2012. He briefed me on the Harvest Fair and sent me off down the street to get enough material to fill a page. A tall order, I thought, but striding out with a show of confidence I didn't feel, I met up with the *Chronicle's* photographer Farnham Nixon and together we lost ourselves in the mass of humanity ambling through dozens – if not hundreds – of stalls. At the turn of the decade, Farnham was taking pictures for both the *Newtownards Spectator* and the *Co. Down Spectator* in Bangor, as well as for the *Chronicle,* which was a mammoth task for one man. He eventually left in the early 60s and 'absconded' to the *News Letter* and *Sunday News* in Belfast.

Stewart relaxing with the late Charles Witherspoon after another successful *Police Six* in 1981

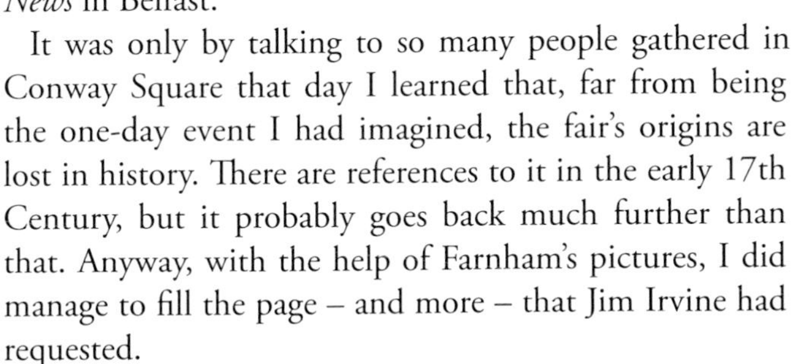

It was only by talking to so many people gathered in Conway Square that day I learned that, far from being the one-day event I had imagined, the fair's origins are lost in history. There are references to it in the early 17th Century, but it probably goes back much further than that. Anyway, with the help of Farnham's pictures, I did manage to fill the page – and more – that Jim Irvine had requested.

Writing UTV's *Crimecall* script with presenter Keith Burnside in 1982

As the 1960s dawned, it was obvious the town was becoming more affluent. Sadly, the two cinemas – the Ritz and the Regent – haven't survived although in the early 60s, they were at the height of their popularity.

One of the perks of being a newspaperman in the late 1950s and early 60s was that you got free admission – not only to cinemas but to most places of entertainment. A colleague of mine, Norman Stockton, and I took full advantage of this. Norman went on to become UTV's Political Correspondent. Television at the turn of the decade was making more and more of an impact on people's lives and the nightly queues outside both local cinemas, which had been the norm, began to dwindle. Even so, with our Press cards, we were able to walk straight in. Saturday morning matinees and live band shows also drew sizeable teenage crowds to the Ritz.

Although Conway Square and the town gradually changed over the 60s, much of it remains familiar. Cafolla's is still there of course, and its ice-cream, in my opinion, closely rivalled Caproni's in Bangor as the best in the country. But the square itself, which used to be a well-marked car park, has long since been pedestrianised and the 'new' one-way traffic system, with roundabouts and

presenter, the late Charles Witherspoon, and when he died a couple of years after suffering a serious stroke in 1982, the programme was taken over by Keith Burnside and re-named *Crimecall.* Stewart continued writing the *Crimecall* scripts for Keith until his retirement in 1995. Keith Burnside is now a news presenter with BBC Radio Ulster.

Stewart has written various short stories, many of which have been broadcast by Downtown Radio and on the BBC's Morning Story slot on Radio 4. In 2011, he published a book, *The Peacock's Tale*, telling of his experiences working for the *News Letter* and also including several of his stories.

As well as occasional writing, Stewart's hobbies include amateur radio and photography.

traffic lights seemingly scattered all over the place, must be confusing to someone who hasn't visited the town for many years. But then – isn't everywhere the same these days?

Reporters in those halcyon days covered all manner of events, most of which never reached the dailies in Belfast. Young Farmers' Clubs were scattered throughout North Down and the Ards Peninsula and I was frequently asked to cover annual meetings and special events – even dances. A small table was always provided for 'The Press' – me – and when votes had to be counted, all eyes looked questioningly in my direction and I would clamber on to the platform to count them. There was more trust in the Press then than now! If I made a mistake somewhere along the line and had the wrong person elected chairman, is it too late to apologise?

Meeting up in their 'local' with Colin Bateman, former *Spectator* reporter/deputy editor and now a best-selling author and TV script-writer

Travelling throughout the Ards in the late 50s and early 60s was a bit of a problem as scheduled bus services did not always match up with your requirements. As a reporter I frequently had to travel to church halls, community centres and venues often far removed from main routes. If public transport didn't suit, I was fortunate to have occasional use of the *Chronicle's* van as the *Spectator* didn't have one of its own in Newtownards. There was always very close co-operation between the two offices and anyway, in many cases, each paper would be sending its own reporter to cover the same event. But there was rivalry too and it was always a feather in one's cap if you managed to get a story the other paper missed.

Stewart Mackay today

Newtownards was, and still is, a great town and while the population has increased dramatically since the start of the 60s, it has always been one of the most newsworthy areas in the Province. Sometimes –just sometimes – I wish I was back in that old *Spectator* office in Frances Street.

Belle Rush

(née McKibbin) remembers... Cyril Lord

Despite his flamboyant and lavish lifestyle, it is practically impossible to find anyone with a bad word to say about Cyril Lord, who provided employment for well over 1,000 people when he opened the largest carpet factory in Europe – at Donaghadee – in the late Fifties.

I worked for CL, as he was known, as his Northern Ireland secretary throughout his 'reign' and well recall how factory staff would stand to attention when he arrived. The Queen herself wouldn't have caused so much commotion as did a phone call to say CL was on his way!

Indeed it was not unknown for him to pull on a pair of wellingtons and wander over the fields to the factory at 3am; if he found someone asleep when they should have been working there was trouble!

Cyril Lord was very well connected and lived an extravagant lifestyle. He owned a house on the Warren Road leading into Donaghadee where he regularly entertained famous guests at no-expense-spared parties. David Frost, Jack Hawkins, Arlene Dahl and Lady Sassoon were among the many visitors and on one particular occasion a last minute commitment prevented Princess Margaret from making a planned visit to his home.

The ostentatious seven-bedroom house had its own permanent chef, a separate house with penthouse

The young Belle McKibbin

Daughter of the late Tom and Mary McKibbin, Belle grew up in Donaghadee with her brother Cecil and sisters Marie and Liz.

After completing a secretarial course she worked for a time for a fabric upholstery company in Donaghadee before taking up the post of senior secretary in the late 1950s at Cyril Lord's new factory in the town.

Belle remained with the company for a number of years as Cyril Lord's Northern Ireland secretary.

She has been married to husband Bill Rush since 1963. The couple, who still live in Donaghadee, have a daughter, Nicole, and four grandchildren.

apartment for guests, servants' quarters, a swimming pool complete with its own underwater vacuum cleaner, and a tennis court and patio with a retractable sunroof. CL drove a Bentley, owned a helicopter, and even had a private jetty built out into the sea in front of the house for his speedboat, which was kept at the harbour and used for occasional trips to the Isle of Man. He also had a luxury home at Belgravia in London and holiday retreats in the South of France and Barbados.

Always the life and soul of community events in Donaghadee, here Cyril Lord can be seen in his boat following a barbecue on the Copeland Islands in July 1961. He was preparing to convey local people and visitors back to Donaghadee. The young musicians include Fred Day, Brian Huddleston, Carson Boyd, Gordon Moore, and Mason Douglas.
70-1-13

He owned four cotton mills in Lancashire, as well as a factory in South Africa, and in time expanded his Northern Ireland business empire to include plants at Newtownards, Bangor and Carnmoney, as well as the Pig 'n' Chicken restaurant at Templepatrick, the Ballygally Castle Hotel on the Antrim coast road and Thompson's Restaurant in the centre of Belfast.

A recruitment advertisement for the Donaghadee factory

In 1959 he was involved in a project to produce the three-wheeled Nobel 200 car and even made a cameo appearance – billed as 'The Carpet King' – in an episode of the *Batman* TV series in 1967, following a chance encounter with a 20th Century Fox executive during a trip to America.

Though small in stature, CL made a big impression wherever he went. He was permanently tanned and all the ladies admired his designer suits, beautiful watch and loved the whiff of his expensive aftershave. When the Bentley arrived and he burst out of it, you didn't know if he was coming upstairs to the office or dashing into the factory. He was meticulous about cleanliness and would take out his silk handkerchief and use it to wipe the looms if he saw as much as a speck of dust.

The Cyril Lord carpet factory in Donaghadee, which was officially opened towards the end of 1960

As far as my own life is concerned, after completing a secretarial course at Newtownards Tech, I had started working for Captain Rhodes, who owned an upholstery fabric factory in Donaghadee and was a good friend of Cyril Lord. I was always ambitious and when I saw an advert in the late 1950s for the post of senior secretary at his new carpet factory, I decided to apply. I was interviewed by Hugh Morrison and two others and although I was still quite young, I got the job. CL had two secretaries in London but I was known as his Northern Ireland secretary – though my main task was as secretary to managing directors Billy McKee and Ian Brackall. Other senior staff included Les Firth and Peter Davies, along with Trevor Halliwell, Holden Pitt, Sander Ferris, Leslie Crawford, John Hobday, Tom Andrews, Charles Valentine, who later became Mayor of Bangor, John Gilliland, Jimmy Gallagher, Jack Macklin, Eric Maginnis and Andy Brown.

Peter arrived here from England, to be joined a few months later by his wife Susan. Peter was totally dedicated both to his work and to his newly adopted community in Donaghadee, where all four of their adored children were born. He is still very much involved in community life and issues in the town.

The carpet warehouse at the Donaghadee factory

These are the people to whom I was particularly close, but there were many others – too numerous to name – who held responsible positions and who were also a pleasure to work with.

Twelve months later I decided to move to Canada for one year and the staff organised a wonderful leaving party.

When I returned home and was asked to come back to my old job, I gladly did.

The tufting machine at Donaghadee

CL already had his holiday home in Donaghadee before he decided to establish the carpet factory there. My friend's father was his gardener so I had known about him from a young age. I very happily lived in Donaghadee with my wonderful parents, Tom and Mary McKibbin, my brother Cecil, sisters Marie and Liz, and, for a time, my niece Danielle.

The already wealthy businessman received massive financial support from the Government towards the development of the 300,000sq. ft. factory on the town's High Bangor Road, and the foundation stone was laid by Cyril Lord himself in 1956. He later said only one other country in the world had offered him even greater incentives to set up business and that was Puerto Rico. The factory even made it into the *Guinness Book of Records* at the time for having the longest brick wall in Europe!

CL was a pioneer of the tufted carpet industry and firmly believed no other company in the world could produce a cheaper carpet. His aim was to sell it at a maximum price of £1 per yard and he hoped to produce about 33,000 yards a week. Shifts ran round the clock from 10pm-6am, 6am-2pm and 2pm-10pm, with the factory providing a massive employment boost for the whole of the Ards Peninsula and further afield.

Wearing the fashions of the latter part of the 1960s, a staff member at work in the Donaghadee factory's spinning department

Synthetic fibres were spun, tufted, dyed and printed in a variety of modern and traditional styles and patterns. Staff adored CL. The factory offered an above average scale of wages, a basic 40-hour week, incentive bonus schemes,

This Cyril Lord delivery vehicle is similar to those in the fleet that made deliveries throughout Northern Ireland

social and welfare facilities, training schemes, a subsidised canteen and state-of-the-art facilities.

By the time the factory was officially opened on 24 November 1960 by the Prime Minister of Northern Ireland, the Rt. Honourable Viscount Brookeborough of Colebrooke, it was employing 1,100 workers. I still have the actual plaque that was unveiled in reception that day.

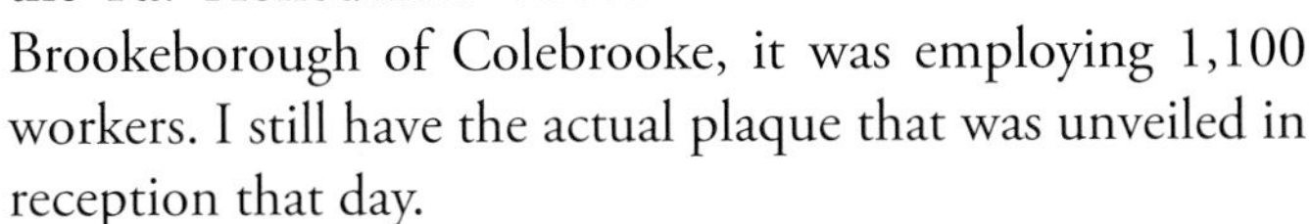

CL also built a huge warehouse and multi-storey office block at Rathgael in Bangor; it now serves as the headquarters of the Department of Education.

In tandem with all this, an extensive TV advertising campaign was launched with the slogan 'Luxury you can afford by Cyril Lord.' He was the first to champion the concept of selling straight from the factory to the public through small high street shops or agents using small samples. Customers measured the size required themselves and sent the information to us. We also had to deal with the resulting complaints when the wrong size or colour was delivered!

Mayor Charles Valentine, who worked in the transport department at Cyril Lord Carpets in Donaghadee, and Mayoress Mrs Valentine hosted a civic reception for Mr and Mrs Cyril Lord at the Town Hall in Bangor on 3 September 1960. Guests, who included senior staff and area sales representatives from the company, heard there was an urgent need for 350 new employees in Donaghadee, along with over 300 more for a new factory that was about to open at Rathgael. Back (from left): Mr Morrison, Mr Billy McKee (joint managing director), Mrs Proctor, Mr Ian Brackall (jointing managing director), Mrs Brennan, Mr Dix, Mr Burnaby, Cllr R. Proctor (Deputy Mayor). Front: Mr A. McNeilly (Clerk to North Down Rural Council), Alderman T. H. Brennan, Mrs Lord, the Mayor, Mr Lord, Mrs Valentine and Mrs A. Levine. *Spectator* picture

When he originally arrived in Donaghadee, CL was married to his first wife, Bessie, with whom he had three children – Jacqueline and twins Peter and Margot. Peter was an adorable wee boy and when he was home from boarding school in the summer holidays he would come to work in the factory under my care. Sadly, he was later badly injured in a car crash as was Margot in a separate accident. Jacqueline later married and moved to America.

After the marriage to Bessie broke up, CL married his second wife, a glamorous editor called Shirley, and they had a son, Richard.

I met my future husband Bill Rush, who later became export director, whilst working at the carpet factory and we married in 1963. On a couple of occasions CL asked if we would stay at his house whilst he was abroad, mainly to look after his two dogs, Kelly and Flanagan. Because CL had difficulty controlling Kelly and hadn't the time to be with his dogs, he eventually asked if we would like to keep him. We were delighted and in time Kelly was joined by Kim, whom we'd got from the same breeder. Those dogs brought us great joy and were with us until they died.

CL had a kindness to him. I remember once being reprimanded after I teleprinted a message I felt was important while he was at a meeting in England. A few weeks later, when he was back in Donaghadee, he handed me a record album and said: "I thought you might like that." However, I do believe I was right, the urgency being in conjunction with Jack and Ah Ping, the adorable Chinese couple who were good friends of ours and who looked after CL and his family's every need when they were here.

Popular Chinese couple Jack and Ah Ping who looked after the Lords when they were in Donaghadee

CL was a man who was way ahead of his time. For example, he launched *Cyrilawn*, an imitation grass selling for 35 shillings a square yard. To get publicity he took over a big hotel in London, laid out a lawn and hired top tennis players to play on it. In 1966 alone the firm's advertising budget was almost £800,000!

He was a very clever man but he could be impulsive. He had these big ideas but it seemed he took on too much too quickly. Everything had to be big and there weren't many people who dared to stand up to him.

Cyrilawn failed to sell and there were other disasters like plans to produce artificial Astrakhan (fake fur) which never took off, while plans to make vinyl flooring also collapsed. His 800 UK retail outlets also proved too costly to operate.

Belle (seated centre) is pictured with Cyril Lord colleagues at a farewell function before her departure for Canada

Cyril Lord Carpets was eventually forced into administration in 1968. It came as a huge blow to everyone; indeed 1,000 employees marched to Stormont to urge the Government to protect their jobs. Fortunately the assets were acquired by Viyella International, which later became Carrington Viyella, and marketing was focused on established retail and wholesale outlets.

By 1974 the factory had no fewer than 1,394 employees and a turnover totalling £184m. However, increased competition and a trend towards laminate flooring led to a decline in business and the factory, by then owned by Shaws, went into liquidation in 2003. The machinery was sold to China and the former factory has since been demolished.

Belle Rush and Peter Davies with the original plaque from the opening ceremony in November 1960

By then I had long since left to raise our wonderful daughter Nicole and we now have four adorable grandchildren and son-in-law Conrad.

We all had so many good times in the carpet factory and numerous lasting friendships were established there. Some of my dear friends were close pals then and have remained so all my life – in particular Kaye Stout (now sadly deceased), Audrey Irwin and Liz Somers, both in Canada, Kathleen Buchanan, Margaret Bell and Liz Gourley, as well as my sister-in-law Margo Cooke, Hazel Reynor, Irene Crawford, Eileen Boyd, Henry Miskimmon,

Hans Arthur, and who could possibly forget the lovely smile of Andrea Kirk on the switchboard. All were part of a wonderful team.

Who was Cyril Lord?

'Carpet King' Cyril Lord was born in Manchester on 12 July 1911 and later served an apprenticeship with a local spinning and weaving firm. He was sent to Northern Ireland by the Board of Trade during the Second World War and spent four years advising the authorities on the conversion of idle flax machines to produce materials for the war effort.

Cyril Lord at the height of his success

Following the cessation of hostilities, Lord took over four cotton mills in Lancashire and built up his successful business empire, which included local carpet factories in Donaghadee and Newtownards.

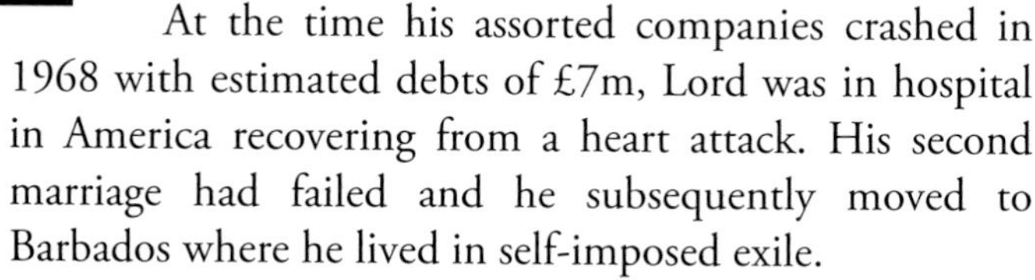

At the time his assorted companies crashed in 1968 with estimated debts of £7m, Lord was in hospital in America recovering from a heart attack. His second marriage had failed and he subsequently moved to Barbados where he lived in self-imposed exile.

He later married third wife Aileen, widow of impresario Val Parnell, whom he had met on holiday in the South of France, and the pair adopted a quiet lifestyle. Lord admitted, in an interview he gave a decade later: "When I was in business, I wanted all the publicity I could get. Now I want to be anonymous. I miss England terribly but I don't want to go back and have to face all that aggravation with the media again."

Lord also maintained his businesses were put into receivership too hastily, saying: "If they had held on for a few more months things could have been all right. You would have thought the Government would have offered to help out, after all the millions we made for the country in exports."

He died in Barbados in June 1984, aged 72.

Joe Millin

remembers... Tea and Scones in Scrabo Tower

My family's connection with Scrabo Tower began shortly after it was built in 1857, when my great-grandparents, Anna and Hugh McKay (who worked in the Scrabo quarry), took up residence in the tower as its first tenants.

On their retirement, their daughter Sarah-Jane and her husband Joseph Millin took over and, despite having neither electricity nor running water, the tower soon became home to their family of 10, including my father Samuel.

By the time my grandparents died most of the family had married and moved away from the tower, leaving three of my aunts, Jean, Lizzie and Agnes, who, following the family tradition, took over the tenancy.

Needless to say, the tower wasn't the best of places for three ladies of advancing years to spend the winter months. During that part of the year they moved to a cottage lower down, at the foot of the track leading straight up the face of the hill. My aunts still had to climb that hill every day through the winter to tend to their small herd of goats and other livestock which remained at the summit.

To bring in a little extra income during the summer months, my aunts started serving teas, scones and fries to walkers, who had slogged their way up from the town, and golfers from the adjoining Scrabo Golf Club which,

Joe Millin as a boy in 1951

Joe Millin was born at Scrabo Road, Newtownards, at the bottom of the lane leading up Scrabo's face. He attended the Model Primary School, Movilla High School and the local Technical College before taking up employment as a metal worker at Gibson's in Belfast.

Recreational pastimes in the 1960s included dancing at the Locarno in Portaferry and playing football.

Joe still lives in Ards; he is married to June and they have a son and a grandson. He enjoys walking and supports Ards FC.

Jean, Elizabeth and Agnes in their cottage at the foot of Scrabo loanen with the silver teapot presented to them by Lady Londonderry in 1957 to commemorate the centenary of the family's connection with the tower.

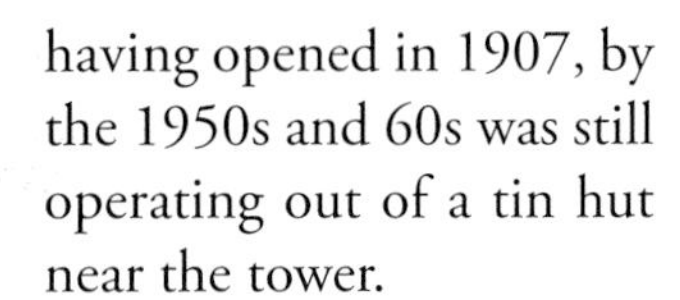

having opened in 1907, by the 1950s and 60s was still operating out of a tin hut near the tower.

I remember as a boy helping out by selling 6d bottles of New City lemonade from a shed beside the tower and by running errands to Maynes' grocers in Newtownards for supplies which then had to be carried by Shank's pony up to the tower. As a lad I was very glad my aunts served tea with goats' milk from their herd as it was one less thing I had to carry up the hill!

My aunts weren't always the only residents on the upper reaches of the hill. I recall a period in the Fifties when they acquired a neighbour who went by the name of John Smith and who made his home in the North Quarry living in a hole (cave would be too grand a term), over which he draped some canvas to make a rough shelter. My aunts used to take him tea and food but I must admit as a young lad I was somewhat afraid of him so I stayed well clear.

John Smith, cave dweller

As he just seemed to suddenly appear, I don't think he was a local man and I doubt that John Smith was his real name, but I've often wondered in the intervening years what became of him.

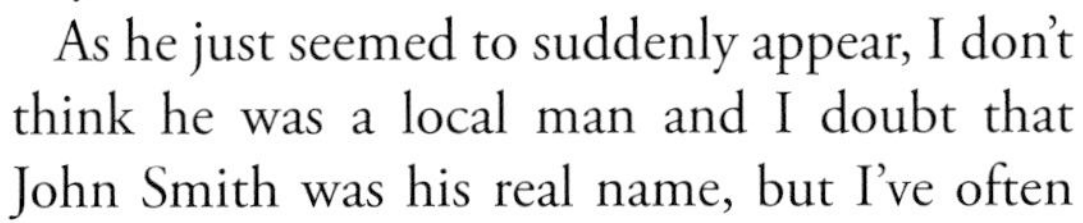

Cave-dwelling neighbours aside, Scrabo Tower was seldom a lonely place with its steady stream of visitors, though of course some days were busier than others.

One of the busiest was always Easter Monday when, in a long-standing tradition, hundreds of people from the town would make their way up Scrabo carrying whin-dyed hard-boiled eggs to be 'trindled' down the slopes. Picnics were hungrily devoured and, inevitably, a football or two would be produced for the youngsters to kick about to the third fairway of the golf course.

Scrabo Tower in the late 60s

I don't ever recall being deterred by the weather on such occasions; indeed on one memorable Easter Monday it snowed and a friend's hands were so badly affected by the cold we had to take him up to the tower, where he held them over a lighted candle to restore some measure of circulation and feeling!

Other busy times were June, when people could pick berries, and September, when the hazelnuts were ready. After that things quieted down again as winter reasserted its icy grip on Scrabo and my aunts moved to their cottage at the bottom of the hill, a yearly ritual until 1966, when they moved out of the tower permanently.

Today Scrabo Tower has been transformed into an exhibition centre which is well worth a visit – though for many older residents any education they receive there will be overlaid with the fond memory of an Ulster Fry washed down with goat's milk tea and the echo of children's laughter as they trindled their eggs on a sunny Easter Monday.

Joe Millin

1963

in the Chronicle

Many homes in Ards were left without electricity as a result of high winds and heavy snow on Sunday 20 January. Treacherous road conditions prevented repair crews from reaching affected areas for a number of hours.

A second blizzard, which began on 5 February, created even greater havoc, with many businesses and factories being forced to close early because of a lack of lighting and heat. Large snowdrifts – said to be the worst in living memory – developed along the Comber to Newtownards road, the Newtownards to Bangor road and along many roads around the Ards Peninsula.

Bus services were severely disrupted and schools were forced to close for the rest of the week. Many social functions were also cancelled due to the inclement conditions.

A snowball fight rages in Newtownards late in January 1963 as winter begins to take an icy grip on the town and district.
54-25-1

It was difficult going for this motorist near McBurney's Corner on the Comber to Newtownards road on 8 February 1963.
55-88-1

Employees of the Cyril Lord factory at Regent Street in Newtownards were told by the Council in February they could no longer run dances in the Queen's Hall after damage estimated at £1 was caused to a seat in the ladies' toilet during a private function attended by 300 people.

As a result of increased competition from overseas manufacturers, hosiery firm Berkshire Knitting (Ulster) Ltd. announced in mid-February it would be introducing wage cuts of between 15% and 30% at its Dundonald and Newtownards factories.
They also planned to introduce a 'tandem' working system, where an employee used two machines in the fully-fashioned knitting section instead of one. That would give such employees a 20% pay increase, but would also result in redundancy for 54 fellow workers. Threatened strike action in early May led to a reduction in the number of redundancies and modifications to the 'tandem' working system.

Mrs Sarah McClements, of Springfield Road, Portavogie, celebrated her 100th birthday on 1 March 1963. Included is her brother John (Mahood), who was 86. *57-29-2*

Mrs Sarah McClements, of Springfield Road, Portavogie, celebrated her 100th birthday on 1 March. She was a native of the village and said she had only left the district on a handful of occasions, mainly at holiday times. One of her near neighbours was her younger brother, John Mahood, who was 86.

Guest of honour at the annual Movilla Secondary Intermediate School prize distribution in early March was Sir John Hunt, who had led the successful British expedition to the summit of Mount Everest in 1953.

The Mayor of Newtownards, Cllr Stanley Woods, takes the salute during a parade of youth organisations to First Newtownards Presbyterian Church in connection with the Charter Week celebrations in late March 1963. *59-98-1*

A Civic Week in Newtownards at the end of March marked the 350th anniversary of the granting of the 1613 Borough Charter by King James I. Various community activities were organised to highlight the growth of the town over the years and its position by the early 1960s as the industrial centre of the county.

Allen West and Co. announced that the company's Newtownards factory would close at the end of May, with the loss of all remaining jobs, due to a recession in the motor control gear industry.

A stone font, believed to be 700 years old and traceable to the 13th Century Priory of St. Columba, was found in the grounds of Walker's Mill by the Rev. Reggie Chisholm, rector of St Mark's in Newtownards. The mill occupied the site of the Old Priory.

A new factory for Wetherdair (Northern Ireland) Ltd. in Ballywalter was opened on 17 May by Commerce Minister Brian Faulkner. It had a staff of 100 local people, mainly women, who were involved in the production of raincoats.

Donaghadee girl Olive Shannon, a student at Regent House School, was one of four national winners in an essay/painting competition organised by Brooke Bond Tea, which attracted 500,000 entries from all over the British Isles. Olive's entry – a painting entitled 'The Storm' – won her a 16-day holiday in Ceylon.

A new primary school in Donaghadee, St Anne's, was officially opened on 25 May by the Bishop of Down and Connor, Most Rev. Dr William Philbin. The celebrant of an open-air High Mass was Fr. J. Magee CC, Downpatrick, a former curate in Donaghadee.

The foundation stone for a new £17,000 hall for Shore Street Presbyterian Church in Donaghadee was laid by long-serving Clerk of Session Luke Semple on 6 July.

Commerce Minister Brian Faulkner announced on 22 July that Johnston and Phillips Ltd. would be taking over the vacant factory formerly occupied by Allen West and Co. Production of electrical equipment was expected to start immediately with 60 workers initially employed by the company.

Local businessman Graeme Mackenzie, who was behind the newly-formed Portaferry Expansion Company, announced they would be introducing a multi-purpose ferry service across Strangford Lough before the end of the year. Mr Mackenzie had just opened The Scotsman, a new hotel and restaurant in the town.

Cadet Roland Shimmons returned home to New Street in Donaghadee on 10 August after a three-week, 8,000-mile round trip to Canada, sponsored by the Air Training Corps. He was a former pupil of Regent House, where he had been a member of 2241 Squadron of the ATC for nearly five years.

It was announced that Newtownards' first and, by 1963, only remaining licensed pawnbroker would be closing on Christmas Eve. Mitchell's in Meetinghouse Lane had opened in 1933 but was pulling down the shutters some 30 years later because of a shortage of staff.
Seemingly, no one wanted to undertake the necessary six-year apprenticeship to be a pawnbroker – along with the Saturday working hours. The business also fell victim to the growing popularity of credit purchases, which made a visit to the pawn shop less of a necessity when money was short.

In similar vein, a call was made at the beginning of September by 17-year-old Derek Harkness, from Carrowdore, for the introduction of a five-day working week. An apprentice at Drysdale's in Regent Street, Newtownards, he launched a petition aimed at employers in the town, having learned that many were in favour of Thursday closing (in addition to Sunday). His own employer, Mr R. H. Drysdale, was fully in favour of the closure, saying it was increasingly difficult to recruit apprentices as no one wanted to work on six days.

Gladys Aylward, whose life as a missionary in China during the 1930s and 1940s was recounted in the film *The Inn Of The Sixth Happiness,* was guest speaker at a packed Queen's Hall on 9 September. Indeed, an estimated 200 people had to be turned away from the event, which was organised by the Worldwide Mission Convention.
As a result of the film, and her appearance on the BBC's *This Is Your Life* in 1963, the story of her journey across bleak mountain ranges in wartime conditions with 100 children aged from four to 16 was known to millions.

Capt. William Long, MP for Ards at Stormont, promised to fight for the reopening of Crommelin Memorial School in Carrowdore, branding its closure at the end of the summer term as "illogical". The 40 pupils had moved to three rural schools close to Carrowdore, namely Dunover, Grangee and Ballyboley. The Ministry of Education had a long-term aim to provide one large primary school in Carrowdore but Capt. Long felt there was room for expansion at Crommelin.

Brookside, the Bangor Road (Newtownards) home of Mr and Mrs Russell Paine, was damaged on 18 September by a large piece of rock blasted from a quarry a quarter of a mile away. Two young children, Timothy (8) and Jonathan (3), were playing outside at the time and the rock, which hit the roof before travelling along the gutter and landing in the garden, missed them by a matter of feet.

Record Round-Up, a weekly music scene column penned by Brian Silvester, appeared in the *Chronicle* for the first time in the issue dated 27 September. Nearly two months would pass before the column's first mention of The Beatles (by way of a reference to the 400,000 advance orders for new album *With The Beatles).*
The very first reference in the *Chronicle* to The Beatles occurred in an advert for an appearance by Tony and The Telstars at Crossgar's War Memorial Hall on 18 October: 'Hear their impressions of The Beatles, Gerry and The Pacemakers, etc.'

David Hamilton of Fruitvale Farm, Cottown, was acclaimed in late September as Northern Ireland's most enterprising farmer after he won the Farmer '63 competition, sponsored by David Brown Tractors (Belfast) Ltd., and organised in conjunction with the Ministry of Agriculture and the Ulster Farmers' Union.

Chronicle readers had a chance to see American singing star Roy Orbison at the Royal Ballroom in Dundonald on 9 October. A special bus was laid on from Newtownards for those wishing to attend the concert – with an all-in price of 7/6d.

The new Ritz Teenage Show opened at the popular Newtownards cinema on 28 September, with more than 350 youngsters aged from four to 16 packing the venue for a mixed programme of cartoons, travelogues, an adventure feature film and stage performances. Those appearing 'live' were singer Brian Rossi along with Lee Parker and The Vibratones, while dancers Tommy O'Brien and Jackie Thorman gave a demonstration of the Twist. The following week saw the attendance increasing to 500.

Eighteen-year-old Irene Wright, from Brae-Ville, Grangee, was elected Miss Ards at a dance in the Queen's Hall organised by the North End Ards Supporters' Club.

The North Down Hospital Management Committee announced in October that it would be introducing new measures at Ards Hospital to prohibit all visitors from smoking. Chief Medical Officer Alexander Calder said he had visited a general ward a few days earlier and found it was filled with smoke. "I thought there was a fire," he declared, adding: "The floor was covered with cigarette butts."
While Mr Calder accepted it would not be right to stop the hospital shop and the trolley service for patients from carrying cigarettes "as this would be an interference with the liberty of the individual," it was nevertheless agreed to return all cigarette vending machines on which manufacturers proposed to charge rentals.

Greyabbey man James Carson retired from his job as head of the Ulster Transport Authority's freight depot in Newtownards. Aged 65, he was the third generation to work in the freight business. His grandfather had transported goods from Greyabbey to Belfast by horse and cart a century earlier.

The Borough Council agreed on 4 November to spend between £10 and £15 on the provision of a glass-covered street map of Newtownards at the front entrance to the Town Hall.

It was announced that the Newtownards household textile manufacturer Irish Tapestry Co. would close at the end of November with the loss of 30 jobs. During a peak period after the Second World War nearly 300 people had been employed at the factory, with the main product being woven bedspreads. They had attempted to move into the candlewick bedspread market but could not compete with larger firms using modern machinery.

Garage worker Fred Freeman, from Parkview in Newtownards, took part in *Take Your Pick,* the popular ITV quiz show hosted by Michael Miles. Offered the chance to choose the key to one of 10 boxes containing mystery prizes, he opted for number 7. He then turned down an offer of £28 for the key – a wise decision as Fred had selected the Treasure Chest containing £90.

The Mayor of Newtownards, Alderman John Algie, sent a telegram on behalf of the people of the Borough to Eric Hughes, American Consul General for Northern Ireland, following the assassination of President John F. Kennedy on 22 November.

"It was with deep shock and profound regret that the news of the tragic death of your highly respected President was received in Newtownards and on behalf of citizens of the Borough I beg to tender sincere sympathy to the members of his family and to the citizens of the USA in their great loss," read the telegram.

It was estimated that at least £20,000 was spent on alcohol in Newtownards over the Christmas period. However, according to local barmen much of the drink was taken off the premises as "more and more people prefer to sit at home watching television with a glass in their hand."

Clergy who attended the institution of the Rev. Hamilton Leckey as Rector of St. Mary's Parish Church, Comber, at the beginning of January 1963. Front (from Left): Mr Leckey; Dr. Frederick Mitchell, Bishop of Down and Dromore; Ven. George Quin, Archdeacon of Down and Rector of Bangor. Back: Rev. W. E. Harris, Diocesan Registrar; the Rev. R. E. Turner, and Canon C. H. Walsh, Rural Dean of Bangor.
52-100-3

Members of First Donaghadee Girls' Auxiliary and friends at a party in the church hall in mid-January 1963.
53-59-3

Canon H. T. Cotter with members of the Portavogie Fishermen's Choir at a Harvest of the Sea service held in Ballyeasborough Parish Church on 27 January 1963.
55-17-1

Bobby Savage (9), of Loughdoo Road, Ardkeen, Portaferry, was among the youngest competitors at the Kircubbin YFC ploughing match at Ballycam, Portaferry, on 15 February 1963.
56-52-2

Bradley McCall QC is pictured at the annual Ards Hospital prize distribution in March 1963 with (from left): Nurse M.T. McCaughrain (silver medal), Nurse H. M.Tompkins (gold medal) and Nurse B.A. O'Hare (bronze medal).
57-79-3

The court scene from *The Merchant Of Venice*, which was presented by the Regent House Dramatic Society in the assembly hall on 28 and 29 March 1963.
60-42-2

Colin Earney, of Graffan Gardens, Comber, enjoys a long cool drink at the Comber Rectory fete in June 1963.
67-52-1

Nine-year-old Frank McCormick and his brother Sam (5), of Demesne Farm, Donaghadee, hold their father's prizewinning mare and foal at Carrowdore Show in late June 1963.
67-99-3

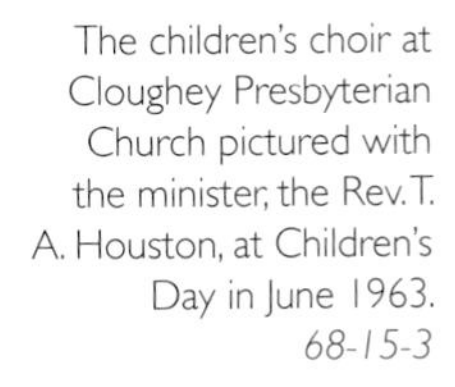

The children's choir at Cloughey Presbyterian Church pictured with the minister, the Rev. T. A. Houston, at Children's Day in June 1963.
68-15-3

Having fun with a couple of old tyres at the Ards District Scout Sports in July 1963 are (from left): John Neill (Second Donaghadee), Gregory Anderson (First Ards), winner of the obstacle race, Alan Holmes (Second Donaghadee) and Peter Francis (Sixth Newtownards).
68-80-1

It was a big day for these Comber children who attended school for the first time in early September 1963. They were pupils at Comber Primary School.
73-98-3

Smiling faces at the opening get-together of the Youth Fellowship at St. Andrew's Parish Church, Ballyhalbert, in late September 1963. Included are the Rev. F. W. A. Bell and the Rev. M. Wilson, Portaferry.
75-92-3

The team from Third 'B' Girl Guides, Newtownards, Regent House Company, who represented Newtownards and Comber District at the North Down County Ceremonial competition in Bangor on 9 November 1963. Back (from left): N. Wilson, S. Gilmore, Captain A. Labe, R. Carson. Middle: H. Brown, M. Dalzell, J. Sloan, B. Cole, E. Moore, F. Weir. Front: B. Heatherington, P. Harper, P. Dickson, M. Wallace and R. Wallace.
79-31-1

A section of the congregation at a recording of the BBC *Songs Of Praise* programme in St. Mark's Parish Church, Newtownards, on 22 November 1963. It was broadcast on 1 December.
79-94-2

Ending the year very much as it began, children from Comber Primary School enjoy a slide during a spell of cold weather just before Christmas.
81-50-3

Sport in 1963

in the Chronicle

Lisbarnett farmer Ernest McMillan, partnered by well-known BBC commentator Raymond Baxter, took part in January's Monte Carlo Rally, although not featuring in the prize list. They drove in an 1100 MG saloon.

After a gap of four months Ards FC finally had a new manager, Hugh Rankin, with the appointment being on a temporary basis to the end of the season. His first fixture was a first round Irish Cup tie against Portadown Reserves, which resulted in a 3-2 victory for Ards.
On the Ards team a week earlier was 15-year-old Maurice Drury, who made his senior debut in a scoreless draw against Portadown.

Mavis Gilmore, a pupil at Glastry Intermediate Secondary School, captained the County Down netball team which won the Ulster Inter-County Netball Tournament in Belfast on 22 March.

Ards Rugby Club won the North Down Cup with a 15-3 victory over Holywood at Donaghadee on 30 April. Scorers were Gordon Kennedy (penalty and dropped goal), Ivan Coffey (penalty), George Ferguson (try) and Billy Herron (try).

Ards Boys won two major trophies within a week in early June – the Irish Youth Cup (with a 3-1 victory over Whiteabbey at Seaview) and the Barry Cup (with a 3-2 win over Lemington Sparta at Ballyclare).

Former Bangor and Distillery player John Neilson was appointed manager of Ards FC to replace temporary manager Hugh Rankin.

Ballyhalbert Yachting Regatta was revived successfully on 15 June after a 25-year break. Behind the venture were Joe Hagan from Kircubbin and Eric Chadwick, owner of the Ship Inn in Ballyhalbert.

North Down's Senior Cup victory over Cregagh on 15 June included an innings of 110 runs by vice-captain Jack McBurney – reportedly the first century by a senior player for many years.

Ards Cricket Club won the Northern Cricket Union's Section D after beating Old Bleach by 119 runs and finishing the league unbeaten (it was the second season in a row that they had achieved the feat). There was a widely held view that the team was too good for that level and deserved to be promoted several league sections.

Billy Kirk made a welcome reappearance after being out of competitive cycling for two years because of ligament trouble, winning Ards Cycling Club's Savage Cup on 4 September. Runners-up were Albert White and Ian Bell.

After just three years in the Belfast and District Senior Table Tennis League, Glenford were the new All Ireland Champions, following a 5-4 victory over Balbriggan on 19 October. It was a special achievement for captain Harry O'Prey, who had previously led the Ards club to the same success. Also on the team were George Cardy and Billy McGimpsey (fourth player Alfie Wright having been unable to travel).

Pictured at a dance in the Queen's Hall early in January 1963 are cup and medal winners, along with officials, from Cyril Lord's Regent Street factory in Newtownards. The team had competed with great success in the 1962 Factory League.
52-95-1

Scrabo Secondary Intermediate School's netball team, winners of the North Down Area Schools' League in March 1963. Back (from left): Jean Bailie, Freda Savage, Elizabeth McBurney, Margaret, Warden, Mrs H. Millin (coach). Front: Margaret Finlay, Sylvia McDowell (captain), Maree Tollerton and Dorothy Houston.
58-24-2

The Ards A Ladies hockey team, winners of the McConnell Shield and runners-up in the All Ireland White Cup in April 1963. Back (from left): P. Moffatt, N. Armstrong, M. Fraser, O. McGladdery, W. Thornton, A. Bennett. Front: J. Sloane, M. Rountree, M. Dempster (captain), A. Keenan and H. Coey.
61-46-2

Glastry Secondary Intermediate School's senior football team won the North Down Schools Intermediate League in May 1963. Back (from left): Mr Pollock, J. Adair, B. Cromie, S. Alexander, K. Lant, Mr J. F. McFerran. Front: S. Thompson, G. Young, D. Davidson, R. Thompson, M. McConnell, R. Thompson (captain). With ball: J. Thompson.
65-52-2

Members of the White Horse Inn darts team from Carrowdore with the trophies they received at a social evening on 2 May 1963. The team had achieved a noteworthy double – the Lower Ards and District League and the Knock-Out Cup. Back (from left): R. B. McKee, T. Stewart, S. Dorrian, J. Burch, D. McCreedy, M. Davison, also Mr A. Beattie, the team's most enthusiastic supporter. Front: R. Boyd, B. Burch, A. Moreland (captain), M. Bennett and S. Muckle.
63-32-3

Broadcaster Ronald Rosser presents the Player of the Year award to Ralph McGuicken, the Ards FC full back, at a North End Ards Supporters' Club function in May 1963.
63-25-2

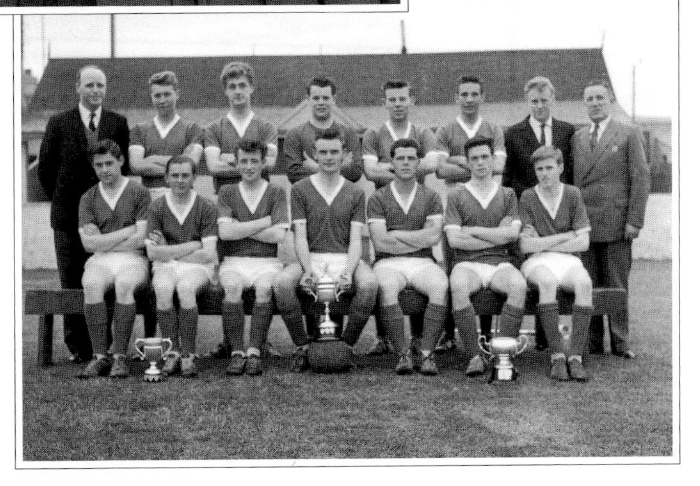

Pictured in June 1963 are members of the highly successful Ards Boys team, winners of the Irish Youth Cup and the Barry Cup. Back (from left): E. Hawkins (manager), Craig, Baxter, Wright, Larmour, Caskey, Murphy, W. Graham. Front: Patton, Mowat, McCready, Houston (captain), Carroll, Gazzard and Hingston.
66-56-2

Donaghadee Olympic football team defeated Tip Top at Londonderry Park in July 1963.
70-81-3

Members of the Castle Espie lawn tennis team, winners of Section Seven in the Belfast and District Junior League in August 1963.
71-96-2

Monday 16 December 1963 marked the official opening of Carrowdore Parish Indoor Bowling Club.
80-87-1

1964

in the Chronicle

Two Newtownards teachers were among a party who spent the first night of 1964 camping 1,000ft feet up in the Mournes. Myrtle Cooke (Scrabo Intermediate) and David Heron (Movilla Intermediate) were attending a mountain activities course for teachers, organised by the Down County Education Committee and based at the Kinnahalla Youth Hostel.

Greyabbey postwoman Agnes McKeag retired on 3 January after a career spanning 21 years. Miss McKeag (68), from North Street, carried out her rounds on foot and by bicycle, covering Ballyboley, Ballyboghilbo and parts of Greyabbey itself. At the time she was one of only six postwomen left in Northern Ireland.

The Newtownards-based firm of Berkshire Knitting (Ulster) Ltd. changed its name in early January to Berkshire International (UK) Ltd.

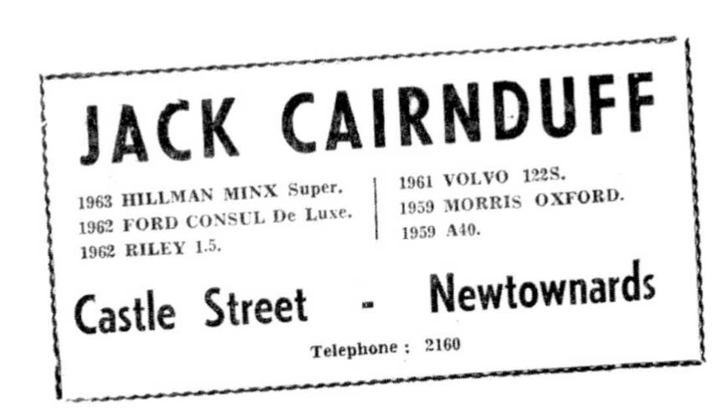

Former British and Empire Bantamweight champion Freddie Gilroy bought the Tivoli Bar at Manor Street in Donaghadee.

Great-grandfather Samuel White, aged 90, of Harbour Road, Portavogie, was proclaimed as one of the most remarkable men living in the Ards Peninsula as he was still riding his trusty 40-year-old Raleigh bicycle "as competently as anyone a quarter of his age." Each week he cycled the four miles from his home to the smithy run by his son, also Samuel, at Ballymacnamee.

Hemstitching firm W. Ferguson (Ulster) Ltd., of East Street, announced it would be closing in mid-January after being an essential part of the industrial life of Newtownards for almost 50 years. This was because of the owner's retirement rather than a fall-off in orders. At one point the company had provided employment for 200 people and as recently as Christmas 1963 the figure stood at 130. The building was taken over by Debretta Ltd., which already had factories in Newtownards, Portaferry and Bangor, with the machinery being sold to other manufacturers.

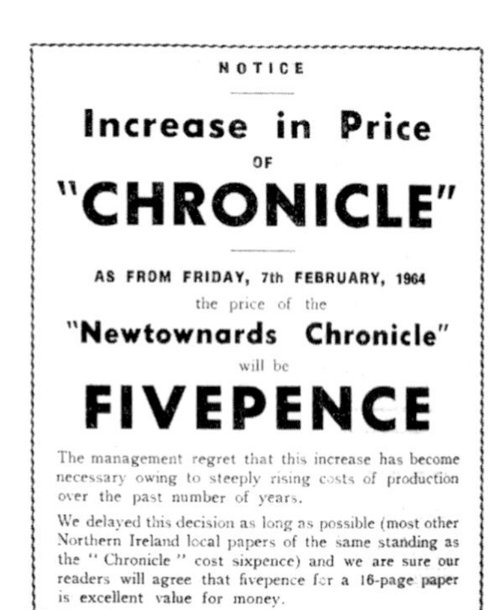
NOTICE

Increase in Price
OF
"CHRONICLE"

AS FROM FRIDAY, 7th FEBRUARY, 1964
the price of the
"Newtownards Chronicle"
will be
FIVEPENCE

The management regret that this increase has become necessary owing to steeply rising costs of production over the past number of years.

We delayed this decision as long as possible (most other Northern Ireland local papers of the same standing as the "Chronicle" cost sixpence) and we are sure our readers will agree that fivepence for a 16-page paper is excellent value for money.

Owing to a steep increase in production costs the price of the *Newtownards Chronicle* rose by a penny to fivepence from the issue dated 7 February. A further penny was added later in the year (27 November edition).

Newtownards Borough Council turned down an application in early February to hire out the Queen's Hall for roller skating. While the applicant explained that the skates had rubber wheels and would not harm the floor, members insisted there remained a risk of damage to the walls.

Ards MP Capt. William Long warned in early February that the livelihoods of 200 Portavogie fishermen were under threat because the only fish carrier service from Portavogie to Portpatrick, which took fish for the Glasgow market, was being withdrawn from 1 March because of the high operating costs.
Speaking at Stormont, he called for financial assistance that would allow the vessel to be retained. However, Capt. Long was advised by Agriculture Minister Harry West that subsidising the export of any commodity from Northern Ireland into Britain was contrary to the terms of the Government of Ireland Act of 1920.

Two Newtownards police officers, Constables John T. Harley and James McIntyre, retired from the force with some 66 years' service between them. Constable Harley, as senior traffic officer at the local station, had the distinction in 1938 of bringing the first traffic car to the town.

The opening hours at Newtownards Post Office were established from 2 March as 9am to 6pm, Monday to Friday, to bring it into line with those of Crown Post Offices elsewhere in Northern Ireland.

Both the Regent Cinema in Newtownards and the Comber Cinema screened the

25 February Sonny Liston v. Cassius Clay world title fight in early March. With Clay (later to rename himself Muhammad Ali) triumphant, it was billed as the "sensational fight film of the century."

The new hall built for Shore Street Presbyterian Church in Donaghadee was officially opened on 7 March by Mrs J. S. McKee and dedicated by the Rt. Rev. Dr. W. A. Montgomery, Moderator of the General Assembly.

Some of the many people who attended the opening of the new Shore Road Presbyterian Church hall in Donaghadee on 7 March 1964. *87-58-1*

Home Affairs Minister Bill Craig assured Stormont MPs in early May that the proposed bridge across Strangford Lough was "not a closed book by any means." He said a preliminary survey had been carried out and three possible sites chosen. The cost of the project was estimated at £2.5m. in 1964.

It was announced that from the beginning of June a five-day working week would take effect in most shops in Newtownards, with all-day closing on Thursdays and Sundays.

Twenty-two candidates stood for election as Councillors and Aldermen in the 1964 Borough Council elections, with Unionist, Liberal, Labour and Ratepayers' Association candidates entering the fray. There were contests in three of the four wards (the exception being Castle). Those returned to office were as follows:
Castle – Alderman John Algie, Cllrs Samuel Gracey, William Orr (all Unionist) and Jack Beckett (Ratepayers' Association).
Glen – Alderman Robert Gaw (Labour), Cllrs Alexander Bailie, Georgina Foulis and James White (all Unionist).
Scrabo – Alderman Archibald Dunlop (Labour), Cllrs Hugh Robert Drysdale (Ratepayers' Association), Joseph McCullough (Labour) and Stanley Woods (Unionist).

Victoria – Alderman William Spratt (Unionist), Cllrs Thomas John Beattie (Unionist), Mabel Doggart (Independent) and Norman Francis (Independent).

Recently retired Sister Alice Johnston received a presentation in Greyabbey Village Hall on 22 May in recognition of her work as District Nurse in the Mid-Ards area for a period of 35 years.

Six hundred people gathered in Newtownards on 6 June to celebrate the centenary of the flax yarn spinning company of George Walker and Co. Ltd., of Castle Gardens Mill. During the course of those 100 years the firm had provided employment for thousands of local people.

Ulster's Pride Women's LOL 110 (Newtownards) members at 'the field' in Ballygowan on Monday 13 July 1964. *96-49-1*

Pictured during a tour of the new fire station in Donaghadee back in September 1964 are (from left): Fire Force Commander G. H. Murphy, Section Leader E. Armstrong, Minister of Home Affairs Brian McConnell and Mrs McConnell, Captain William Long MP, Mr James Finlay, chairman of the Northern Ireland Fire Authority, and Mrs G. M. Stone, chairman of Donaghadee Urban District Council. *99-72-1*

Ballygowan was host to the first all-county Twelfth of July demonstration, with Orangemen, bands and supporters numbering some 40,000 packing into the village, somewhat enlarging its usual population of 480. Because the Twelfth fell on a Sunday, the 274th anniversary of the Battle of the Boyne was delayed until the following day.

Eighteen year-old Yvonne Armstrong, a shorthand typist from Carrowdore, was a first heat winner of the Miss TV Post beauty competition at Bangor's Pickie Pool, qualifying for the final on 14 August.

Donaghadee's new fire station, the 43rd to be erected in Northern Ireland since 1950, was officially opened on 28 August by Home Affairs Minister Brian McConnell. Built in Union Street at a cost of just over £13,000, it could accommodate two vehicles and also provided a well-appointed recreation room for the firemen.

Sixteen-year-old Cynthia Murphy, from Circular Road, Newtownards, received a Vox electric guitar worth £22 after winning a talent competition, promoted by the Ivy Benson Band, at the Villa Marina in Douglas, Isle of Man.

Newtownards Rotary Club came into being on 15 September at the Queen's Hall, venue for the Charter Dinner. It was attended by representatives from Rotary's 19 other clubs from both sides of the border. Newtownards president Andrew Malcomson was presented with the Charter by Felix J. Hughes, of Dublin.

Bill Haley and The Comets appeared at the Queen's Hall on 18 September. Also on the bill was the Johnny Mitchell Showband. The concert was promoted by Newtownards Young Farmers' Club and tickets cost 7/6d.

The former Regent House School at Regent Street was transformed in early October into a car showroom, garage and filling station operated by William H. Spence and Co. The old assembly hall became the repair and service department, while the headmaster's office formed part of the showroom.

The new Baptist Church in Frances Street was officially opened on 3 October. The first church, which opened in 1924, was made of corrugated iron and was located in Greenwell Street. Among the speakers at the Frances Street ceremony was Pastor William Wilson, first secretary back in 1923.

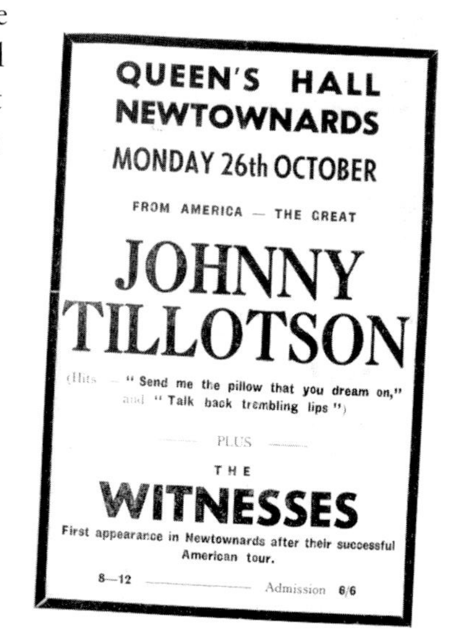

Miss Agnes Brown, originally from Cardy, Greyabbey, celebrated her 100th birthday at Ards Hospital on 19 October. She received congratulatory messages from the Queen and the Governor of Northern Ireland, Lord Wakefield.

Jennifer McCaig, of Nendrum Way, and Janette Malloy, of Comber Road, were among the Newtownards fans who flocked to see The Beatles at the King's Hall in Belfast on 2 November. "We didn't really expect to hear much of the singing," said Jennifer, "but the amplifying system was so good that even with all the screaming and yelling around us we could hear everything perfectly."

Newtownards Chamber of Trade sent a letter of protest to the Ministry of Commerce following the decision of Canadian Technical Tape Ltd. in mid-November to switch its planned factory from Newtownards to Bangor. A site had already been identified but tests showed it to be unsuitable – the Chamber's view was that further locations should have been examined.

An outbreak of fowl pest on a farm at Ardkeen near Portaferry at the beginning of December was the first in Northern Ireland for 15 years. The discovery led to the slaughter of 15,000 infected chicks, with a watch being kept on a dozen more farms in Down, Armagh and Antrim.

Plans for a municipal swimming pool in Newtownards received a boost in early December when the Borough Council revealed that a deal had been completed for a supply of water from the Enler River.

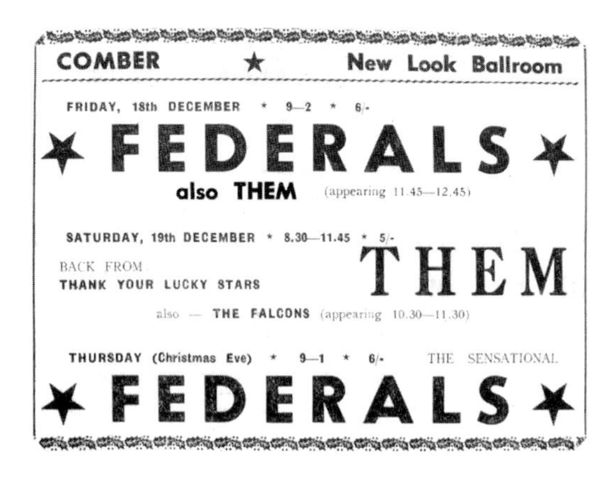

Them – the Belfast band that included a young Van Morrison – appeared at a number of local venues in the run-up to the Christmas holidays. Fresh from performances on two top UK television programmes, *Thank Your Lucky Stars* and *Ready Steady Go,* they took to the stage at the Queen's Hall, Newtownards, on 12 December and the Comber Ballroom on 18 and 19 December.

Members of First Donaghadee BB who won the Ards Group Novice Squad Drill competition in early January 1964. Back (from left): G. Gilliland, B. Irwin, A. Martin, A. Gilmore, H. Reynolds. Middle: G. Elliott, J. King, E. Jenkins, M. Martin, A. McCullough. Front: B. Campbell, Staff Sgt. J. Fraser, the Rev. J. E. Glenfield (chaplain) and J. Dunnon. *82-60-1*

Cup winners following the Newtownards Young Farmers' Club ploughing match in January 1964. Back (from left): W. Davidson, R. McKee, E. McBlain, A. Barr. Front: R. Savage, M. Stevenson, L. McMillan. R. Crosby was unable to attend. *87-67-2*

As was the practice at the time, children 'had their tonsils out' at the first hint of a sore throat. This fate befell all six featured in this picture, which was taken at the end of January 1964. Five of the young people were from the same Ardkeen family, and they all had their tonsils removed on the same day, which must have been something of a record for Ards Hospital. At the front are Marie McKibbin (11) and brother Samuel (9). Back: Nathaniel McKibbin (12), Annie McKibbin (16), holding a niece, nine-week-old Mary Agnes Strain, and Hugh McKibbin (14). The McKibbin children's parents were Mr and Mrs James McKibbin, of Ballygela. *84-36-2*

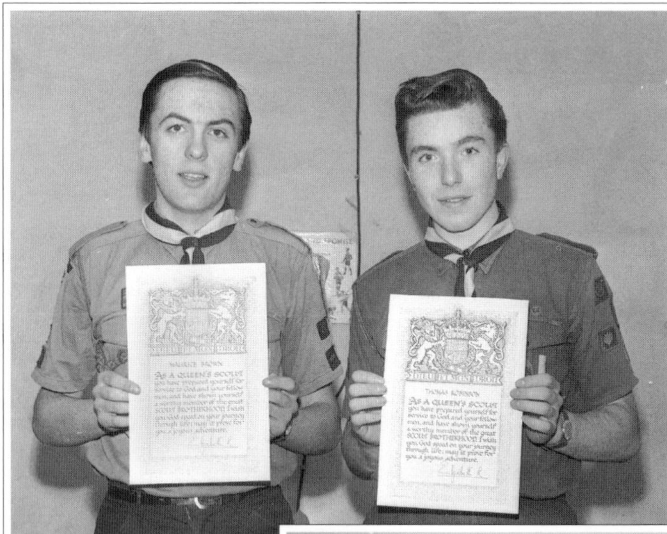

Two members of First Newtownards Scout Troop, Maurice Brown (left) and Thomas Robinson, received their Queen's Badges in January 1964.
83-99-1

Children from the Model Primary School in Newtownards who received awards for their efforts in collecting money for Dr Barnardo's Homes in February 1964. The awards were handed over by Miss Laura Graham while Miss A. Wright was in charge of the collection at the school.
85-81-1

Members of the Ballywalter Boys' Brigade vaulting horse team at the Company's display in early April 1964.
89-36-3

Members of the Newtownards Keep-Fit class going through some exercises at the local Technical School in April 1964. The class, which was over 40-strong, was under the supervision of Mrs P. Walker.
89-77-1

Prizewinners at the Ballygowan Presbyterian Church Girls' Brigade annual display in late April 1964 were (back, from left): Ann Burgess, Veronica Kirk, Irene Gibson, Sandra George, Mary Lemon, Linda Kelly, Eileen Craig. Middle: Lorraine Smyth, Jean Gourley (officer), Mary Eid (Captain), Mrs D. Crawford (who presented the awards), Jean Garrett (officer), Susan Dalzell. Front: Roberta Smyth and Avril McCarroll.
90-73-1

Special award winners at the First Portavogie Life Boy Team Display in May 1964. Back (from left): Wilbert Thompson (senior drill down), Samuel Beattie (Squad Cup), John Warnock (Perpetual Cup for best all-round boy) and Gary Kenning (junior drill down).
91-33-1

Fourth Newtownards Girls' Life Brigade cadets who competed for the Battalion Cup in choral speaking, physical education and singing games, gaining the highest combined points total, at the Ards Battalion competitions in May 1964.
91-83-1

Teams from Second Newtownards Girls' Life Brigade (Greenwell Street Presbyterian Church) with the Verse-Speaking Cup and Physical Education Shield they won at the Ards Battalion competitions in the Palmer Memorial Hall in May 1964.
91-64-1

Greyabbey LOL No. 1592 members with their new banner, which was unfurled by Mrs David Johnston on 13 June 1964.
94-31-2

John Moore (sen.) attended his 59th 'Twelfth' demonstration in Ballygowan on 13 July 1964. He is pictured (centre, back) with sons Billy, Victor and Jackie and grandsons Moore Porter and Tom Moore.
96-57-2

Sixteen-year-old Jim Ferris, of Parsonage Road, Portaferry, with the ship he built using 600 lollypop sticks. He completed the task in late July, having commenced it five months earlier.
97-75-1

Having a welcome cup of tea and a rest after helping on Miss Pyper's farm at Ballyhalbert are Jim Baillie, Jack Dickie, Jim McIlwaine and Hugh Foley.
97-77-1

Kenneth Neill, of Kenmuir, General's Walk, Millisle Road, Donaghadee, with his miniature garden exhibition which won first prize at the Donaghadee and District Horticultural Society Show on 15 August 1964.
99-25-1

First day back at school for pupils of Cottown Primary School in late August 1964.
99-44-1

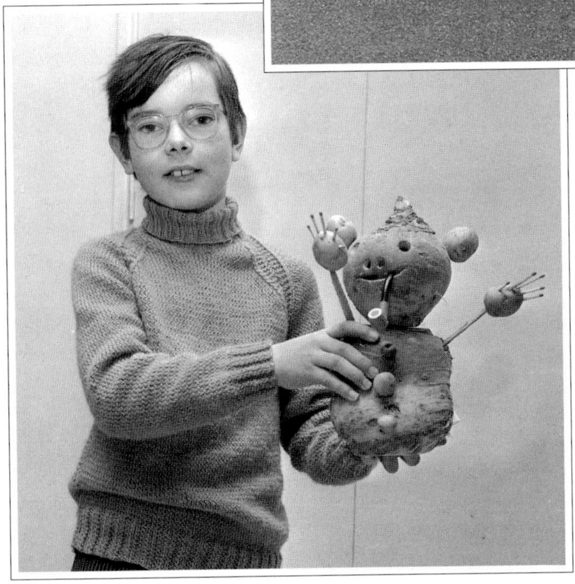

Helen McKelvey, of Lucerne, Greengraves Road, Newtownards, with the turnip lantern that won her a first prize at the Newtownards Young Farmers' Club show and sale in the Queen's Hall on 17 October 1964.
102-32-1

Members of Ballymiscaw Young Farmers' Club who staged the play *Beside The Seaside* in Craigantlet Orange Hall in early November 1964. Picture includes Margaret McGladdery, Emily Thompson, Jim White, Ronnie Ardill, Josephine McCormick, Ann Reid, Hazel Jamison, John Berry and Mrs Carson, along with producer Mrs Ballagh, stage manager Mrs Lyttle and prompter Iris Morrison.
103-2-1

Children from Killard School who were entertained at a Christmas party organised by staff at Johnson and Phillips in Newtownards in early December 1964.
105-31-3

Students of Regent House School in Newtownards who performed in George Bernard Shaw's *Pygmalion* in mid-December 1964.
105-80-2

Sport in 1964

in the Chronicle

The Ards Senior Ladies Hockey 1st XI secured the Senior League Championship following a 2-2 draw with Victorians at Drumglass on 1 February. They followed this up a fortnight later with a 7-0 victory over Stranmillis College in the Ulster Shield final at Deramore Park. It was the first time they had accomplished the League and Shield 'double', remaining unbeaten in competitive games throughout the season.

Brenda Armour defeated Glenford team mate Margaret Finlay on 15 February to win the Irish Girls Table Tennis Championship.

Ards Senior Ladies Hockey Club 1st XI followed up their double-winning success by claiming a place in the All Ireland Women's Hockey Cup final following a 4-3 semi-final victory over Pembroke Wanderers on 4 April. A week later they defeated Munster side Old Ursulines 3-0 to lift the cup.

Newtownards won the Belfast and District Amateur Billiards Intermediate League with victory on 15 April over Lawnbrook in the last match of the season.

Ards became All Ireland Table Tennis Champions in early May following victory over Dublin side Crofton.

1st Donaghadee Boys' Brigade achieved a noteworthy league and cup double in the Belfast BB Soccer League, beating Third Carrick BB 8-2 in the final league game.

Woman Constable Elaine Bowman, from Pound Street in Newtownards, won the women's singles in the finals of the Police Table Tennis Championships in mid-

May. They were held on the Isle of Wight. She repeated the feat in 1965.

Newtownards British Legion Darts Club defeated Larne 4-3 in the final of the British Legion-organised Alan McKibben Shield.

Edward Gaw and William Curragh, both members of Ards Bowling Club, won the City of Belfast bowling title against stiff opposition on 25 July.

The Donaghadee Improvements (Action) Committee, in co-operation with Ballyholme Yacht Club, revived local yacht racing by staging a regatta on 25 July. The event attracted large crowds to the town, although only 18 yachts took part.

Leeds United beat Ards 6-0 in a pre-season friendly at Castlereagh Park on 7 August. The visiting side featured a number of well-known players, including Paul Reaney, Terry Cooper, Billy Bremner, Jack Charlton, Johnny Giles and Albert Johanneson.

Donaghadee Cricket Club secured the first major trophy in their 13-year history, the Junior Qualifying Cup, on 15 August with an 88-run victory over Belfast High School Old Boys.

Ards FC sacked manager John Neilson on 12 October after he refused to resign the post. He had signed a three-year contract six months earlier but there was general dissatisfaction within the club about a poor run of results, coupled with the serious financial position it was in. Jimmy Tucker took over as trainer-coach with team selections being made by a three-strong committee.

Denise Fitzell, of Newtownards College of Further Education, was selected to play for the Northern Ireland Schoolgirls netball team against various English schools and county teams in Liverpool on 31 October.

Former Ards FC manager George Eastham was coaxed back to the club in late November having signed a three-year contract that included the provision of a house for him in the town. The appointment followed a 5-0 home defeat by Glentoran. His first fixture ended in a 3-3 draw with Derry City. Eastham, who had managed the team between 1953 and 1958, would see out the decade at Castlereagh Park.

The Regent House team defeated Orangefield Boys 9-0 in the first round of the Schools' Cup on 18 January 1964.
83-57-3

The Comber under-13 basketball team defeated Holywood 48-30 in the final of the North Down competition in March 1964. Back (from left): K. McKee, T. Lowry, S. Evans, W. Bennett, M. O'Prey. Front: D. Minnis, D. Cromie (captain), K. McBriar and T. Edgar.
87-98-3

The Newtownards Technical School team, winners of the Senior Technical School Cup in April 1964. Back (from left): Drew Darley, Davy Roberts, George Hamilton, David Miskelly, Martin McIlveen, David McIlveen. Front: Mr McMullan, Drew Davison, Bill McAvoy, Alan Charles (captain), L. Henry, Derek McAleese, Mr A. L. Orr (principal).
89-78-3

Members of the First Millisle Boys' Brigade football team who were defeated by Third Ards BB in the final of the North Down BB League Knock-Out Cup at Castlereagh Park on 9 May 1964.
91-73-3

The Londonderry Primary School football team won the Newtownards and District Primary Schools Cup in early July 1964.
96-24-1

Members of the Donaghadee 1st XI, winners of the Junior Qualifying (Cricket) League in September 1964.
100-52-2

Lady Mairi Bury, Commodore of Newtownards Sailing Club, officially declares open the new clubhouse on 15 August, watched by Vice-Commodore Stanley Woods, Rear Commodore Angus Jardine and honorary secretary Dr David Park.
99-20-2

Mrs L. Browne with guests at her Lady Captain's Day at Kirkistown Golf Club in mid-August 1964.
99-12-3

Girls from Regent House School in Newtownards take a break during a netball practice in October 1964.
102-42-2

1965

in the Chronicle

The Amphicar *107-47-2*

While debate raged over the urgent need for a ferry service – or indeed a bridge – to link Portaferry and Strangford, local farmer and landowner Major William Brownlow had his own solution to the problem. Thanks to his newly-acquired Amphicar, he was able to drive off the pier into the sea and within minutes had reached the other side where he could attend to the livestock on his farms. The Amphicar could reach speeds of 60mph on land and 7.5mph in water. A cabriolet-style four-seat vehicle, steering was via the two front wheels on land, switching to unbreakable plastic twin propellers for the sea journey.

Having installed an IBM 1440 computer at their new factory extension in Donaghadee, Cyril Lord Carpets Ltd. advertised for "young ladies with punch card experience, who want to work at good salaries in ideal conditions."

Breadserver Adam Burrows, of Queen's Square, Newtownards, retired in mid-February after a career spanning some 42 years with Messrs. Bernard Hughes Ltd. As well as Newtownards itself, his route took him as far as Millisle and Carrowdore, Killinchy and Derryboy.

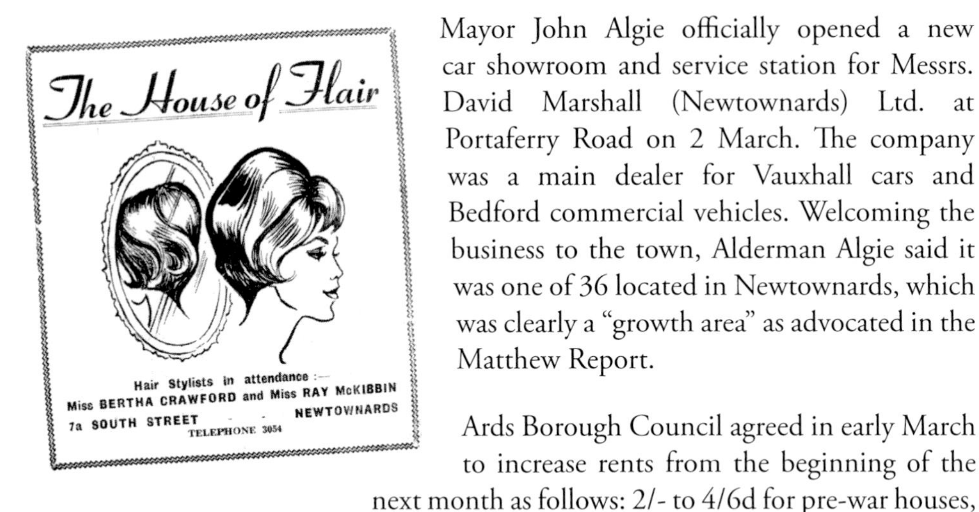

Mayor John Algie officially opened a new car showroom and service station for Messrs. David Marshall (Newtownards) Ltd. at Portaferry Road on 2 March. The company was a main dealer for Vauxhall cars and Bedford commercial vehicles. Welcoming the business to the town, Alderman Algie said it was one of 36 located in Newtownards, which was clearly a "growth area" as advocated in the Matthew Report.

Ards Borough Council agreed in early March to increase rents from the beginning of the next month as follows: 2/- to 4/6d for pre-war houses, 3/6d to 6/9d for post-war houses, and 1/- for garages. The rises were needed because of a deficit in the Housing Revenue Account and also the demand for new house-building programmes.

North Down Rural Council received a complaint in mid-March about the presence of freshwater shrimps in the Portavogie water supply. Members were told that closer control would be possible once a new chlorination plant was installed.

Miss Mary O'Neill (right) makes a presentation at Glastry Secondary Intermediate School on 19 March 1965 to Mrs Elizabeth Warnock to mark her retirement after 42 years at Ballyhalbert Primary School. *112-60-1*

Mrs Elizabeth Warnock (née Caughey) was presented with farewell gifts on 19 March following her retirement after teaching at Ballywalter Primary School for more than 42 years. She was a native of Ballyhalbert and her home at Braehead was within sight of the school, which she had joined back in 1922.

Capt. Terence O'Neill paid his first official visit to Newtownards as Prime Minister when he attended a meeting organised by the Ards Unionist Association in the Queen's Hall on 25 March. He was greeted at the town boundary by the Dr Wright Memorial Pipe Band and escorted to the Town Hall where he was received by Mayor John Algie.

Former Scrabo Intermediate School pupil Helen McKee won a fashion design competition sponsored by the Brand Fashion Group in Belfast. Helen, from High Street in Newtownards, who was a third year student at Belfast College of Art, received a 100-guinea cheque from Irish fashion designer Irene Gilbert as her prize, as well as a study tour to London and Paris.

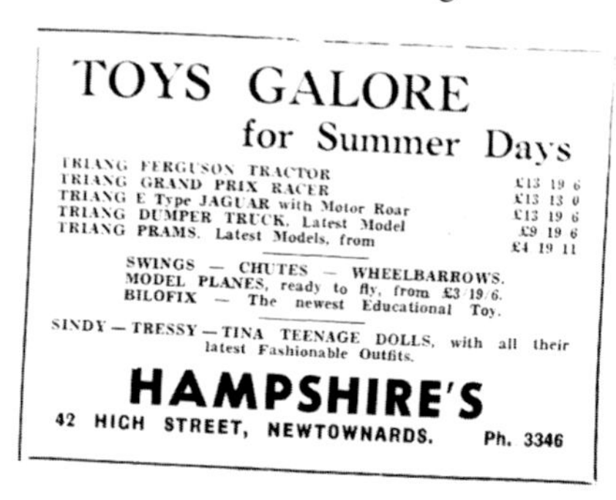

The National Trust purchased the village of Kearney, between Ballyquintin Bay and Cloughey, in late April with funds raised through its Enterprise Neptune coastal appeal. The agreement included not only the village but also a mile and a half of foreshore and covenants relating to 284 acres of land. It meant the stretch of coast on the eastern side of the Ards Peninsula would remain free from building development and would be open and available to the public "at all times."

The curator of the Ulster Folk Museum at Cultra expressed an interest in putting on display a rare Victorian-era octagonal pillar box, bearing the Royal initials VR, which stood at Frances Street in Newtownards. It was thought to be at least 100 years old. The move, with the Council's permission, took place at the end of July.

Promising the "biggest and finest store in Newtownards", Lipton's opened a new self-service supermarket in High Street, opposite the Town Hall, on 18 May. The manager was local man Ivor Powell, who for the previous 14 years had managed the Maypole Dairy, also in High Street.

Prime Minister Terence O'Neill was back in Newtownards on 17 May to attend the golden jubilee celebrations for local firm Black and Co. based in Thomas Street. Capt. O'Neill also paid a whistle-stop visit to Portaferry where he called at the Gammon Pritchett and Wetherdair factories.

Employees of Black and Co. (Newtownards) Ltd. presented a painting by renowned artist Kenneth Webb to the directors of the firm to mark its 50th anniversary in April 1965. Behind the painting are (from left): William Black, James Chambers and Harold Black (directors), Richard McKee (engineer) and, to the right, Rebecca Kennedy (winder). Mr McKee and Miss Kennedy had worked for Black and Co. for 45 years and 41 years respectively. *114-59-2*

Donaghadee Harbour Master George Wilson Ashe retired at

the end of June from the position he had held for 35 years. Aged 64, his roles had included maintaining the harbour and serving as lighthouse attendant.

Veteran Ballygowan postman James Ross was presented with the British Empire Medal on the occasion of his retirement at the end of July. A First World War veteran who had served with the Royal Irish Rifles, he had joined the Post Office in 1926. The final 20 years of his career were spent in Ballygowan.

Two Newtownards men, Cllr James White and Mr Blakely McGimpsey, were guests of honour at a dinner held on 2 September to mark their 50 years of membership of the Orange Institution. They were members of Scarlet Crown LOL 1919.

Residents of Ballybarnes Cottages at Bradshaw's Brae demanded a piped water supply and flushing toilets. Their water was supplied from back garden rainwater tanks and a single tap at the front of the eight 60-year-old houses. They claimed dogs licked the tap and strangers would use it when passing their homes.

A new body, the Ards Committee of Oxfam, held its inaugural meeting in the Good Templar Hall, Newtownards, on 21 September. Chairman was Mr H. W. Gallagher and the secretary was Miss Caroline McDowell.

A member of a famous Donaghadee seafaring family, Seaman William Nelson, was one of the 10 men who survived a collision in the Thames Estuary on the morning of Tuesday 28 September. Tragically, nine other men lost their lives when the 2,258-ton hopper *Sir Joseph Rawlinson,* and a tug, *Danube VIII,* collided in fog some seven miles off Shoebury Point in Essex.
Seaman Nelson (30) was the son of the late Hugh Nelson, who as coxswain of the Donaghadee Lifeboat played a heroic role when the cross-channel ferry *Princess Victoria* sank with considerable loss of life in January 1953.
With only seconds to spare, the survivors of the *Sir Joseph Rawlinson* – one of five ships employed to dump London sewage 40 miles out in the North Sea – managed to jump into the water from the hopper as she keeled over and sank. The vessel had been holed below the water line. The men were picked up by the tug, which eventually landed them at Gravesend.

Major traffic control changes in the centre of Newtownards were being planned by the Borough Council in mid-October, in conjunction with Government officials

and the police. Top of the agenda was a one-way traffic route stretching from Gibson's Lane in Regent Street to Factory Lane in Frances Street, and from the Old Cross in High Street to Gibson's Lane in Mill Street. Castle Street would also be one-way as far as Market Street and there would be no through traffic at Conway Square (with two bottleneck openings on the north side being closed).
Members of Newtownards Chamber of Trade gave their approval in principle to the proposals.

Chart-topping band The Kinks appeared at the Queen's Hall, Newtownards, on 6 November. It was part of a three-day Irish ballroom tour, also taking Romano's in Belfast, the Top Hat in Lisburn, Milanos in Bangor and the Adelphi Ballroom in Dundalk, co-promoted by local entrepreneur Trevor Kane.

Newtownards man Joe McCormack, of Victoria Avenue, won the £50 treasure chest when he took part in ITV's *Take Your Pick* quiz programme. He was employed as a postal and telegraph officer in London.

Capt. William Long retained his Ards seat with a convincing 5,702 majority over Labour candidate Ed Bell in the Stormont election held on 24 November. The incumbent MP received 7,442 votes to his opponent's 1,740. There was a 45 per cent turn-out by voters.

Portavogie welcomed its first lifeboat with the arrival in early December of the 41ft. *Glencoe,* which replaced the former lifeboat at Cloughey. However, to maintain the link the new vessel was known as the Cloughey-Portavogie Lifeboat and was initially manned by the old Cloughey crew, pending the recruitment of new men from Portavogie.

Brenda Irvine (17), of Corry Street, Newtownards, won the title Miss Blaxnit 1965 during a dinner-dance at the Queen's Hall on 17 December. Runners-up were Doreen Gunning, of Edith Helen Road, and Yvonne Jeanette Lloyd, of Frances Street, both Newtownards. In June 1968 Mrs Gunning would win the title of Newtownards Civic Queen.

Newtownards Chronicle reporter Adrienne Bratty is pictured with Rolling Stones co-manager Andrew Loog Oldham (centre) at a press conference in January to announce the band's forthcoming appearance in Belfast. Also included is *County Down Spectator* reporter Jack Ledgerwood, who hailed from Newtownards.
107-20-1

Newtownards man Thomas Nightingale, of Mill Street, who was born on 6 January 1875, celebrated his 90th birthday at the home of his son-in-law James Crockard. Mr Nightingale had six daughters, two sons, 17 grandchildren and two great-grandchildren, and all of them lived locally.
107-26-2

Pictured at a farewell dinner in the New Mount Royal Hotel, Donaghadee, on 5 February 1965 is James Adair, who was heading back to Perth, Australia, after a six-week holiday with his family in Newtownards. Prior to emigrating he had lived at Mark Street. Included are members of the Adair family circle.
108-99-1

Donaghadee Salvation Army Juniors received their Sunday School awards from Lt. Col. Violet Roberts in the Salvation Army Hall, Newtownards, on 8 February 1965. Included are Capt. and Mrs Beeson.
109-16-2

The Donaghadee Young Farmers' Club debating team won the senior section (21-25 years) finals of the YFCU group debating competition, held in Belfast on 6 March 1965. From left: Billy Martin, leader, Maureen Wightman and William Brown.
111-71-1

Junior members of First Ballywalter Brownie Pack with their leaders in March 1965.
111-44-3

Queen's Badge winners at First Donaghadee Boys' Brigade's annual inspection and display on 12 March 1965. From left: Sergeant S. Moore, Corporals G. Hamilton, B. Frazer, S. Ardis, R. Dunnow and Lance Corporal J. Jenkins.
111-89-3

Donaghadee Wolf Cubs took part in the St George's Day parade in April 1965.
115-36-3

Carrowdore Girls' Life Brigade members dressed for their 'Down Memory Lane' production at the annual display in May 1965.
116-77-3

Cup winners at the Regent House sports in late May 1965. Back (from left): Mrs I. Managh, Rosemary Guy, W. H. Parker, I. J. Morrison, S. I. Thompson, J. A. Gwynne, R. H. Barker, W. R. J. Elliott, Jaye Camlin, Mr M. Caves. Front: Yvonne Savage, Elizabeth Boyd, Ann Burns, C. H. Lowe, Angela Lemon, J. C. Kelly, Angela Duke and Ann Elkin.
117-81-2

Members of the new Eighth Down Scout Troop attached to St Patrick's Church, Portaferry, were invested in June 1965. Included are Troop founder Fr. O'Hanlon, CC, Scoutmaster Harry Murray and leaders.
118-78-3

Mayor Samuel Gracey starts the annual Scrabo walk and race in Conway Square on 12 June 1965.
119-42-3

Stephen Orr (7), from Moyle Hill, Ballywalter, met an American cowboy film star of the 1940s when Sunset 'Kit' Carson paid a visit to the McKelvey Pavilion at the Ards Hospital on 11 June 1965. Sunset had appeared in a large number of 'B' westerns, including *Rough Riders Of Cheyenne, Santa Fe Saddlemates, Sheriff Of Cimarron* and *Firebrands Of Arizona.*
119-57-3

First Newtownards Wolf Cubs and leaders with the County Down Wolf Cub Challenge Flag and the District Wolf Cub Cup, which they won in June 1965.
119-84-3

A section of the Corpus Christi procession leaving St Patrick's Parish Church, Ballyphilip, Portaferry, in mid-June 1965.
120-45-2

The Greyabbey Girls Choir gave their first public performance before a large audience in the Village Hall on 18 June 1965. Their new uniforms were dedicated by the Rev. J. P. McAteer.
120-36-2

The Children's Day choir at Portavogie Presbyterian Church in late June 1965 with the minister, the Rev. T. A. Houston, Sunday School teacher Mr William Charles Adair, organist Mrs Palmer and an unidentified guest minister.
120-58-3

Prizewinners from Comber Primary School's fancy dress parade, which formed part of the school's sports day on 25 June 1965.
121-14-1

Prizewinners and officials of Comber and District Racing Pigeon Club after their prize distribution and dance in the Andrews Memorial Hall on 8 October 1965. Included is Mrs D. G. McKibben, wife of the treasurer, who handed over the prizes.
129-51-2

Voluntary workers from Christ Church in Carrowdore who were helping to renovate the Wolsey Hall in November 1965.
130-26-1

Mr William Orr (seated) is pictured in November 1965 with the Rev. G. McK. Eagleson and members of the Strean Presbyterian Church choir after receiving an easy-chair to mark his retirement from the choir after 50 years' service.
131-23-3

Children from Millisle Primary School at their end-of-term Christmas pantomime in mid-December 1965.
133-80-3

Pupils attending Portavogie Primary School presented a nativity play and sang assorted Christmas carols at the school on 21 and 22 December 1965.
134-25-2

Members of the Scrabo Secondary Intermediate School gymnasium club in December 1965 with sports master Mr W. Menagh.
130-38-3

Sport in 1965

in the Chronicle

Ards FC inside forward Ray Mowat gained a unique double honour in February when he was awarded an amateur international cap and a youth international cap, both fixtures being against Wales. Later in the month the 17-year-old was watched twice by Preston North End manager Jimmy Milne, but the club subsequently rejected a "four figure" offer for Mowat.

Carroll McBride and Clifford Thompson of Ards Table Tennis Club were chosen to play for Ulster in an inter-provincial series in Cork on 22 and 23 January, with Gary Bowman, also from Ards, the reserve.

Indoor bowling was becoming increasingly popular by early 1965, with First Newtownards Presbyterian Church Bowling Club attracting 40 members within a short time of its formation. Club president was the Rev. A. Adams, Major A. L. Orr was chairman and Mr Ken Sloan was secretary.

Ards Ladies Hockey Club player Rosalind Armstrong gained her first Irish international cap on 6 March after being selected to play on the right wing against Scotland.

Fifth Ards Boys' Brigade won the Bangor and District (Soccer) League after defeating Fifth Bangor 3-0.

Following an 8-5 win over Collegians, Ards II were proclaimed champions of the Junior League's second division. The Ards points were scored by Walter Montgomery (try) and Derrick Nash (penalty and conversion). The team gained 25 out a possible 26 points and were five points ahead of their nearest rivals.

Regent House reached the semi-final of the Schools' Cup for the first time in their history, following an 8-3 victory over Sullivan Upper on 9 March. They played Campbell College in the semi-final three days later, losing the match to the eventual cup winners by 14 points to 3.

Former Ards player George Eastham – son of the manager of the same name and then playing for Arsenal – was selected to play for England. He subsequently won 19 caps for his country.

The Corner House darts team from Newtownards won the Comber and District Darts League in late June following their victory over the local British Legion.

Regent House 1st XV were defeated 14-3 by eventual winners Campbell College in the semi-final of the Schools' Cup on 12 March 1965.
111-79-3

Comber Secondary Intermediate School's netball team reached the quarter-finals of the schools' netball league in March 1965. Back (from left): Frances McClements, Jean Whitford, June McKeag, Myrtle Cooke, Rosemary Porter. Front: Irene Hall, Pat Watton (captain) and Ann Fisher.
112-13-1

Members of the Glastry Secondary Intermediate School football team with sportsmaster Mr J. McFerran in early April 1965.
112-67-2

North End A were the undefeated Newtownards Temperance Darts League champions in April 1965. They also won the Knock-Out Cup, the Pairs Championship, the Average Cup and High Score.
114-25-3

First Ballywalter Boys' Brigade footballers were defeated by Seventh Bangor in the final of the North Down BB League Knock-Out Cup at Castlereagh Park, Newtownards, on 1 May 1965.
115-84-1

Ballycran finished as runners-up in the Down Camogie Championship after defeating Portaferry on 26 July 1965. Back (from left): Margaret Magee, Teresa Lennon, May Lennon, Rita Caughey, Margaret Caldwell, Wilma Ritchie, Margaret Doherty, Olivia Bell. Front: Ann Caldwell, Rosaleen Smyth, Claire Doherty, Kathleen Magee, Eilish Lennon, Moira Caldwell, Maeve Caldwell and Brigid Doherty.
124-56-1

The Down hurling team who played Antrim at St Patrick's Park, Portaferry, on 3 October 1965 in a Hurling League of Ireland (Division II) match.
128-96-1

The team from Scrabo Golf Club who won the Holt Shield competition in October 1965.
130-21-2

Entertainment
in
The Ards
in the
Sixties

Jim Palmer

remembers... The Scene

Jim Palmer

Born in East Belfast, there was an early move to Dundonald but also weekend visits to Ballyhalbert, so when Jim Palmer moved to Ards in 1971 he was only a half blow-in but with a good working knowledge of Ulster-Scots.

Graduating as a teacher in 1969, Jim taught in Belfast for four and a half years before moving to Comber for a further 33 happy years; for most of those years he had a big involvement in the local youth service.

The Scene column lasted for some 30 years but

"I'LL give you two weeks' trial, son." That was *Newtownards Chronicle* Editor Norman Boal's offer to me back in January 1969, as I took over *The Scene* from my brother Wilbert.

At least Wilbert had some sort of track record as a columnist, having been the assistant to the writer of the *Dundonald Pars,* the legendary Sam McAughtry. My experience, on the other hand, was reading Shakespeare for A-Level and at College, but Shakespeare I most definitely was not!

Actually, referring to Norman as the Editor does him an injustice because, living on the *Chronicle* premises, he was also caretaker, cleaner, paymaster, manager of the printworks, and he wrote all the Ards FC reports for our paper and all the local and national ones as well. I would take over his soccer writing duties on his death in 1985.

Among his many talents Norman was a senior soccer referee and he also had an inbuilt Jim Palmer radar system which he turned on when I was owed money and would arrive at the office only to discover he had mysteriously disappeared – much to the amusement of staff members like Jimmy Boal and Gordon Orr.

The trial he gave me was to last some 30 years and guaranteed me enough memories to fill several books.

As a 21-year-old, and very much a product of the Sixties,

Newtownards Chronicle Editor Norman Boal

as far as I was concerned being appointed a pop columnist was akin to a kid being handed the keys to the local sweetie shop! My Press card could get me into any dance, show or cabaret and afforded me the opportunity to interview all the big names who came to play in the Province.

In 1969, for example, I was able to both introduce Roy Orbison onstage in Bangor and also to have a lengthy one-to-one interview with him. What a singer and what a gentleman.

I also had chats with The Troggs' Reg Presley, Carl Wayne and fellow members of The Move, Tiny Tim, who told me his talent(!) was "a blessing from Heaven," plus Dave Dee, who had top radio dee-jay Emperor Rosko playing the tambourine at his Bangor show.

The problem was that, entertainment-wise, Newtownards was nowhere near the centre of the Universe for most of the area's young people, who usually had to travel to either Belfast or Bangor to find their music scenes. It may have been the Swinging Sixties, but I reckon it would be fair to say the "Swinging" part of things rather by-passed our town.

That's not to say the late Sixties as a musical era was dead in Ards because we had the Saturday dances run in the Queen's Hall by Trevor Kane – although during '69 no one was quite sure in what musical direction to travel. Thus we had the full range, from American country star Hank Locklin to great pop bands like The Cousins, Newmen, College Boys, Teddie Palmer and The Apollo, to name but a few.

But if you wanted to see The Freshmen, Dickie Rock or The Dreams then you had to travel further afield.

Interestingly, the Queen's Hall closed its doors during July and August with promoter Kane re-opening it as the 'Freakeasy' and featuring all the top local and Belfast groups, which was much more like it for us youngsters.

the soccer reporting from 1985 continues with both the *Chronicle* and *Spectator* newspapers, while reports for others over the years have ranged from *The Sun* to the *Daily Telegraph*.

Married to Elizabeth in 1974, they have two daughters, Gillian and Ruth, and the family home remains in Newtownards, overlooking the now derelict Castlereagh Park – former home of his beloved Ards Football Club.

Teddie Palmer in the 1960s

Belfast-based Dino was the dee-jay although he was replaced early in 1970 by a certain Prince Jim who bore an unmistakable resemblance to myself... but that's another story!

Norman Keenan's Gumm were big personal favourites, as were Virtue who featured my friend James G. Meredith plus Robert Apps and various others.

Another local outfit were Words Of Love from my late father's home village of Ballyhalbert while, from Newtownards itself, Shades Of Blue were playing local gigs too.

In my newspaper column I'd complained about the lack of support among dancers and music enthusiasts for local venues. That was especially true of the Orange Hall which Gil Moore opened as 'Family House'. Over six weeks he brought in top groups like Vintage, Dolls House, The John Smith Band and Sam Mahood's Big Soul Band, yet by the end of April 1969 the House had closed its doors.

On the other hand the middle-of-the-road market was pretty healthy. Falls' Bar, with my good friend Ian in charge, ran regular cabaret nights with compere Jimmy James and acts such as The Raparees, while The Steeplechase featured TV performer Brian McCann each weekend as resident frontman and later that splendid local singer Brendan McSherry.

Safari, a super Ards group with guys like Ernie Nichols and Junior McGreegan on board, could be found at The Jubilee on North Street, while the Tyrone Tavern in Frances Street offered Thursday to Saturday music from maybe The Skyliners one week and Shades Of Folk the next.

Playing around the private dances were outfits such as the James McVeigh and W. McBride Bands, The Big Four, The Snowdrifters and assorted traditional olde time fiddlers, but safe to say they didn't quite fit into the Palmer Scene.

But, of course, there were things happening out of town too. Portaferry's Locarno Ballroom was a very popular dance with a mix of pop and country bands. It was run

The Exiles as they appeared on the Isle of Man in 1966. From left: Ivan Pepper (bass guitar), Ronnie Morris (organ), John Smith (drums), Teddie Palmer (lead vocals), Albert McKenzie (rhythm guitar) and Dave Storey (lead guitar).

by the Milanos group with Bangor staff Denis Wright and Norman Murphy looking after this one as well.

Hinds' Bar was right across the road and with ten o'clock closing mine host Hugh often encouraged me to stay for a late tipple after the doors had officially closed. I was easily encouraged!

I can recall one night sitting with members of Brian Coll's band who told me that teetotal Brian didn't allow them to drink spirits before the show. As ordered, not a drop passed their lips, but as regards the copious amounts of Carlsberg Special, that was another matter!

Some wonderful nights were enjoyed there with great outfits like Gene and The Flames, Joe Duffy and The Carling Showband, Simon Scott And The Plattermen, while there was also a Miss Down contest with a two-week Spanish holiday up for grabs. It was run over four weeks with the Jimmy Johnston Band doing the honours on the first night.

Not too far away in Comber the Andrews Hall hosted Friday night dances run by local pig farmer Hubert Gabbey. Hubert was a lovely guy who employed the same bouncers as the Queen's Hall – and you couldn't have found a tougher trio in Northern Ireland as they showed some time later when they saved me from grievous bodily harm as I was leaving the Freakeasy. One carried a chair leg up his jacket and, yes, I saw him use it!

I remember one night Hubert being in a state of panic as the Soul Foundation took the stage without their legendary lead singer Sam Mahood. Sometime later the hall doors burst open with Sam being held up on either side, assisted onto the stage and then giving his usual storming performance.

Among the regulars were my favourite group The John Smith Band – led by schoolteacher John from Comber and certainly good enough to be pros as members Alistair 'Haggy' McKenzie (Suzi Quatro) and Paul Lyttle eventually proved.

There were other happenings too with the Imperial in the 'Dee starting a Thursday dance late in '69 with The Secrets opening. But it was a sign of the times when the venue advertised "No mod dress" and "Come along nurses and young farmers!"

Millisle Young Farmers featured Colm and The Sundowners, a country band from Portaferry who were great pals of mine and enjoyed a lot of success.

There was a Strangford Festival in the summer featuring Pat McGeegan (Barry McGuigan's dad) and his Skyrockets, Robin and The Signs, top cabaret man Tony G. Ford and Candy Devine, later to be a Downtown Radio star. She married Don McLeod who, amongst other accomplishments, ran the dance in Crossgar.

So 1969 drew to a close, along with my first year as Prince Jim and only 29 years to go… my adventure had only just begun and what a start it had been!

Patrick (Paddy) Bell

remembers... Ballywalter Flute Band

It is said that everyone who remembers the assassination of President John F. Kennedy on 22 November 1963, also remembers where they were when they first heard the news. For me it was the balcony of the Ulster Hall in Belfast, on the occasion of the 46th annual Championship of Ireland bands contest, run by the North of Ireland Bands Association.

The competition was held over four days and my band, Ballywalter Flute, had been placed second in the intermediate section with the test piece *Opera Gems*, under the baton of conductor Jack Brown.

I don't know for sure but I would be willing to risk a small wager that Northern Ireland has more flute players per head of the population than any other country in the world, and a large part of the reason for this is, of course, the number of flute bands.

Back in the 1960s most flute bands were affiliated to the Northern Ireland Flute Band League and the North of Ireland Bands Association, which also included brass, accordion and military or concert bands. These bands were constructed with a full range of harmony parts and were capable of playing everything from Beethoven to The Beatles.

Contests were organised to promote musical improvement and much of the classical and popular

Patrick Bell

Patrick Bell, known to many as Paddy, is a retired professional musician and flute teacher from Ballywalter. His early musical influences were from his father John and from his friend and mentor Jack Brown.

At the age of 16 he was offered the opportunity to study flute at the Guildhall School of Music in London with Professor Geoffrey Gilbert, principal flute with the Halle and London Philharmonic Orchestras, but he had to decline the offer due to domestic circumstances.

Patrick held the position of principal flute with the bands of the Royal Ulster Constabulary and Police Service of Northern Ireland for 25 years, and was flute tutor with the South Eastern Education and Library Board as part of their Advanced Teaching Service.

He has played for many members of the Royal Family, including Her Majesty the Queen and Diana, Princess of Wales, and has performed at many leading venues throughout the United Kingdom.

Patrick is also a lifelong member of Ballywalter Flute Band, both as a player and as their conductor (from 1991-2005). During this time they won three world championship titles and numerous other awards, and broadcast regularly for BBC radio. His musical arrangements are widely used by bands in Northern Ireland and Scotland.

He now enjoys making music with Family Folk, a group which, true to its name, consists of his daughter Karen, sons Alan and Stephen, brother-in-law Lawrence Brown, and nephew through marriage Stuart McCrea.

Patrick also plays guitar, harmonica, tin whistle (sometimes two at once) and banjo, and has recently been given a set of lowland pipes. As he says, you're never too young to learn!

repertoire was arranged for this purpose. There are many sophisticated arrangements, both by professionals and by gifted amateur musicians, and the standards that have been achieved are quite remarkable. Many musicians have graduated from this system to become professionals and some have become internationally renowned.

Ballywalter Flute Band had its origins in the local company of the Boys' Brigade. In 1953, under the visionary leadership of Jackie Brown, they became an independent organisation, and in 1955 they entered their first NIBA contest, competing in the junior 2nd grade and finishing in third place. They won the grade in 1958, which prompted a move into the junior 1st grade, which they won in 1962. Promotion to the intermediate section resulted in a win in 1965, while the following year the band competed in the senior section, for the world title, for the first time, gaining a creditable fourth place.

Thus, in a period of just over 12 years, the band had progressed from humble beginnings to competing with the best, at the highest level. Jackie was later to see his dream fulfilled, even though he had retired from conducting due to ill health, when the band won world titles in 1991, 1994 and 1998.

In the 1960s I was a member of a quartet from the band which appeared on the popular Ulster Television programme *Teatime With Tommy*, hosted by pianist Tommy James. The quartet, which also included Jackie Brown, George Bryce and Jim Spratt, played part of Rossini's *William Tell Overture* (yes, the *Lone Ranger* bit!) and a selection from *The Sound Of Music*. In those days of black and white television we were told not to wear white shirts because of the dazzle and also that light blue would actually look like white on the screen. The same quartet also appeared on the follow-up series *Return Visit*.

Ballywalter Flute Band often promoted fundraising concerts in the local parochial hall, which featured some very well known celebrities like the famous comedian James Young, who lived in Ballyhalbert – in the house which still bears the name he gave it, *Camelot* – and Peter Tomelty, the superb lyric tenor from Portaferry, who was

Ballywalter Flute Band in May 1963: Back, (from left) Raymond Lemon, Hugh McConnell, James Donnan, Willie Beattie, Wilfred Corkum, Desmond Monan, Robert Acheson. 3rd row Harry Flynn, Gibson Adair, Gordon Whyte, Patrick Bell, Francis McKay, George Bryce, Jackie Brown. 2nd row David Monan, Ronnie Birch, Leslie Robinson, Tom Beggs, Mervyn Dunbar, Ronnie Barclay, Robert McCready, Lawrence Brown, John Walsh.. Front row: Sandy McKay, Hugh McCready, John Birch, John Fergie, Hubert Lemon, Sam Monan.
64-4-1

one of the stars of TV's *With A Fiddle And A Flute*.

I also remember a concert by The Pattersons folk group in the lecture hall. They were very popular at the time, even appearing on *The Morecambe and Wise Show*. Billy Patterson, the eldest brother, was a sergeant in the RUC, stationed in Greyabbey.

Members of Ballywalter Flute Band who won in the solo, duet, quartet and sextet sections of the Northern Ireland Flute Band League contest, which was held in Belfast in April 1965..
114-43-3

Incidentally, did you know that Peter Tomelty's famous brother Joseph, the celebrated actor and playwright who wrote *The McCooeys* for BBC radio, took the surname from St McCooey's Wells at Ballyquintin Road near Portaferry. It's nice to see there is now a blue plaque at his humble home, 22 Shore Street, Portaferry.

Back in 1963 Ballywalter Flute Band had obtained its own bandroom on the Well Road, on land owned by

Gerald Calvert, who charged us the enormous sum of one shilling a year ground rent. The entire project cost £250 and the hall was opened by Lady Dunleath.

The hall, sadly no longer there, served the band very well for many years and contained one very interesting piece of furniture – a piano which had belonged to James Galway's mother. It was given to Mervyn Gaw, a member of the band and postman to James Galway's father, who lived on the West Winds Estate in Newtownards. Mervyn had no room for it in his house so the piano was brought to the bandroom. James Galway's parents are interred at Comber Cemetery, while his cousins Doreen and Phyllis live in Millisle.

I have written at length about Ballywalter Flute Band because of my personal association with it but I also want to pay tribute to the other bands from the towns and villages of the Ards, to the high standards they have achieved, to the musical education they have provided, and to the fellowship they have promoted within the community as a whole.

Holy Trinity Parish Church in Ballywalter has always had a very healthy musical tradition, much of this being due to the interest and influence of Patron Andrew Mulholland, namely Lord Dunleath of Ballywalter Park. One of only two Patronages in the Anglican community, the church was extremely fortunate to have him as a fully active member. He was very supportive of the arts, and particularly music, and his great passion was for church organs. Indeed the majestic Mulholland Organ in the Ulster Hall bears the family name.

Lord Dunleath was an enthusiastic member of the church choir where he sang bass, and it is said he could whistle the melody of a hymn while humming the bass part at the same time. No doubt it was his influence, and extensive knowledge of classical organ repertoire, that attracted many of the country's top organists to Holy Trinity over the years, while the post of organist and choirmaster has been held by such luminaries as Ian Barber, Desmond Hunter, Norman Finlay, Billy McDonald, Alfie Burrows, John Boal, Stanley McCready and Michael Richards, and continues to attract the talents of people like Joe McKee, Paul Briggs and John Murdoch.

Lord Dunleath was responsible for many classical music events in the church; these were followed by a reception at his stately home, Ballywalter Park. He was an agreeably eccentric man. I remember, after playing at one of these, how he gathered together all the men who had taken part at the top of his magnificent staircase, where we found to our amazement dozens of empty tin cans.

"Now, on a given signal from me," he said, twitching in excited anticipation, "we shall kick the cans down the stairs to frighten the ladies!" Such was his sense of humour.

Ballywalter Parish also includes the lovely little church of St Andrews at Balligan, Inishargie, and in 1968 the Balligan Consort was founded principally for the purpose of performing choral evensong, which it continues to do twice a month, along with other classical repertoire, to an extremely high degree of musical excellence.

In the grounds of Bangor Abbey, in a corner just inside the gates and adjacent to the Newtownards Road, stands a headstone to author W. G. Lyttle, who wrote several notable local books set in the Ards Peninsula. *Betsy Gray, The Smugglers Of Strangford Lough* and *Sons Of The Sod* are his best known works, so when in the Sixties we started a little folk group we decided to use one of the titles as the name. Thus The Sons Of The Sod was born.

The Sons of the Sod (from left): Denis Gibson, Michael Doherty, Paddy Bell and Lawrence Brown although the original group also included Jack Brown and John Walsh

The group, which was moderately successful, played in the villages of the Ards and beyond, and at the same time caught the attention of James Young, who by then was at the height of his popularity. On two occasions we were guests in his homes, once at his house off the Knock dual carriageway and again at *Camelot* in Ballyhalbert, where he cooked us all sirloin steaks, 'singing' as he did so.

The purpose of our visit was to be introduced to Pat McKay, an entertainment producer, who at that time was putting on shows in Belfast's acclaimed Boom Boom

Room. His idea was that we would sing and play as we walked down a spiral staircase, accompanied by dancing girls. For commercial reasons Jimmy wanted to change our name to The Fisher Boys, saying it would have the double inference of placing us geographically by the sea and possibly being related to each other.

I don't think we were ready for all that and nothing came of it but we appreciated the gesture – and the steaks were excellent!

The tale of Ballywalter's drunken monkey!

Back in the 1960s we lived next door to Robbie and Sammy McCready, two elderly brothers who were inseparable. They worked together digging ditches and laying hedges for the farmers, supplementing their income by keeping hens and growing vegetables.

During the summer months they went to Wallace's Rocks to catch crubins – for those who don't know the word, these are wonderfully flavoured edible brown crabs which come inshore during the summer months and hide in holes in the rocks for protection while they cast their shells and allow their soft new shells to harden.

Robert McCready

After Robbie married his wife Sarah, she moved in and all three shared the same house. They were simple people with few home comforts and meagre furnishings. To help bring in some extra money Sarah reared young piglets which she kept in a tea chest beside the fire! She gave them all names and cried her eyes out when the lorry came to take them away. However, after a suitable period of mourning there was always a new batch to take their place.

Alec McCracken, a local man who had joined the Merchant Navy, brought a monkey home from a trip to South America and gave it to Sarah as a present. It had a somewhat unpredictable disposition, so she kept it tethered to the leg of a chair. At weekends the monkey enjoyed a bottle of Guinness along with Robbie and Sammy, and was always in the best of humour on these occasions. However, on one fateful Saturday evening McCracken, ever the mischief maker, laced its drink with cherry brandy. The dramatic results were in equal measure frightening and amusing.

Some men become irritable and ultimately aggressive when they drink 'shorts' and it seems that drunken monkeys are no different. In a very short time, and in a state of gathering fury, it broke free of its tether, bit Sarah violently on the left leg, and took off out the front door in a bad-tempered rage. Reverting back to habits learned in the Amazon rain forests, it scampered up the spouting and careered over the slate roof until it reached the ridge. Screaming with anger, it ran panic-stricken along the ridge until it collided with James Henry Dunbar's chimney and fell headlong into the darkness!

James Henry was a simple and God-fearing man, by then the wrong side of middle age, who always wore an old sailor's cap with a once shiny peak. He liked nothing better than to while away the hours by the fireside reading the comics – or at least looking at the pictures. Thus he sat in innocent amusement, a smile playing on his lips, and wrinkling the well-furrowed corners of his eyes, completely engrossed and unaware of the impending doom to follow.

In a cloud of soot and smoke, and with a hellish bloodcurdling scream the monkey emerged from the open lum! Now totally black, from its drawn-back ears to the tip of its prehensile tail, its bared white teeth stood out in stark contrast, gleaming in the flickering flames of the firelight.

"It's the divil!" yelled James Henry, as the monkey's fearful glaring eyes burned into his soul, and thinking his time had come he bolted out the door and ran for his life up Ballywalter Main Street!

Peace and quiet was eventually restored when James Henry could run no farther and the monkey was recaptured, but James Henry was never as near the open fire again – and he kept one suspicious eye on the lum as he read *The Beano*.

The monkey never drank cherry brandy again, and everyone was relieved when Alec McCracken went back to sea!

Anne Iveston

remembers... Ards Choral and Orchestral Society

Anne Iveston

Anne Iveston (née Paisley) was born in Belfast. Donaghadee was always regarded as her second home as the family spent their Easter and summer holidays there when she and her three sisters were growing up.

During World War 2 they lived permanently there for two years and it was then that Anne attended Regent House School in Newtownards and continued to be a pupil there when the family returned to Belfast.

At the age of eighteen she became a student at Stranmillis Training College

Thursday night was music night – at least for Ards Choral and Orchestral Society. In 1947, the year the choir was formed, Thursday afternoon was the 'half-day' holiday for shopkeepers and other businesses in Newtownards so it was deemed an appropriate night for rehearsals as singers would have time to relax and then attend practices with good voices in the evening.

With the arrival of the Sixties, Viscountess Mairi Bury continued to be Patron and Mr J. Martin Poots was president. Musical Director Ernest Browne retained the conductor's baton and was preparing to rehearse Mendelssohn's *Elijah* for the Spring concert of 1960. His 'day job' was teaching mathematics in Regent House. Some people believe there is an affinity between mathematics and music; Mr Browne certainly had the ability to support this opinion.

"Soh – a needle pulling thread", those memorable lines from *The Sound of Music*, always remind me of chairman Eric Kerr. He was well known for his tailoring skills in Newtownards, but on Thursday evenings he joined the tenor section of the choir and read the music from a Tonic Sol-fa score – as did some others who had been trained this way at school. Copies of these scores had to be hired from the 'Tonic Sol-fa' library in England.

'Grace by name and gracious by nature' was how the

chairman described Miss Grace Lyttle, the Society's honorary secretary all through the Sixties and beyond. She was the ideal person to undertake such an onerous job but to her it was a labour of love; the success of the Society was paramount.

She became a friend to visiting soloists, organised transport and musical scores and offered them hospitality in her own home, where she and her sister, Renee, made them very welcome. Grace was well known to soloists all over Northern Ireland, including William Loughlin (from Londonderry), Irene Sandford, Mattie Waugh, Eric Hinds, Uel Deane, Janette Simpson and many others. They all appreciated her friendliness and efficiency and always looked forward to being welcomed by her on final rehearsal and concert nights.

Here is a verse from a humorous poem about the Society, written by Mr Browne and sung to the tune of *The Mountains of Mourne*:

And now, Mary dear, you'll be wantin' to know
About the brave boys that look after the dough.
There's Master Bob Morrison with Brother Loane
Why they'd even charm money or blood from a stone.
And now don't be jealous dear Mary my sweet
While I mention a lassie ye hardly could beat
She's the hard-worked Hon. Sec. with a sweet smiling face.
And everyone knows and admires 'Our Grace'.

Robert Morrison was the honorary treasurer, entertainer, member of the bass section and, as the poem says, 'Master', given that he was a schoolmaster in the town's Victoria Primary School. Another talented bass, Mr W. H. Loane, assisted him as auditor. Who better than a bank manager to do that particular job?

Mr Morrison was also adept at writing poetry. 'The Harvest Fair' was a masterpiece, describing what happened in Newtownards Square on 23 September every year. He identified some fictitious, local-sounding characters who might have called in to buy their 'yellow man' or look for bargains. William McDonald set this poem to music

and later qualified as a primary school teacher. Her teaching career began at Templemore Avenue Public Elementary School in Belfast.

Anne married Bill Iveston in 1953 and once more returned to live in her favourite place, Donaghadee. After teaching part-time in various schools and bringing up their family of four Anne became a permanent member of the Regent House Preparatory School staff in 1970 and remained there until her retirement.

In 1975 she was invited by Ards Borough Council to become a founder member of the Ards Arts Committee and held the position of chairman on various occasions. She represented the committee and liaised with the Arts Council in Belfast. One of her great loves was organising lunchtime classical concerts in the Londonderry Room at the Town Hall. Many up-and-coming young artists welcomed the opportunity to perform and gain experience. On her retirement after almost 30 years, Ards Arts Committee decided to have an annual musical event called the 'Anne Iveston Musical Evening' which takes place in November in the Queen's Hall.

Anne became a member of the Ards Choral and Orchestral Society in 1954 and here she remembers some of her friends who sang with her in the Sixties and recalls some of the music they performed.

and it was a popular item for Mr Morrison to perform at Choral soirees.

Newtownards people, on hearing the name McDonald, would occasionally remark: "Is that one of the musical family of McDonald?" William was indeed one of that famous family. He was accompanist to the Society and played the continuo on organ or harpsichord at performances of oratorios such as *Soloman, The Messiah* and *Elijah*.

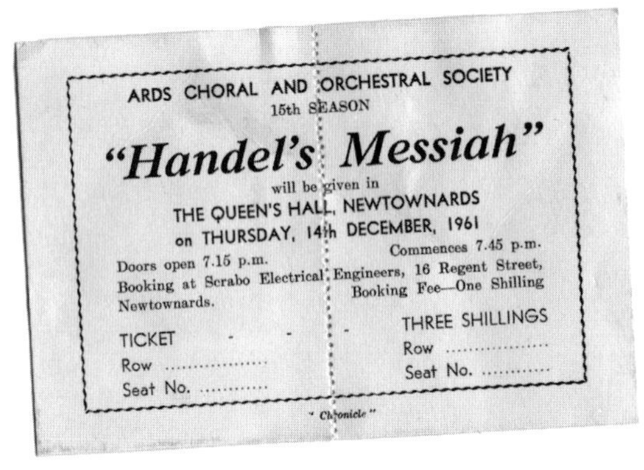
ARDS CHORAL AND ORCHESTRAL SOCIETY
15th SEASON
"Handel's Messiah"
will be given in
THE QUEEN'S HALL, NEWTOWNARDS
on THURSDAY, 14th DECEMBER, 1961
Doors open 7.15 p.m. Commences 7.45 p.m.
Booking at Scrabo Electrical Engineers, 16 Regent Street, Newtownards. Booking Fee—One Shilling
TICKET - - - THREE SHILLINGS
Row .... Row ....
Seat No. .... Seat No. ....
"Chronicle"

These instruments were kindly loaned to us by Lord Dunleath from his collection at Ballywalter Park and William was able to re-tune them so they were in perfect condition for the concerts. He was well known throughout the Province and both the BBC and the Arts Council for Northern Ireland called upon his expertise in tuning pianos and organs. Ards Choral was fortunate to have him as accompanist during the Sixties and to benefit from his considerable musical ability.

The orchestra, comprising amateur players, was always a great support to the choir. They rehearsed every Thursday evening between 7 and 8pm, with the choral practice then running from 8 to 10pm. Some professional players would augment the orchestra for the final rehearsals and performances, with Mrs Keem Perry serving as leader on those occasions.

Three members of the Copeland family were weekly participants for orchestral practice, namely Messrs H. Copeland (violin), J. S. Copeland ('cello) and P. Copeland (clarinet), along with Mrs D. Crowe (violin), Mrs E. Crowe ('cello), Mr W. McDonald ('cello), Mr R. McDonald (trumpet), Mrs E.W. Browne (violin), Mr K. Browne (trumpet), Miss Rosalind Armstrong (oboe), Miss Joyce Heaney (clarinet), Mr J. Brown (flute) and Mrs W. S. Kingan (violin).

The Society's 'Coming of Age' was marked in 1968. Much thought and effort was put in by committee, choral and orchestral members to make it a year of celebrations. After much discussion it was decided to perform *Hiawatha* (Parts 1 and 2), the concert being held on 25 April. This work, by Samuel Coleridge-Taylor, was popular with Chorus members as they had performed it in 1963. The story of Hiawatha unfolds from 'The Wedding Feast' through to the 'Death of Minnehaha'. The composer must have appreciated the story in Longfellow's poem as he called his own son Hiawatha.

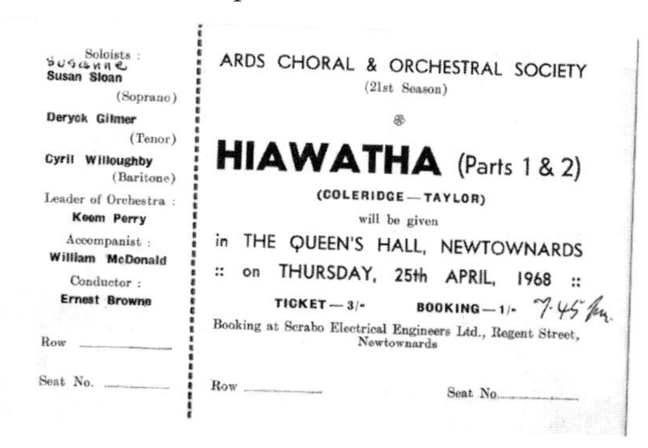
Soloists :
Susanne
Susan Sloan
(Soprano)
Deryck Gilmer
(Tenor)
Cyril Willoughby
(Baritone)
Leader of Orchestra :
Keem Perry
Accompanist :
William McDonald
Conductor :
Ernest Browne
Row
Seat No.

ARDS CHORAL & ORCHESTRAL SOCIETY
(21st Season)

HIAWATHA (Parts 1 & 2)
(COLERIDGE—TAYLOR)
will be given
in THE QUEEN'S HALL, NEWTOWNARDS
:: on THURSDAY, 25th APRIL, 1968 ::
TICKET—3/- BOOKING—1/- 7.45 pm.
Booking at Scrabo Electrical Engineers Ltd., Regent Street, Newtownards
Row
Seat No.

There was further exciting news for the Society during the anniversary year when, in September, rehearsals moved to the Londonderry Room at the Town Hall. Previously they had been held in Regent Street Presbyterian Church Hall, where the Society had been formed 21 years earlier.

Making a welcome return to the committee was John Brown. He was an enthusiastic supporter of Ards Choral, not only as a singer but also as an organiser of social events. A warm welcome was also extended to new committee member Laura Gilliland, a talented singer, pianist and organist.

Another name that comes to mind was founder member Jim Robinson, who worked diligently as a committee member, social committee member and sang in the tenor section. The baritone voice of Clarence Godfray enriched the bass section and he was chosen many times to sing solo parts. He was librarian for some time in the Sixties but unfortunately for Ards Choral he had to leave as he and his wife moved to Ballymena for business reasons.

Back in 1962 David Caughey had made his debut among the basses. This was the beginning of his long and dedicated membership of the Choral Society. In later years he served as treasurer, chairman and president.

Messrs John Brown, Jim Robinson, Clarence Godfray and David Warden, along with Miss Elspeth Irvine and some others formed a small drama group within the

Ards Choral in1968 – the year of their 21st anniversary

Society. All were 'characters' in every sense of the word and often performed their self-written playlets, giving much laughter on Choral social evenings.

It was then a case of goodbye to the Sixties! The Society did the honours once again by performing Handel's *Messiah* in December 1969.

Messrs Albert Stead and David Caughey were two new members elected to the committee at that time. The last committee members on duty until the mid 1970s were: chairman, Mr E.C.L. Kerr; hon. treasurer, Mr R. Morrison; hon. secretary, Miss Grace Lyttle, along with Mr D. Caughey, Mr J.S. Copeland MBE, Mrs W.H. Gilliland, Mrs W. Iveston, Miss M. Johnston, Mr W.H. Loane, Miss H.I. Thompson and Mr A. Stead.

Thursday night is still music night for Ards Choral Society. May it continue into future decades entertaining audiences and, above all, giving great pleasure to all its members.

Muriel Day

remembers... The Eurovision Song Contest

I was absolutely terrified as I stepped onto the stage in Madrid that Saturday evening in March 1969. There I was, the girl from Newtownards, the first female ever to represent Ireland in the Eurovision Song Contest.

My three backing singers were so nervous they'd threatened to go home, but after a few bars we settled into it. Millions were watching us live across Europe and there were over 5,000 in the audience of the beautiful Madrid Opera House. Noel Kelehan was our musical director and it was just incredible to sing with a 66-piece orchestra.

Muriel Day early in her career

My song, *Wages Of Love*, had been a runaway success at the earlier National Song Contest in Dublin. Eight contestants took part, including Dana – who of course, went on to win Eurovision the following year – Dickie Rock and Patrick McGeegan, who was boxer Barry McGuigan's father. Of the total 60 votes available from 10 juries all around the country, I received 30. Next closest to me was Dana, who received eight points for her song *Look Around*. I was in shock – that was me bound for Spain!

RTE gave me some nice clothes – all very modest, including an Italian leather suit – to take to Madrid. I had already got into trouble for my mini-skirts, which were part and

Muriel Day was born at Scrabo Road and describes growing up in Newtownards as 'a joy.' The only daughter of James and Margaret Galway, she had one brother, also called James, who still lives locally with his wife Irene.

She attended the nearby Model Primary School and later Glenlola Collegiate in Bangor. After leaving school, she worked in Cecil Wilson's drapery shop at Conway

parcel of the era we were living in. I had worn one for the National Song Contest, but after winning I was told in no uncertain terms: "Ireland is a Christian country – please lower your hemlines."

They gave me this awful mid-calf white satin straight up and down dress to wear for Eurovision. I politely accepted it and took it with me, but I told them the white wouldn't look good on TV.

I had this wonderful dressmaker in Belfast called Alice Campbell, who made all the clothes for my stage performances. Alice designed and made the whole wardrobe for my week-long stay in Madrid, including a three-piece suit in the Spanish colours. RTE were happy we did so well and never said anything afterwards about the green mini-dress I actually wore for the final!

Amazingly, Eurovision that year had four winners, when each received the same number of votes – it had never happened before, nor indeed since. Lulu won with *Boom Bang A Bang* for the United Kingdom, as did the representatives from Spain, France and the Netherlands. Ireland came joint fourth, though some record books have us down as finishing seventh or eighth.

When we returned to Dublin Airport we got the most wonderful reception and over the next few days there were lots of photo-calls, TV shows and interviews. When we visited Cork the streets were lined for miles just to see me. I was going to do a concert but there were so many people the Gardai had to pass me over their heads. And we hadn't even won!

Indeed it was there in Cork that my involvement in the National Song Contest came about. I had been singing with the Dave Glover Showband for years – and married Dave in 1962 – but the band finally broke up in the late Sixties when Dave decided to start doing cabaret. Dave and I were performing in Cork for a week when this huge storm broke out on the Monday night. Butch

Square in Newtownards but left when she joined the Dave Glover Showband.

Muriel previously sang in the choir at Strean Presbyterian Church where she came to know and received valuable advice from Ottilie Patterson, who later became a world famous jazz singer.

Ottilie and war hero Blair Mayne – who became the subject of the book *Colonel Paddy* – were among the most famous people to come out of the Ards area. Muriel never met Blair Mayne, though her parents knew him and her mother's dentist was his brother.

Tragically, Blair Mayne was killed when his sports car hit a telegraph pole at Mill Street in Newtownards in December 1955. His body was found by Muriel's uncle, James Alexander. A statue of Blair Mayne was erected at Conway Square in 1996 in honour of his wartime bravery.

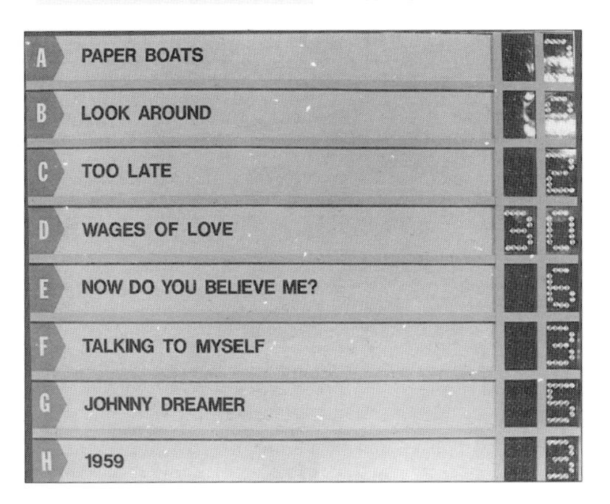

Muriel's song *Wages Of Love* was well ahead at the Irish National Song Contest, which preceded the Eurovision final

Moore, who played with the Capitol Showband and had himself represented Ireland in the 1965 Eurovision Song Contest, had been on his way to the US with his then fiancée but their plane was grounded due to the storm. They checked into our hotel, came to hear Dave and me playing in the lounge and afterwards joined us for a drink.

Muriel performs with the Dave Glover Showband.

Butch asked if I had ever thought of doing Eurovision and I said nobody had ever asked me. He asked if he could get me an audition would I go and I said "Yes." Before he left for the States he phoned and arranged an audition for me in Dublin on the Wednesday.

A guitar-playing friend of ours did me two quick-fire arrangements of *Harper Valley PTA* and *You Don't Have To Say You Love Me* and I took those two pieces of music to RTE. There were about eight people sitting behind a table with notebooks. There was no microphone, just Noel Kelehan on a baby grand piano. I sang my two songs, left and returned to Cork to finish the rest of the week. On the Friday I got a call from RTE to say they had a song for me. They'd chosen *Wages Of Love*, written by Michael Reade, and the up-tempo, bouncy tune went on to win the National Song Contest.

At that time I was also the first female from the North to represent Ireland in Eurovision and I'm happy to say the decision didn't get a negative reaction at home. However, there wasn't the same fabulous reaction in the Republic, but after all it was *their* entry. I was appearing on Gay Byrne's *The Late Late Show* when someone said I had no right to represent them. I pointed out it was a songwriter's contest and any singer could enter.

By then I was in my late 20s and already had a fairly lengthy musical career under my belt. My father James was a drum major in a pipe band and also a drummer in the Army, while my mother Margaret (née Moore) came from a very musical Bangor family, so I grew up surrounded by music.

As a child I was in the Girls' Brigade and was asked to sing at a few little concerts. I built up a reputation for singing and, aged about 15, one of my first shows was in the Orange Hall in Newtownards, where Frank Carson was also appearing. He was very funny even then.

Muriel (seated, right) awaits the results of the National Song Contest in 1969. Included is Dana who went on to win Eurovision the following year.

I began singing duets at small concerts with Newtownards man Roy McCord, who played the guitar. Then Ivan Patterson, who lived across the street from me on the Scrabo Road, got together with Hugh Blake and my cousin Jimmy Moore and together we formed a skiffle group called The Saints. That was good fun; Ivan was a great singer and guitar player.

I was 19 at the time and had a boyfriend but we broke up because I was singing so much on a Saturday night and couldn't go out with him. Three weeks later he turned up and, saying he wanted to prove he wasn't against me singing, showed me a newspaper advert for Dave Glover who was looking for a girl singer. I applied and sent a photograph but never heard anything back.

Sometime later someone told Dave there was a "wee girl called Muriel" singing in Donaghadee and he came to hear me. I thought he'd been very rude not replying to my earlier application and I didn't particularly want to be introduced. However, we did finally meet and he arranged an audition in Belfast. He offered me the job and also suggested I change my surname from Muriel Galway to Day as it sounded better.

He went to see my mother and told her he needed me to sing on Sunday nights but she turned him down. He explained that Sunday was the best night of the whole week and it was part and parcel of the deal. He finally talked her into it but then she demanded I come home every night.

That too proved impossible because sometimes the band stayed in hotels. She was far from happy but relented in the end.

The band was based in Belfast and I was the only member not from the city. We played Orange Halls on a Saturday night and Parochial Halls on a Sunday and very often the same people came to both shows. A lot of people followed the band and before too long it became my full-time profession as we were working four or five nights a week, from Belfast to Cork and from Dublin to Galway.

We would often leave in the afternoon, travel five or six hours to a gig, dancing would be from 9pm until 2am, and by the time you'd spoken to people afterwards it could be 3.30-4am before we were on the road home. I enjoyed every single place we played; I just loved everything I was doing.

The audience also loved my clothes. Alice was so far ahead of her time in her designs; she was amazing. I used to make four changes a night because I could. The girls would be waiting to see what I was going to wear for the next set.

Dave was always harder on me than anyone else as he didn't want them to think he was playing favourites. He was tough but fair. As we became better known, there were lots of TV appearances and I was even featured singing *Twisterella* in the acclaimed British film *Billy Liar* in 1963.

Muriel performed with The Night Squad in Canada during the early 1970s.

By 1970 Dave had formed a new band but he and I were parting. I thought the best thing was to move to Canada, where there was work waiting for me. I left in 1971, taking three of the band members with me – the guitar player, the bass player and the drummer. We formed a new band called The Night Squad and based ourselves in Kingston, Ontario.

It was a new audience and they loved our energetic style. We played a lot of Sixties British music by the likes of Dusty Springfield, but after a while we were playing material by Diana Ross and Aretha Franklin. While in Canada I married band member Eddie McCann, from Belfast, though we later parted.

After 20 years abroad I returned to Northern Ireland and, having qualified in Canada, set up my own business as a laser therapist, treating people with addictions. Having been away for so long, not many people remembered me. However, a neighbour in Newtownabbey, Joe Trainor, arranged some gigs in clubs where I was rediscovered by promoter David Hull. He then organised showband shows in the Waterfront Hall and all over Ireland. The first concert I did was in the Waterfront in 1997, the year it opened. It helped to put me back on the map.

Muriel Day today

I now have a wonderful manager called Malcolm McDowell and I still regularly perform, doing a mixture of country, pop and jazz. After the 1969 Eurovision Song Contest, Peter Warne (who wrote *Boom Bang A Bang* for Lulu) penned a song called *Nine Times Out Of Ten.* It was released on a Northern Soul compilation album and is presently enjoying a revival with tens of thousands of hits on the Internet. It's 40 years old and is still filling dance floors. Incredible! Because of that, I was recently asked to perform in a Northern Soul club in Wales and there are other exciting projects in the pipeline.

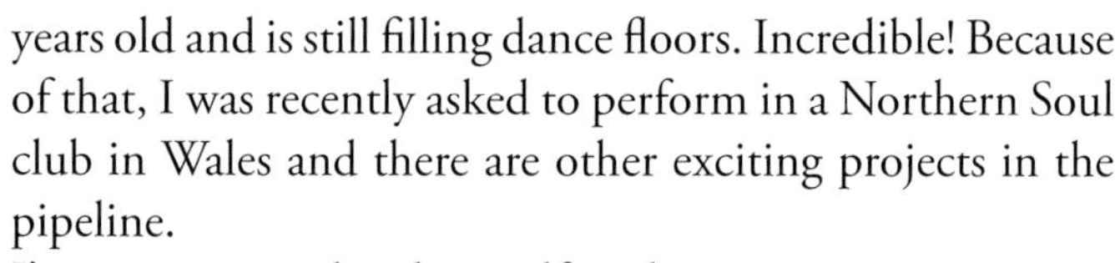

I've never considered myself to be a great singer; I just think of myself as an entertainer. I have been blessed and if I'm healthy enough and the voice lasts, I'll do it until I drop!

James G. Meredith

remembers... Teenage Life

I can't imagine what it would be like today, but as far as I'm concerned growing up in Newtownards during the Sixties was so inspirational – we had freedom. I don't remember facing any of the limitations or controls placed on children today although I do remember being told to be home before it got dark, but that was about it!

There was so much innovation and change, with everyone simply wanting to make things better. But first, a few observations. We survived being born to mothers who smoked and/or drank while they carried us. They took aspirin, ate blue cheese dressing, tuna from a can and didn't get tested for diabetes.

Then, after that entire trauma, our cots were covered with bright-coloured lead-based paints. We had no childproof lids on medicine bottles and when we rode our bikes we didn't wear helmets. And let's not forget how popular hitchhiking – seeking lifts from complete strangers – was back then.

As children – if we were lucky – we rode in cars with no seat belts or air bags; we drank water from the garden hose and not from a bottle. We sometimes shared our soft drinks with four friends, from one bottle, and no one actually died from this. Who remembers ever washing an apple before eating it? We ate buns, white bread and real butter, but we weren't overweight because we were always playing outside!

James G. Meredith

James G. Meredith was born on 23 April 1951 at Newtownards Hospital, joining a large family (six older sisters and two older brothers) in a small house at the town's Church Street. He attended Londonderry Primary School, Scrabo Secondary School and Newtownards Technical College, as well as Felden House in Belfast, where he took a City and Guilds pre-apprentice course in electrical engineering.

Although he would subsequently become a semi-professional and full-time professional musician, he was also employed over the years at a variety of local businesses, including Savages Butchers in Regent Street (before leaving school), Dick Jefferson's pub (after leaving school), Blaxnit Hosiery, Canadian Technical Tape (Bangor) and 3M UK.

As well as listening to late night radio stations such as

A young James in Mill Street, Newtownards

Radio Luxembourg, an early pointer to his musical future was his involvement in the ABC Cinema's Saturday morning talent competition for minors in 1963. The Newtownards-based group Virtue followed in 1968, along with, variously, Lawrence Thomson, Michael Richmond, Philip O'Connor, Jim Doak and Robert Apps.

By 1972, after playing extensively in Germany and Denmark with Tapestry (which had its origins in Ballymena), James returned to Northern Ireland, settling in Bangor.

A career highlight arose when James was invited to join Sunshine in 1978 following a stint in The Fresh Boogie Band and a number of different semi-professional line-ups. Eight weeks later Sunshine took part in the BBC-produced *A Song For Europe* at the Royal Albert Hall in London, the

We would leave home in the morning and play all day, as long as we were back when the streetlights came on. No one was able to reach us all day and guess what… we were actually okay.

We would spend hours building our go-karts out of scrap prams and then ride them down the hill, only to realise too late we'd forgotten about the brakes. We didn't have iPads, PlayStations, Nintendos, Xboxes or video games. There were no DVDs and our television sets with their tiny screens and a couple of stations certainly didn't have Surround Sound speakers.

We had no mobile phones, text messages, personal computers, the Internet or online chat rooms. However we did have friends and we went outside and found them! We fell out of trees, got cut, broke bones and teeth and there were no lawsuits from those accidents. We ate worms and mud pies literally made from dirt, and the worms did not live in us forever!

We made up games with sticks and tennis balls and although we were warned it would happen, we did not put out very many eyes. We rode bikes or walked to a friend's house and knocked on the door or rang the bell, or just yelled for them! Football teams had trials and not everyone made the team. Those who didn't learned to deal with disappointment. Imagine that!

The idea of a parent bailing us out if we broke the law was unheard of. They actually sided with the law!

Looking back all these years, I believe the Sixties produced some of the best risk takers, problem solvers and inventors of all time. There was an explosion of innovation and ideas. Yes we had the freedom, failure, success and responsibility, and we just learned how to deal with it all.

For me, Newtownards in the early Sixties was all about music and at that time the only bands we knew were pipe, flute or accordion marching-type bands. The local groups were mostly of the skiffle or showband variety, with the members all dressing in colourful suits and playing the top hits of the day.

There was a huge variety of showbands throughout Ireland at that time, mostly playing country and western

The Saints skiffle group

music or strict tempo dance music, which I suppose had in time replaced the era of the ballroom big bands.

Obviously the American rock and roll stars proved very popular with teenagers everywhere in the late 1950s and early 1960s. The UK quickly followed with its own groups and big name artists like Adam Faith, Cliff Richard and The Shadows, Lonnie Donegan, Frankie Vaughan, Helen Shapiro, Petula Clark and Frank Ifield. Gerry and The Pacemakers and The Beatles had only just started to emerge and they also wore suits!

By the late Sixties/early Seventies colour television was becoming the standard and the music media – vinyl – was also switching from mono recording to stereo. Of course, our local record shop, Scrabo Electrical, stocked all the latest Top 20 chart singles and albums.

Almost every Saturday morning in 1963, at the tender age of 12, I would head off with a sixpence tucked safely in my pocket and carrying my modest six-string acoustic guitar which I'd bought in the Arcadia Book and Card Shop at High Street in Newtownards. My destination was

purpose being to select the United Kingdom's entry for that year's Eurovision Song Contest. Their song *Too Much In Love* finished eighth out of 12, the winning entry being *The Bad Old Days* by Co-Co.

James later reformed The Fresh Boogie Band and worked at a number of local venues with a view to eventually becoming professional again.

James and his wife Ann still live in Bangor. Although James is now retired from the management position he held at 3M UK, he is still very much involved in the music world, with much of his work being done in his home studio.

James's local music nostalgic website 'Memory Lane Ards & Bangor' can be found at **www.ardsbangor.com**

James at Lisleen Place, Newtownards

the ABC Minors Matinee with its weekly talent competitions at the town's Ritz Cinema (now Wright's Arcade).

I can still remember standing centre stage and singing *I Like It*, which around that time was a No. 1 hit for Gerry and The Pacemakers. Eventually, after weeks of knock-out rounds, I got into the finals. First place went to Margaret Brown, second was Fred Benson, while third and last place went to me!

The song which began with the words "We are the boys and girls well known as Minors of the ABC," was always the finale at the shows in the Newtownards cinema.

Long before I started buying albums and singles, I spent much of my time listening to Radio Luxemburg and then, a little later, the pirate station Radio Caroline, picking out the chords and learning how to play my favourites.

It wasn't long before I realised I wanted to become a musician. What could be easier (not!) even though at that time I hadn't even seen or heard a live group other than the late great Brian Rossi and The Wheels at the Ritz Matinee Show. I guess I was just a little too young for the Young Farmers' Hall or the Queen's Hall.

Wearing my Ben Sherman shirt and best pair of jeans, I was almost ready – but what about the Mods and Rockers? Over in England you had to be one or the other during the Sixties, otherwise you got a hiding from both groups! Mods on their Lambrettas or Vespa scooters with the extra mirrors and the Rockers, also known as 'ton-up boys' with British-made motorcycles, were all part of the macho culture at the time.

So I opted out, preferring the company of my school friends around the Scrabo Estate, rather than the cool guys at Cafolla's in the town square.

The first complete song I learned was *The House Of The Rising Sun* by The Animals. For those who know it, this meant using everything but bar chords. From that moment on I just listened and learned songs from the masters at that time, otherwise known as The Beatles.

During my early years at Scrabo Secondary School I teamed up with my friend Fred Benson, who also had a guitar. We rehearsed lots of popular songs with harmonies. After a short time I started rehearsing with a few other friends, including Bobby Hastings and Dennis Boyle, at the old Scout Hall on Nursery Road (near what became the Ards Shopping Centre). We would also travel by Ulsterbus to Conlig Hall with all our gear packed on board.

James with Lawrence Thomson

Then along came our first gig; I don't remember ever receiving any money. At 16, I even sang solo and played acoustic on Saturday nights in the back room of the Royal Bar in Frances Street.

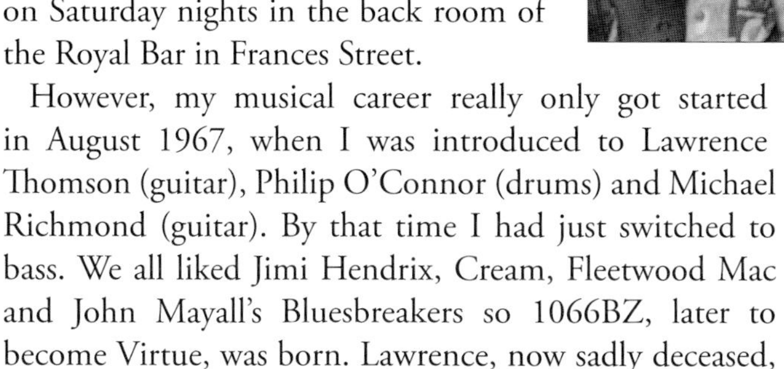

However, my musical career really only got started in August 1967, when I was introduced to Lawrence Thomson (guitar), Philip O'Connor (drums) and Michael Richmond (guitar). By that time I had just switched to bass. We all liked Jimi Hendrix, Cream, Fleetwood Mac and John Mayall's Bluesbreakers so 1066BZ, later to become Virtue, was born. Lawrence, now sadly deceased, was an exceptional musician and singer with his own style of playing.

A little later we played the first half at Greyabbey Village Hall, mostly Hendrix and Cream material, and then on came a Donaghadee-based group, The Suburbans, featuring the one and only Gary Moore on guitar – what a player!

From that moment on I just knew it was what I really wanted to do.

The members of Virtue: Robert, James and Lawrence

James G. Meredith

Unfortunately, we simply didn't get the exposure through gigs, most likely because it was only the start of the Rock era and our music didn't appeal to audiences who really just wanted to dance. After all, we really only had dance halls at that time.

Our first real break would come a little later in the decade when, on 10 January 1969 at Cloud 9 in Bangor's old Co-op Hall, we supported The John Smith Band. Other great local Blues/ Rock and Soul groups that played there included Sk'boo, Creative Mind, Sam Mahood and The Method, a band we saw many times.

Jean Douglas

(née Gourley) remembers... Miss Northern Ireland

I couldn't quite believe my eyes when I stepped out the front door of the family home at The Square in Ballygowan on my wedding day on 15 September 1965. It seemed the whole village had come out to greet this very surprised 21-year-old.

Jean and John Douglas on their wedding day

My husband-to-be John Douglas and I had planned a quiet wedding and never for a second expected anything like this. Television crews and national newspaper reporters were among the crowd. The reason for their interest? At the time I was the reigning Miss Northern Ireland.

My mother had originally suggested we walk the short distance to Ballygowan Presbyterian Church but like all brides I wanted to arrive in a fancy car. Though it's the bride's prerogative, I hadn't intended to be late but we could barely make our way through the crowds and in the end I was 20 minutes late.

Our wedding picture and the crowds that turned out made front page news in the *Belfast Telegraph* and headlines

Jean – or Jane as she was officially christened and how she was known during her beauty queen days – was the only daughter of Robert and Alice Gourley. She was the middle child, having two older and two younger brothers.

The family ran a grocery shop and village inn at The Square in Ballygowan, known as the Railway Bar. The village was a halt on the Newcastle line and when the train stopped some passengers would quickly nip into the nearby bar for a swift drink, hence the name.

Eager to follow her older brothers to school, Jean was allowed by headmaster Jacob Hare to start at Ballygowan Primary School at the tender age of three. Despite her ambition to become a hairdresser, Jean's mother insisted a more practical option was to attend Belfast School of Commerce where she trained in shorthand, typing and book keeping.

Her first job was as junior shorthand typist with potato merchants James McVeigh and Sons, based at May's Market in Belfast. She later entered the Civil Service and became a doctor's secretary at the Royal Victoria Hospital, a post she held until her children were born.

Jean met John Douglas, who hailed from near Comber, at Sunday School

in the *Daily Express, Daily Mail* and *Daily Mirror*. They declared: 'Village Stops for Beauty Queen.'

The *Express* reported that "Shopkeepers, butchers and bakers left their counters, policemen left the beat and children abandoned their classroom to surround Ballygowan Presbyterian Church."

It was estimated that over 400 well-wishers had turned out to catch a glimpse of me in my satin and lace wedding dress.

There was even a TV crew perched on top of the church gates. I remember the cameraman asking if he could come to the reception. I told him "No" but he said he wasn't sure if he had enough suitable footage as he was being jostled so much by the crowds.

Later that evening as we waited at Aldergrove Airport to leave on our honeymoon we looked at the TV and our wedding came on the news. I hoped nobody would recognise us! It had been an unbelievable day. Only that I still have the newspaper cuttings and pictures of the crowd to prove it, I would wonder "Did that really happen?"

Ballygowan was a small place back then and the occasion certainly caused quite a stir.

My first proper introduction to beauty competitions came at the age of 17, in January 1961, when I was accorded the title Miss Ballygowan at a dance organised by the Ballygowan branch of the Mid-Down Unionist Association. There weren't many places to go in the village at the time but there was the Young Unionist Club which organised various trips away so I went along for the social aspect.

A competition to find Miss Young Unionist was being organised and each club had to put forward

Jean Gourley was acclaimed 'Miss Ballygowan' at a dance organised by the Ballygowan branch of the Mid-Down Unionist Association in the local Orange Hall on 20 January 1961. Runners-up were Maree Peak and Mrs K. Gibson.
18-1-2

someone. I was asked if I would do it and initially said "No" but I was talked into it. The politician Sir Robin Kinahan and his wife were the adjudicators for the final in the Ulster Hall and I couldn't believe it when I won the darn thing! I was presented with a bouquet of flowers by Sir Robin and received a cheque for £5.

The prize also included a trip to London to attend a Conservative weekend and ball where I met future Prime Minister Ted Heath and quite a few other politicians. Some members of the Ballygowan branch went along too as did Young Unionist John Taylor, who would later serve as MP for the Ards area. It was my first trip to London, which for a 17-year-old was a marvellous experience. We were shown all around the city and the House of Commons. I remember wearing a beautiful cobalt blue gown to the ball.

Jean winning the Miss Bangor title in 1965

So that's what started it off. I later went on to pick up a total of 18 titles. These included Miss Bangor, Miss Portrush, Belfast Dairy Queen, Miss County Down in the Rose of Tralee (I sang as my party piece and wore a green dress) and Mary of Dungloe festivals, Miss TV Post and Miss Ulster Television.

In 1965, I was chosen as Miss Northern Ireland at the Plaza Ballroom in Belfast and went forward to the Miss UK competition in Blackpool. The following year I represented Northern Ireland again, at the Miss Great Britain competition in Morecambe.

Jean takes part in 1965's Miss Northern Ireland competition

For those competitions a chaperone, an older motherly figure, was assigned to look after five or six girls and make sure we had everything we needed. A lot of the English girls were on a circuit doing different competitions and knew each other and I sometimes felt a bit of a country cousin. Most of the girls were nice and the pair became childhood sweethearts. They started dating seriously when Jean was 16 and John often accompanied her to the beauty queen competitions. Dance halls were the hub of social life then and Friday night was the big night out. A highlight for Jean was hearing Reg Presley and The Troggs play at Milanos in Bangor.

Following their marriage, Jean and John's first son, Richard, was born in 1966, followed later by the arrival of second son Mark and daughter Victoria. Indeed, Jean was already married and a mum when she represented Northern Ireland in the Miss Great Britain competition.

When the children were older, Jean returned to work as a book keeper for an estate agent. She and John are both now retired, still living in the Ballygowan area and enjoy spending time with their family and six grandchildren who all live nearby.

Son Richard, a music teacher, and wife Lynsey have two children, Callum and Anna. Mark, an accountant, and his wife Libby have three sons, Andrew, James and Harry, while daughter Victoria, also an accountant, is married to David Gibson and they have a baby daughter, Jessica.

Jean's brother Jim still runs the family bar, now known as The Roundabout. Her other brothers, Douglas and Tom, still live locally while, sadly, youngest brother Roy passed away a few years ago.

One of Jean's most treasured possessions is a Bible engraved with her name, which was presented to her by the Presbyterian Church in Ireland to mark 18 years'

but there was rivalry among them. Sometimes I got fed up with it – it could be a wee bit false. I could take so much then thought: "I'm going!"

Usually you had to arrive a week before the actual competition and attend various functions, dinners and sight-seeing trips. Something was laid on each day. I remember being driven around in horse-drawn carriages and in a cavalcade of cars in Morecambe. The weather always seemed to be good back then.

Quite often we were given a long evening dress to keep. We were supplied with swimwear in a bid by companies to promote their designs and would get our hair done for free in salons. Any prize money I won was spent on buying more clothes.

I remember meeting quite a few different stars, including Tommy Trinder, Beryl Reid, Jimmy Ellis, Larry Cunningham and comedians Freddie 'Parrot Face' Davies and Frank Carson.

There were quite a few television appearances along the way, especially when I was crowned Miss Ulster Television. I went to Bristol for the final of Miss ITV and we had the most tremendous weekend.

During my time as Miss Northern Ireland I had to have my sash with me at all times and was asked to attend different functions, football matches, open petrol stations and adjudicate on various May Queen competitions, etc. It was quite an honour.

One thing led to another and I was approached and asked to do modelling (I modelled swimwear and underwear for Triumph) and photographic work – though I would have to say I was quite amateurish at it!

During those whirlwind years the thing that gave me most joy and fulfilment was my continued involvement with Girls' Brigade. I first joined the Ballygowan Company when I was seven,

Jean when she entered the Girls' Brigade aged seven

became a captain when I was 20 and am very proud to have been involved ever since.

The Girls' Brigade is a Christian youth organisation for girls of all ages, backgrounds and abilities. It offers a programme of fun activities and events for girls and leaders where they can meet, have fun, compete and share friendship.

The Girls' Brigade Star, the highest award in GB, was won by four members of 59th NI Company (Ballygowan Presbyterian Church) in April 1962. Standing (from left): Patricia Watson and Irene Long. Front: Sub-Officers Jean Gourley and Jean Garrett. *31-81-1*

Ballygowan has a thriving company attended by around 150-160 girls and led by 14 officers. As well as undertaking assorted badge work, the company has proved hugely successful in other areas such as the Duke of Edinburgh Award scheme, PE and choral speaking competitions.

Some years ago I undertook a two-year course in rhythmic gymnastics and was able to teach my nieces; they in turn were then able to teach it to their daughters. Three generations of our family are now involved in Ballygowan GB. My daughter Victoria and nieces Lorraine, Jane and Rose are all officers. I would like to think it was partly because of my influence that they became involved.

Veronica Kirk and Mary Lemon were presented with their Girls' Brigade Stars at the annual Ballygowan GB display in May 1966. Included is their captain, the recently married Mrs Jean Douglas. *141-16-1*

Things have changed such a lot since my time as a teenager. There are so many more negative influences out there now. I would encourage any girl to become a part of the Girls' Brigade. It's trying to keep girls on the straight and narrow. It's very hard to get young people of any age to go to church these days but in GB there is a spiritual side to it and it's a nice way to keep girls within that family.

Sometimes, because of my experiences, I find I can give some advice. Everyone has disappointments in life and I feel it is so important to teach the girls that you don't always have to win – that taking part is what matters.

It's learning how to overcome the disappointment that's

attendance at Ballygowan Sunday School (aged 3-21) without a single absence. On one occasion she even left hospital following a serious ear operation to attend before having to return to her hospital bed for further medical care.

Following a lifetime of dedicated and proud service, Jean is now the President of Ballygowan Girls' Brigade. While she no longer teaches she is still very much involved, describing GB as her "whole hobby."

And while the girls may not realise it, Jean's beauty queen legacy lives on. A solid silver cup, donated by the Milk Marketing Board after she was crowned Belfast Dairy Princess, is still presented each year at the annual display to a girl from the Ballygowan Company.

important – to be able to congratulate the winner and be happy for them. Sometimes, you have to pick yourself up, dust yourself down and away you go again.

Looking back on the beauty queen days, while it was all very exciting at the time, it's something I don't really talk about now. I don't honestly think it altered my ego.

I don't look back and say, "I'm sorry I did that," but I don't know if I would do it again. Today there aren't the same opportunities and girls are much more career-orientated. I wouldn't be against any girl becoming a beauty queen as long as she has the right frame of mind because you can easily get carried away. You have to keep a level head.

But I definitely have no regrets whatsoever about my time spent in the Girls' Brigade. I have loved every minute of it.

All in the family – Jean Douglas (centre) is surrounded by her nieces and great nieces, all members of Ballygowan Girls' Brigade. Clockwise (from back, left): Lauren Gourley, Lorraine Mayes (née Gourley), Rose Lemon (née Gourley), Sophie Gourley, Victoria Gibson (née Douglas – Jean's daughter), Hannah Mayes, Rebecca Gourley, Erin Mayes, Rachel Gourley and Jane Shields (née Gourley).
Picture by Bob Torrens, Newtownards Chronicle

Margo Burns

(née Harron) remembers... Music

Little did I realise when I visited my friend's home in Donaghadee back in 1960 to ask her brother to tune my guitar, that it would change my life dramatically and result in a musical career that has spanned over 50 years and taken us all over the world.

I didn't even know how to play that guitar but it had been left to me by my father, a soldier I'd never met, and so someone suggested asking Trevor Burns to tune it. I went to my friend Nan Burns' house at New Street to ask her brother but he was upstairs rehearsing with friends with the idea of putting a band together.

Margo with The Hep Cats (from left): Gordon Moore, Trevor Burns and Carson Boyd

Margaret Harron was born in Donaghadee and raised by her grandparents, Eddie and Daisy Harron, who lived at East Street.

After The Marvettes disbanded, Margo and husband Trevor continued as Take Two and began touring further afield as a cabaret act, working top-class venues around the world, including South Africa, Rhodesia

Nan and I had been mates for years and in the Girl Guides together and we were all at the Secondary Intermediate School at Northfield, later Donaghadee High, though Trevor, who was a prefect, and I hated each other!

When I arrived, their mother Lily was playing the piano. Mrs Burns was a well-known pianist in bars around Donaghadee at the time, while her husband, Bertie, was the local barber. I asked her: "Do you know the song (now Zimbabwe), Botswana, Nigeria, Sri Lanka, Australia, America, Singapore, Spain, Italy and Portugal.

On returning to the UK in 1978, the couple were asked to join top club band The Rock 'n' Roll Circus who had recorded several albums and had notched up Top 10 singles in South Africa and on the Continent. This led to two years' touring across Britain and Europe.

Following a visit to the Abercorn Nightclub in Belfast with The Rock 'n' Roll Circus, Margo and Trevor were offered a residency by owner Dermot O'Donnell. After 20 years on the road, they decided it was time to settle and happily agreed. Along with resident band Nitelife, Margo recorded the single *Behind The Footlights*, which became a big hit, reaching Number One in the local charts in 1981. This led to radio and TV appearances with Gloria Hunniford and on *The Gerry Kelly Show*.

After four years off the road, a strong desire to return to touring saw Margo and Trevor rejoining The

Margo in 1960

Scarlet Ribbons?" She told me to sing the words and she would play the tune.

When Trevor appeared she insisted: "You need to get her in the group!" He replied they didn't want a girl!

Trevor and my cousin Carson Boyd, from Bow Street, had already formed a skiffle band called The Hep Cats in 1959, appearing with the famous Pierrots in the hut on Donaghadee seafront. Many of those Pierrot entertainers boarded with the Burns family for the summer season. Back then it cost thruppence to sit on the deckchairs and a penny to sit on the wall to watch the show – if they could catch you!

After about a year, with skiffle on the way out, they decided to get into rock 'n' roll. Carson knew I was going to be singing at the Ashleigh Ballroom in Millisle and suggested he and Trevor should go along to hear me. The pair cycled to Millisle, heard me sing *Blue Moon* and in the break Trevor asked if I fancied joining them. I asked if they knew any Connie Francis songs. Trevor lied convincingly so I agreed and The Marvettes were formed.

I played rhythm guitar, which Trevor had taught me. He also played guitar, as did Elvis-lookalike Robbie Miskimmin, from Moat Street. Carson was the drummer, while Gordon Moore, from Bow Street, played bass.

Future members would be Fred Day, from Meeting House Street (guitar), Brian Huddleston, from Meadowbank (saxophone), and Wilson Beck (bass). He came from Ballysillan in Belfast and was the only band member not from Donaghadee, travelling down on his scooter.

Margaret and The Marvettes didn't have quite the right ring to it so Trevor suggested I change my name to Margo and I've been known as that ever since. My mentor was Belle Crowe, wife of Walter Davidson, who was our manager at that time. As well as singing with the Melotones Showband, she and Walter had a caravan in Groomsport. Thanks to Belle's advice on my look, I dyed my hair blonde, started wearing make-up and modernised my wardrobe.

Ian Hamilton, from Moat Avenue, was managing us earlier on and we decided it would be a good idea to hire

Margo and The Marvettes in Belfast in 1960: Fred, Wilson, Carson, Trevor, Brian and Margo

Sam Hill's large upstairs room in the town, which could hold 50-60 people, and stage a dance there every Saturday night. It was always packed and although there was no alcohol we sold soft drinks and the profits helped to pay Sam's rent.

The band rehearsed each Tuesday and Thursday night in Trevor's attic until an eviction notice was served on him because of the noise from the electric guitars and amplifiers. Rehearsals then shifted to the Orange Hall at Manor Street until the neighbours complained again and eventually we moved to a more isolated hall on the Shore Road near the Dunallon Hotel.

Soon we were regulars at the Queen's Hall in Newtownards, playing all the hits of the day, and then we got a residency at the Fiesta Ballroom behind St George's Market in Belfast. It wasn't long before Trevor noticed that each time I got up to sing the crowd stopped dancing to watch. As a result he suggested I stop playing guitar and concentrate on the vocals.

We shared the bill, doing alternate sets, at the Queen's Hall with the Monarch Showband which had Van Morrison on sax. Soon we were touring all over Ireland supporting the top showbands of the day. We also played with Shane Fenton and The Fentones – Shane later became Alvin Stardust – Kenny Ball, Acker Bilk and Eden Kane, as well as up and coming stars Roy Orbison and Johnny Cash.

The American artists were often heading to the big US Army bases in Germany but as the Musicians' Union wouldn't allow them to play in England they regularly interrupted their journey to perform in Ireland.

Once we were sitting with Johnny Cash in the dressing room of the Top Hat Ballroom in Lisburn and he asked us where we came from. We told him and he repeated "Dunadee" and then "Donadee" – he just couldn't pronounce Donaghadee correctly. As he took a sip of

Rock 'n' Roll Circus.

During a week-long holiday in 1987 visiting Trevor's sister Nan, who was living in Majorca, Margo was asked up to sing in a popular bar in Santa Ponsa. Margo proved such a hit that she and Trevor were signed up to do a summer season the following year.

They became massively popular and, in all, spent 14 summer seasons entertaining in bars all over the island, returning home to Donaghadee each winter.

The introduction of all-inclusive holidays saw a marked downturn for the bar trade and the couple decided that, after more than 50 years in the entertainment business, it was time to slow down. They are now semi-retired and have returned to live permanently in Donaghadee.

They occasionally perform at charity events and Trevor, also a talented artist, recently formed rockabilly duo The Deemen with friend Davy Angus.

whiskey he pulled out a map and wrote down the name, saying he had just realised how green Ireland was and he wanted to write a song about it. And he did – it was *Forty Shades Of Green*, which was included on his 1963 *Ring Of Fire* album and opens so memorably with the lines:

I close my eyes and picture
The emerald of the sea
From the fishing boats at Dingle
To the shores of Donaghadee

Roy Orbison was another gentleman and a very funny guy. When we first met him in 1961 he had blonde hair but when he returned a year or two later his hair and clothes were black and he was wearing those trademark dark glasses. He had changed his whole persona.

We toured extensively all over Ireland in our salmon pink and yellow Austin J2 van, previously owned by the Melotones Showband and by then emblazoned with our name, abbreviated to 'Margo and Marvettes.' We would get in from work at the Cyril Lord carpet factory in Donaghadee, where Trevor was a forklift truck driver and I was a gill spinner, have our dinner and then set off in the van.

I remember once doing a gig in Cork, not getting home until 5am and then having to start work at 6am. I was still wearing my sequinned dress but just pulled my overalls on over the top.

While Sunday was a day of rest in the north, it was a big night out down south and our band was in demand in dancehalls all over. That meant our Sundays were always spent on the road. We longed to have a Sunday roast but instead we just ate in the van. I well remember tying sausage rolls to the van's heater to warm them up!

We were working full-time at Cyril Lord's, still rehearsing on Tuesdays and Thursdays, and then doing gigs most other nights. It took a lot out of us and eventually we realised we couldn't do both any more. In September 1963 the band held a meeting and we decided to give up our jobs, turn professional and head for the bright lights of

London. Needless to say, our families weren't too happy about us going off into the unknown but, all the same, I set off with £40 in my pocket which my grandmother had given me.

We packed up the van, which had curtains I'd made as I knew we'd be sleeping in it, and caught the same Liverpool ferry as George Jones and Van Morrison with the Monarch Showband, who were heading to Germany. A storm hit as the boat was being unloaded in Heysham. They got their van off first so we told them to go on ahead and we'd meet them in London. It was a couple of hours before we finally got our van off the ferry. We had no map and ended up at Matlock in Derbyshire. We got to London about three days later but by then had lost all contact with the other band.

We found hotel accommodation at Seven Sisters in London. However, we couldn't all afford to stay there so we used to take it in turns with three sleeping in the van and three sleeping in the hotel. I used to order a big breakfast in the morning and then share it with the others in the van. They were fun times but it was hard going.

We managed to get a few gigs at some Irish halls but that was about all. We weren't really that happy so after about a month we decided to head home, knowing our old jobs at the carpet factory were still there for us.

Along the way we stopped for fish and chips at Finsbury Park and left the van parked outside. A man named Jim Fox then walked in, asked for Margo and The Marvettes and enquired if we could help him out. When we told him we were on our way home he replied: "Have you not heard the news? JFK has been assassinated." He had a hall full of people at the Harlesden 32 Club and the band he'd booked hadn't turned up. So we followed him to the club, set up our gear and both he and the audience loved us. He urged us to stay and got us a Friday night residency at the Gresham Ballroom in Holloway Road.

We rented a flat for £12 a week where we could all stay – that was a lot of money back then. Times were certainly tough; stallholders in Wood Green Market used to keep us vegetable leftovers so I could make soup or a stew for us.

Christmas night 1964 was spent at the US Airbase in Alconbury, Cambridgeshire. From left: Les, Fred, Margo, Trevor, Carson and Brian.

It was called survival.

Entertainment-wise it was very much dog-eat-dog in London. Competition was fierce with an estimated 8,000 groups in the city at that time and everybody was fighting for all sorts of work. You would turn up for an audition and there would be about 30 bands there. We met Lulu and The Rolling Stones and also shared the bill at the Gresham with Tom Jones right at the start of his career, when he was performing under the name Tommy Scott and The Senators.

Soon we started playing the American army bases in England and Germany and began to change our whole style of music. We got in with some black airmen who brought us records featuring music we'd never heard of, from the likes of Diana Ross. We switched from rock 'n' roll to soul and Motown. Being an all-white band and singing black music was a novelty. They used to call me the 'blue-eyed soul sister.'

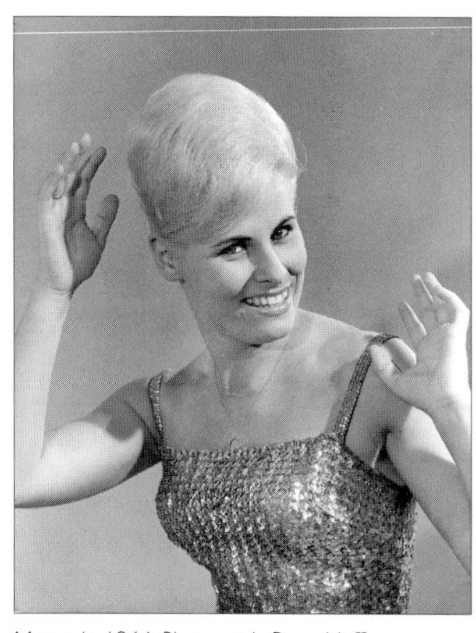

Margo in 1964. *Photograph: Dezo Hoffman*

We got to tour with top American acts like The Drifters, whose *Under The Boardwalk* was a chart-topper at the time, Ben E. King, The Orlons and Hank Locklin.

Sadly, back then there was still segregation among black and white soldiers. We were once performing at a base in Germany when a riot broke out. We had to run off stage and were locked in the dressing room for our own safety. We couldn't believe it. We were there to entertain but ended up being caught up in the middle of a fight.

We also toured theatres, dancehalls, nightclubs and casinos all over England, Scotland and Wales and joined the cabaret circuit working with all the stars. We were like gypsies, on the road all the time. Sometimes we would do a social club and then go on to play in a nightclub as they started later. Once, after playing an army base in Germany, we packed up our gear and travelled 400 miles to perform in another on the same night.

We made several television appearances along the way, although I actually turned down a chance to leave the band and go into television with renowned presenter Muriel Young. We also cut a number of records. In 1964 we recorded three singles for Shel Talmy on the Parlophone label. On the first single, *Start The World Spinning Again*, the label changed my name to Sherry Weine. I also recorded under the names Liza Dulittle and Maggie Brown. At one time my picture was on the side of red London buses.

In terms of The Marvettes, Wilson Beck was first to leave the band, in late 1964, while we were still in London. He was replaced as bass player following a successful audition by Les McSheffrey, who was originally from Holywood and was working as an electrician in the Finsbury Park Astoria.

Trevor and Margo on their wedding day in September 1965

In the middle of all this activity Trevor and I decided it was about time we got married and so we returned home to Donaghadee for our wedding in the local Parish Church on 18 September 1965. I had bought my dress and two bridesmaids' dresses in London and brought them home with me – thankfully they all fitted!

We returned to England with the band moving to Manchester to be closer to the cabaret scene. In the late Sixties we were asked to perform at the Manchester City football ground, in front of a 62,000-strong crowd and before a televised derby match between City and United. George Best came on and quickly scored the first goal.

During the Sixties fashions and hairstyles changed so

Margo and Trevor

much – in my case progressing from my silver lamé suit to hot pants and then to glamorous long sequinned dresses. It was difficult back then to buy suitable dresses so I designed my own and had them made for me.

Over the years we've found that one thing always leads to another. It's not what you know, it's who you know. For us it's always been a matter of being in the right place at the right time.

We had our ups and downs – we had fabulous times and some bad times but I would never have changed it. Life could have been very different. We could have been stuck working in the factory for years. It's long gone and where would we be now?

Joe Dorrian

remembers... Amateur Theatre

The arrival of the Sixties saw Newtownards enjoying a thriving amateur theatre tradition, with local companies putting on plays, concerts, musicals and other shows. A variety of organisations, including the Young Farmers, Boy Scouts and Boys' Brigade had been treading the boards since the early years of the 20th Century.

My own stage connections were with the various societies connected to St. Patrick's and, in particular, the period of the 1960s. It all came about with the arrival of a new curate – a human dynamo called Fr. Eamonn O'Brien. This young man was mad keen on shows and soon was organising us all into a Choral and Dramatic Society with his trademark enthusiasm.

St. Patrick's had a tradition for putting on plays and musical shows in various forms going back to the early part of the 20th Century. A group of 'old hands' formed the basis for this new musical and drama group and young recruits were queuing up to join. Fr. O'Brien was our producer and he brought in several of his clerical friends to help. Fr. Frank Kennedy was to be our musical director and Fr. Malachy Murphy headed up our 'backroom boys and girls' as stagehands, scenery makers, costume makers and make-up artists.

Auditions were held for singers and actors, rehearsals were started and we then set out on the theatrical journey

Joe Dorrian in the 1960s

Joe was born Charles Joseph Dorrian, on 24 October 1944, at 9 James Street, Newtownards, and has lived all of his life (so far) in the town. His parents were Owen and Mary Dorrian and he has two sisters, Colette and Mairead, being the middle child.

He was educated at St. Finian's Boys' Primary School and later at Newtownards Technical School. In 1960 he took a summer job in the Ulster Print Works and stayed for 17 years. He had a number of different

Members of St Patrick's Choral and Dramatic Society at a rehearsal in the hall for a variety concert in early February 1962. *27-95-1*

that would take us to many parts of Northern Ireland, as well as to the Waterford Festival of Light Opera. But that was in the future.

The original format involved an opening number with the entire chorus (the first was *There's No Business Like Show Business*) then a short one-act play (the first was W. W. Jacobs' famous horror story *The Monkey's Paw*), followed by a themed musical scene (our first was an Irish scene with suitable songs). In addition, there were a number of short, front-of-curtain numbers during the performance to allow for scene changes and then the show ended with the very popular *Black and White Minstrels*, as seen on BBC TV (very non-PC nowadays but perfectly respectable then).

This style was followed for a number of seasons with plays such as *Roadside*, a comedy, and a 'serious' comedy called (I think) *The Doctor's Dilemma*. The scenes included a South Seas one, an Italian one and a Cockney one with songs from Lionel Bart's musicals *Blitz, Fings Ain't What They Used T'Be* and *Oliver*. The 'Minstrels' remained an immensely popular finish.

The first of these concerts was so successful it was decided to rerun some of the choral numbers and bring along guest artists to entertain at a guest tea to raise money for charity. The first was Brendan O'Dowda, who was extremely popular at that time with his many performances of the songs of Percy French, composer of *The Mountains Of Mourne*. A special gala performance was held in the presence of the Governor of Northern Ireland, Lord Gray.

Other guests in the following years included Ivor Emmanuel and his wife Patricia Bredin. Ivor was a well-

occupations in the Print Works but eventually became a work study engineer, having obtained his qualifications by day-release and 'night tech' studies.

With an interest in politics, Joe joined the Alliance Party and was elected to serve on the newly-created Ards District (later Borough) Council. He served for only one term as he had decided to join the Royal Ulster Constabulary and felt he needed to sever his political links in the cause of impartiality. Joe served in the RUC from 1977 until his retirement in 2001, having attained the rank of sergeant.

Almost all Joe's service was in Belfast, including a five-year stint with the Community Relations

known Welsh tenor with a television programme (in Welsh) called *Land Of Song*. He was also in the film *Zulu* as the leader of the soldiers' choir. Scottish television programme *The White Heather Club* was extremely popular in Northern Ireland and several members of this troupe, including the beautiful and talented Moira Anderson, joined us for shows.

We also did a bit of touring with our productions. Our dress rehearsal was always 'out of town' in the County Armagh village of Crossmaglen. While it later had a checkered reputation during the Troubles, in our day it was a quiet little place starved of live entertainment. I remember the first time we went there was in January 1963 – we picked the first weekend of the 'Big Snow' and had to almost dig our way out of the county!

Another venue we played was the Borstal in Millisle; you should have seen the faces of the 'inmates' when our young ladies came on stage wearing their grass skirts for the South Seas scene. We played in a number of other places in Belfast and as far away as Cookstown and were well received everywhere.

In our third or fourth season we went for an all-musical show (no opening playlet) and produced what was essentially a pantomime, *Pinocchio*, based on the famous full-length animated film. Permission had to be obtained from the Walt Disney organisation to use the music and songs from the film. These included *When You Wish Upon A Star*, *I've Got No Strings*, *An Actor's Life For Me* and *Give A Little Whistle*. It was great fun putting on this show, but it was very hard work.

The time came when Fr. O'Brien felt we were ready to put on a full-scale musical and so we went into rehearsals for a production of Jerome Kern's *Showboat*. This was first produced in the 1920s and is considered a landmark in Broadway musicals. Songs in the show include such classics as *Only Make Believe*, *Can't Help Lovin' That*

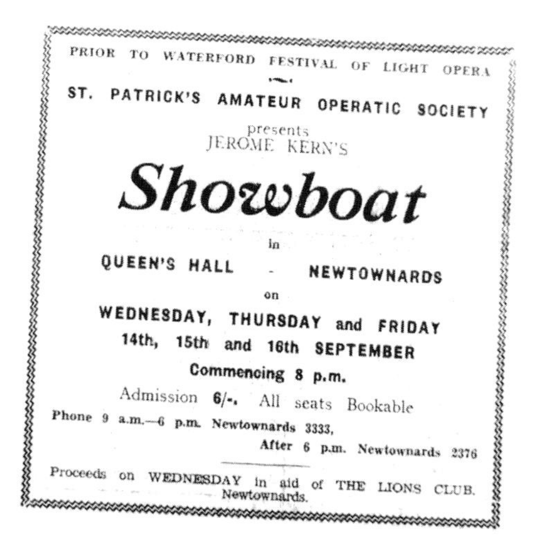

Branch in West Belfast.

He has been married to wife Dorothy since 1967; they have a son, Richard, and a grandson, Charlie.

Joe enjoys reading, studying history, photography and cruising. He and Dorothy enjoy all travel and have visited many countries. Their favourite destination in Europe is Italy and they have visited some 26 of the States in the USA.

This picture was taken during a dress rehearsal for *South Seas Scene* around 1964. Included are (back, from left): Joseph McCormick, Eugene McLarnon, Brendan Auld, Joe Dorrian, Sean Auld, Seamus Murray, John Mooney, Duncan McLarnon, Harry McMullan, Lawrence Braniff. Richard Murray, Willie Auld. Middle: Dympna Gilmore, Olive Meredith, Billy McKenna, Beatrice McBride, Billy Roley, Marjorie McLaughlin, Julie Gibson, Eileen O'Reilly, Frances Carson, Mary McLaughlin, Freda McLaughlin, Mairead Dorrian, Celia Hargan, Anne Murray (others not known). Seated: Marie West, Theresa West, Marie O'Neill, Marie Waugh. Moira Quinn and Deirdre Gilmore.

Man Of Mine, *Bill* (which, by the way, had lyrics by P. G. Wodehouse), and the show's most famous song, *Ol' Man River*. It was filmed twice — once in the 1930s and again in the 1950s.

Showboat was by far the most ambitious project we had attempted and, in order to raise the quality of the musical side, famous Belgian-born choirmaster and conductor Leon Rittweger was brought in as musical director. Mr R. was a talented and charming man, who was also a very hard taskmaster and who accepted nothing but our best efforts. He brought with him a young man to act as piano accompanist for our rehearsals. This was none other than Derek Bell – later known worldwide as the harpist with Irish traditional musical ensemble The Chieftains. Derek was the one Terry Wogan once said looked like a bank manager who had wandered on stage by mistake. This was because Derek invariably dressed formally in a three-piece suit while the others were in jeans and sweaters.

The show proved a great success and we took it to the 1966 Waterford Festival of Light Opera, where we were well received and obtained a number of prizes for individual performances. It was considered an excellent production for a first-time company.

In 1967 for some reason (which I cannot now remember) it was decided to put on a 'straight' play (no musical numbers) and the famous farce *The Happiest Days Of Your Life* was chosen. It played to packed houses in the Queen's Hall and also brought to an end my involvement in the company at that time. I was getting married and a new job involving shift work meant I was unable to give it my full attention. At this time the others in the troupe were beginning rehearsals for the musical *Sunny*, but it also coincided with Fr. O'Brien's transfer to another parish. This left such a great gap in the production side that *Sunny* was abandoned.

Joe Dorrian

Later the stalwarts reconstituted the society as The Patrician Players and continued with the tradition, but, as already stated, I deeply regret that my new job excluded me from taking part. Someone else from that excellent group could give the history of that period.

I also regret that I am somewhat vague about the chronology of the shows, but it was some 50 years ago and my memory isn't what it was. I also deliberately decided not to include a list of the people who took part in our shows – mainly because it would be invidious to accidentally leave out any of the actors, singers, dancers, musicians, stagehands, costume makers or make-up artists who together made such wonderful entertainment.

You know who you are — so take a little private bow.

Ivor Edgar

remembers... The Cinemas

Ivor Edgar

Ivor Edgar was Senior Master and is now Archivist at the Royal School, Dungannon. His roots, however, are in Newtownards.

He wrote *Red and Blue Heaven*, the history of Ards Football Club, of which he is now a director. He also contributed the Dungannon section to *The 1608 Royal Schools*, which was published in 2008 to mark their 400th anniversary.

Married to Anne, also from Newtownards, they have two sons and three grandsons. After his family, Ivor enjoys travel, gardening, Rugby League, football and cricket.

In 1964, when Ronnie and Marie Bailie got married, they moved into a house in Newtownards, in North Street. For the Bailies it was ideal, being located precisely halfway between the Ritz and the Regent.

"We had a television set all right," Ronnie recalls, "but we loved going to the pictures. Our big night was Saturday. We would buy the *Chronicle* as soon as it came out, see what was on, decide which picture we preferred, and enjoy our night out. And the best part, you know, was going to Charlotte Heron's for a fish supper afterwards!"

Little did Ronnie know that the 1960s would be the final decade of the cinema as he and generations had known it: change was already in the air. But for now, let us return to those innocent days of yesteryear, and look at 'the pictures' back in 1960.

There was no shortage of choice if you felt like going to the pictures, or 'the flicks' (never 'the movies'), with two cinemas in Newtownards, the Picture House in Comber, the Regal in Donaghadee, the Amethyst in Kircubbin, the Tatler in Ballywalter, and the Portaferry Cinema. No multi-screens then, but you could, when the Ritz and the Regent were changing the programme every second day, see six films a week (or 12, if you counted the 'wee' picture). You also got trailers for the pompously-worded 'forthcoming attractions', the Pearl and Dean ads, and the newsreel, either *British Movietone* or the stirring march and cock-a-doodle-doo which heralded *Pathé News*.

In 1960 the Saturday programme, at least in the two Newtownards cinemas and in Donaghadee, started at 2.30 in the afternoon and if you weren't asked to leave you could stay until the cinema closed at 10.30 that night. It also meant you could arrive halfway through the main picture and leave at the same point during its second showing (thus adding the phrase "This is where we came in" to the nation's vocabulary).

The Ritz in the mid-Sixties when it screened a programme of Elvis Presley films all week. *Newtownards Chronicle* picture

Filmgoing had its own rituals back in the 1960s. For a start there was a choice: the cheap seats down at the front, the back stalls, and, for the affluent, or for courting couples, the balcony, where the usherette would discreetly illuminate the steps with her torch as she showed you to your seat. Later the same torch would flash its warning if the management suspected any untoward behaviour, whether among the courting couples or the more riotous inhabitants of the front stalls.

Certainly drinks and confectionery were available beside the pay box, where the stainless steel ticket machine shot out its passports to glamour, but there was also the-girl-with-the-tray. Elegantly she would process to the front of the cinema and turn to take up her position facing the audience to purvey orange drinks and ice creams.

And in the 1960s everyone smoked – or so you might have thought, watching the smoke curl upwards through the projector's beam, as patrons enjoyed that now forbidden indulgence, lighting up in imitation of the heroes and heroines on the screen!

At the turn of the Sixties those seven picture houses from Comber to Portaferry each had their own character, not to say idiosyncrasies. The Comber Cinema was the newest of them, built as recently as 1957 to replace the old Picture

REGENT NEWTOWNARDS Phone 2269
Continuous daily from approximately 2 p.m.
To-day—AL CAPONE, 2.10, 5.39, 8.50; WOLF LARSEN, 4.08, 7.19
Monday, January 25 — Three Days
BRIDAL PATH
Technicolor
A WOMAN'S TEMPTATION
Thursday, January 28 — Three Days
BROTH OF A BOY
SUBWAY IN THE SKY

COMBER CINEMA, COMBER
Continuous daily from approximately 6 p.m. Sat. continuous from approx. 3 p.m. Phone 220
Sat.—YOUNG INVADERS, 2.30, 5.48, 9.06; THE GREEN EYED BLONDE, 4.15, 7.33
Monday, January 25 — Two Days
COMPULSION
DESERT HELL
Wednesday, Jan. 27 — Two Days
SAPPHIRE
Eastmancolor
Friday, January 29 — Two Days
NO TIME FOR SERGEANTS

REGAL, DONAGHADEE
PHONE 3144 Monday—Friday: Cont. daily from approx. 3 p.m.
To-day—WAR SHOCK, 3.15, 6.02, 9.03; MAN OR GUN, 4.42, 7.29
Monday, Jan. 25 — Two Days
NEVER STEAL ANYTHING SMALL
KELLY AND ME
Wednesday, Jan. 27 — Two Days
STRANGER IN MY ARMS
HIS BUTLER'S SISTER
Friday, Jan. 29 — Two Days
THE 39 STEPS
CATTLE DRIVE

THE CINEMA PORTAFERRY
Sat.—THE REVENGE OF FRANKENSTEIN. Sun.—CATTLE EMPIRE
Mon. and Tues. Jan. 25 and 26
THE VIOLENT PLAYGROUND
Thurs. and Sat. Jan. 28 and 30
SHAKE HANDS WITH THE DEVIL
(Saturday continuous from 6 p.m.)
Fri. and Sun. Jan. 29 and 31
THE FASTEST GUN ALIVE

TATLER BALLYWALTER. PHONE 259.
PLEASE NOTE—Change in Showing Times: Doors open 7 p.m. Programme starts at 7.30 (Monday—Friday) Continuous from 6 p.m. (Saturdays)
To-day—NEVER STEAL ANYTHING SMALL; NO NAME ON THE BULLET
Monday, Jan. 25 — Two Days
THE SECRET LIFE OF WALTER MITTY
Technicolor — Also
THE THREE OUTLAWS
Wednesday, Jan. 27 — Two Days
THE RELUCTANT DEBUTANTE
Color and C/Scope — Also
UNDERWATER WARRIOR
Friday, Jan. 29 — Two Days
SHAKE HANDS WITH THE DEVIL
Also
HIGH JUMP

AMETHYST CINEMA KIRCUBBIN
To-day—THE LONG KNIFE
Monday, Jan. 25 — Two Days
THE SQUARE PEG
Also CAVE OF OUTLAWS
Wednesday, Jan. 27 — Two Days
SEA FURY
Also HOTEL SAHARA
Friday, Jan. 29 — Two Days
IMITATION OF LIFE

ABC RITZ NEWTOWNARDS PHONE 2249
To-day—SOME LIKE IT HOT; THIS IS MALTA
Monday, Jan. 25 — Two Days
THE MYSTERIANS
Eighteen and Anxious
Wednesday, Jan. 27 — Two Days
THE SIEGE OF PINCHGUT
Invitation to Monte Carlo
Friday, Jan. 29 — Two Days
ALIVE AND KICKING
THE YOUNG AND THE GUILTY

All seven local cinemas advertised their shows in the *Newtownards Spectator* at the beginning of 1960

House. The cinema boasted 400 seats, the most sought-after being the double seats down both the sides! In Newtownards, the Ritz and the Regent were sizeable halls, seating over 1,500 between them. The Ritz, formerly the Palace, was a fine 1930s art deco building. Part of the ABC chain, it reintroduced Minors' Matinees on Saturday mornings in 1963, charging 6d a head for a mix of films and live entertainment for children.

The tip-up seats were surprisingly vulnerable. Victor Moore, then working in Donaldson's garage at the Old Cross, remembers broken ones being brought in for welding practically every Monday morning!

The Regent, Newtownards' other cinema, regularly ran late night film and variety shows. In 1961 a young Frank Carson was part of the entertainment, as was an unbilled turn by legendary Ards FC centre-forward Mick Lynch. Another popular stage favourite was the hypnotist Edwin Heath, whose gift for persuading otherwise sedate members of the audience that they were hip-swivelling Elvis Presleys always drew the crowds.

On Saturday nights, around ten past eight, the observant cinemagoer might notice a minor exodus. There was nothing wrong, it was just that those slipping out knew that the boy who sold the *Ireland's Saturday Night* would be taking up his position on the steps of the Regent, and the 'Ulster' was as important an element of Saturday night out as the fish supper.

Throughout the 1960s the Regal Cinema emphasised Donaghadee's continuing reputation as a holiday town by offering Midnight Matinees throughout July and August. Further down the Peninsula, Ballywalter's Tatler was a surprisingly sizeable cinema for a village, a 400-seater with a balcony. It just squeezes into this chapter, closing in early

November 1960 after what was presumably a last desperate throw of the dice – showing *The Ten Commandments* for a full week at increased prices in late September.

The Amethyst, in Kircubbin, owned by the Mills family, survived less than a year after the Tatler closed. Kieran McCarthy remembers sitting there on a stormy night and hearing the waves crashing against the wall just beyond the cinema. That left only the Portaferry Cinema to fly the flag for the Low Country for most of the 1960s. It was unique in the Ards, not only because it opened on Sundays, but also because, up until 1962, when owners the Hinds family opened the Locarno Ballroom, the cinema doubled up as a dance hall, with the seats being taken out on Wednesday nights to create a dancing area!

Laura Carr (the owner's daughter) is pictured at the Regal Cinema in Donaghadee more than half a century ago. *Photograph courtesy of Rex Armstrong.*

But despite dances and the occasional concert, the main business of the picture houses was, of course, to show pictures. So what were we in the Ards watching in the 1960s? The decade began with *Psycho* and ended with *Midnight Cowboy*. In between we watched epics like *Lawrence Of Arabia*, *Zulu* and *El Cid*, sang along to *My Fair Lady* and *West Side Story*, were thrilled by *Bullitt* and *The Birds*, mildly titillated by *Tom Jones* and *The Graduate*, and charmed by *Mary Poppins* and *The Love Bug*.

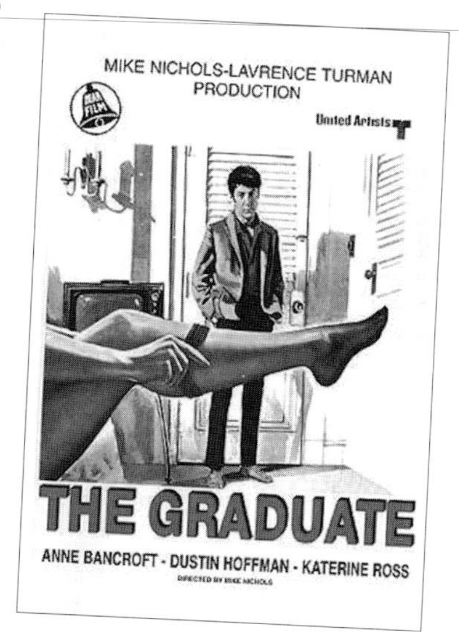

From *Carry On Constable* to *Carry On Again Doctor*, the series amused us no fewer than 15 times that decade. Westerns could still produce crackers like *The Man Who Shot Liberty Valance*, but a trend towards more thoughtful, psychological films and 'comedy' Westerns like *Cat Ballou* led many to believe the genre had had its day until the remarkable *Dollar* films of the late 1960s, which catapulted Clint Eastwood to fame.

Spy films became popular, with *Dr No* the first of six James Bond films released during the period.

Elvis made no fewer than 26 films in the Sixties, from *Flaming Star* to the justly forgotten *Change of Habit*. Cliff

Richard starred in *The Young Ones* and *Summer Holiday*, and for a time each new pop star was given his own vehicle, with Billy Fury in *Play It Cool*, Adam Faith in *Beat Girl*, and, of course, *A Hard Day's Night* and *Help!*, featuring The Beatles.

Early in the 1960s there was a rash of 'naughty' pictures with an X Certificate to egg on the customers. 'Strictly Adults Only' was included in the advertising if the title wasn't specific enough, but there was little need for elaboration with a title like *Around The World With Nothing On* ("They'll catch their death of cold" was my grandmother's wry observation).

Films of the 'adult' variety were very much a sign of desperation. Certainly the industry, at the end of the 1960s, was still capable of producing moneyspinners like *Butch Cassidy And The Sundance Kid* and *Easy Rider*. The trouble was that it couldn't produce enough of them to entice the public into cinemas.

Nor could the picture houses in the Ards get them quickly enough. Films on the ABC chain had to have a first run at the Ritz in Belfast, then move on to the suburban Strand or Majestic before being shown in Newtownards. As car ownership grew it became easier to drive up to Belfast to see a film in the city centre while it was still brand new, and local cinemas suffered as a result.

Other forms of entertainment appeared. UTV, with its brasher, more populist style, came to our screens in 1959, immediately grabbing huge audiences. When colour was added later in the Sixties there was bound to be a bloodletting.

In 1960 there were seven cinemas in the Ards, but by 1970 only three remained. In 1960 the Ritz and the Regent abandoned afternoon showings for good. The nearby Metro, in Dundonald, had already gone in 1959 after only a few years' existence, while by 1961 both the Amethyst and Tatler had succumbed. The closure of the Regal towards the end of the 1960s left Donaghadee without a cinema.

For me the closure of the Ritz in Newtownards was a savage blow. On 4 November 1967 they showed *Legions*

Of The Nile and *Three Coins In The Fountain*, and then closed the doors for ever. Comber, Portaferry and the Regent all survived for a time, but in the end they went as well. Cinema, in a different form, survived, but the days of the dress-suited manager, the smoke-filled auditorium, the red plush curtains, the girl with the tray, the double bill and the 'full supporting programme' had gone forever – but as Bob Hope had sung some 30 years earlier in those very picture houses: "Thanks for the memory".

ACKNOWLEDGEMENTS

The author wishes to thank Leslie Adams, Ronnie Bailie, Len Ball, Michael Edgar, Donald Elliott, Kieran McCarthy, Victor Moore and Noel Spence for their help.

Kathleen Dorrian

remembers... Kircubbin Dance Hall

Kathleen Dorrian has spent all her 67 years in Kircubbin. Her mother, Eileen, ran a small grocery and confectionery shop at the top of the Main Street – known as 'Eileen's Corner' and a great meeting place for local people – until her death in 1970, when Kathleen took it over.

She continued to run the shop alone for another eight years. The time came to close it and get a job with a steady income, so she went to Woolco and later Wellworths in Newtownards, where she worked for 19 very happy years, many of those as supervisor.

Kathleen resigned in 1996 and then worked for two

For 'big' events in 1960s Kircubbin, the community would descend on the Herron Hall, situated at the north end of the village in the area known as The Green. I remember the late great comedian Jimmy Young bringing his show to the hall, as well as singer Bridie Gallagher, a big star at the time. It was standing room only for such events, but for teenagers like me the main focus of entertainment was at the other end of the village.

To the casual passer-by travelling up Roden Street in the early 1960s, the unremarkable tin hut with a corrugated iron roof wouldn't have merited a second glance. However, come Friday night, when its green door opened to welcome dancers from the length and breadth of the Peninsula, it became Kircubbin's very own 'Ballroom of Romance', attracting customers from Portaferry, Greyabbey, Ballywalter and Portavogie to dance the night away.

Established by Paddy Finnegan in the early 1950s, the dance hall was a simple structure comprising a fairly long narrow room with a stage at one end, behind which was a small changing room for the 'artistes'. The wooden floor was always kept in very good condition and sprinkled liberally with Lux soap flakes to smooth the way for the dancers who waltzed, foxtrotted or quickstepped their way around it.

The dances were held on a Friday night – that being pay

day for most of the people in the area – but, especially for girls like myself, preparations began much earlier in the week. Back in the early Sixties drindle skirts, with their underlying petticoats to give them their distinctive shape, were very much the fashion for teenagers. To make them sit out properly you had to starch the petticoats – although if you couldn't afford starch, soaking them in sugar syrup before hanging them on the line to dry achieved the same result (though at the expense of a tough battle with the swarms of flies attracted to the sweet smell of the drying garments!).

Come Friday night, while the men got ready by having a quick brush-up and shoeshine before going down to the pub for a couple of pints, the girls indulged in more intricate preparations. Hair was done up to the latest style with curlers, etc. always left in place to the last possible minute for best effect, makeup was carefully applied, diligently washed and ironed tops and skirts were put on, then, with a last check that nylon seams were straight, stilettos were pulled on and we were ready for the off.

The dance officially started at 9pm although usually things didn't really get going until around 10 or 10.30, when the young men (and many not so young) arrived from the local pubs. Inside the hall the format for the dance was the same as anywhere else at that time, with the men all lined up or sitting at one side of the hall, while the ladies adopted a similar formation on the other side. When the music started the latter would initially all dance together, until one by one the men would join the fray with potential partners and the dancing would continue until 2am with the bands performing the popular music of the time.

Many and varied were those who played at these dances and to be honest I can only remember a few names. The Johnny Flynn Showband, The Hawaiian Band from Portaferry, The Debonaires and Ray McCourt's Band all made regular appearances, with our own local band, the far from originally named Kircubbin Skiffle Group, becoming a near permanent fixture during the interval while the main act took a well-earned rest.

The line-up of the Kircubbin Skiffle Group was Sammy

years, part-time, in the St Vincent de Paul charity shop in Kircubbin. Her partner, Billy Sharpe, subsequently reopened the corner shop as a 'Fruit and Veg.' and Kathleen now spends her time helping him.

Her hobbies include reading, photography and going on holidays. She has been on four British and Irish Lions tours – twice to South Africa, once to New Zealand and once to Australia – all of which she describes as "happy times".

Eight years ago Kathleen started the village's Digital Photography Club; it now has 10 very enthusiastic members and annual displays in Portaferry Library, Dundonald Library and recently Comber Library.

Cooney, David Mawhinney, Hugh James Smyth and the late Jimmy Doherty. As they all lived close to the hall, Tom Finnegan allowed them to practice there during the week. Their big chance came when Tom asked them to play during the breaks and it became a regular gig for them. Sammy Cooney continued playing music after the other members went their separate ways and he became a very popular singer in local clubs and pubs for many years.

Needless to say, the local lads were not the only ones who learned their trade in Finnegan's Dance Hall. I well recall how, in the early 1960s, a rock 'n' roll band from Newtownards used to come down on a Tuesday night to practice there. The name of the group has long been forgotten in the mists of time but they charged teenagers just sixpence (2½p), covering the price of their petrol, to jive away from 7-9pm. It didn't bother us that very often we kept dancing to the same song as they rehearsed it, since both performers and dancers were perfecting their moves during those happy nights we spent in the hall.

While dancing might have been the headline act at the hall, there was always a strong subtext to these activities and that subtext spelt out r-o-m-a-n-c-e! Indeed, I know of many long-lasting romances which started at these dances, although strict supervision ensured that arrangements of the heart weren't entered into quite as lightly as perhaps they are today. To escape the aforementioned supervision, initial tentative contacts made in the dance hall often had to be followed up with a certain amount of subterfuge such as Sunday walks round the 'four roads' when careful choreography ensured potential partners could 'bump into' one another without arousing suspicion!

The hall was going strong from the 1940s to the late 1960s. When not being used as a dance hall, many different groups were accommodated there. Sales of work were held in it on a Saturday near Christmas, while Kircubbin's young farmers used it as a meeting place for a short time.

However, all good things have their time and by the late Sixties the venue's popularity was starting to wane with the greater availability of transport to further afield venues and the opening of more modern dance halls in Newtownards and Portaferry. At the end of the decade the dances were moved to a hall behind Finnegan's bar and the tin hut was empty.

In time it was taken over and used as a second-hand furniture store by a Mr Henry McPeak but the venture didn't last too long and the hall again lay unwanted and unloved until Messrs Danny Doherty and Cahal Doherty reopened it as a small clothing factory. This gave very welcome work to women in the area but you can't help but wonder if, during some boringly repetitive task, the ladies would glance around the building and in their minds they would hear again the faint echoes of music and laughter from their youth.

In time the clothing company moved to larger premises in Portaferry and in the 1990s the old hall was demolished due to health and safety concerns. Today a very nice family home is located on the site and only fond memories remain of that old tin hut in Kircubbin.

1966

in the Chronicle

Almost half the pupils of schools in Newtownards were off during the last week of January because of an influenza epidemic. At Regent House 50 pupils were sent home due to illness in just one day. In other schools classes had to be amalgamated because teachers as well as pupils were absent. Verbal Reasoning (11-Plus) tests for primary school pupils were postponed for three weeks.

James McCormick, president of Ballywalter Young Farmers' Club for 36 years – and thus the longest-serving YFC president in the entire movement – was presented with gifts on 4 February to mark his retirement. He received an inscribed silver tray and a travel voucher from vice-president Hilda Knox.

Shadow Chancellor Reginald Maudling spent much of Saturday 12 February in Newtownards, including visits to the headquarters of the Ulster Flying Club at the local airport and to the Town Hall, where he was welcomed by Mayor Samuel Gracey. The visit was organised by North Down MP George Currie.

Mary Jamison, from Movilla, retired in February from the staff of flax spinners George Walker and Co. after a career spanning 51 years. She had worked in the finishing department.

St Finian's Primary School in Newtownards was re-opened and blessed on 15 February by Most Rev. Dr. William Philbin, Bishop of Down and Connor, following an extensive renovation programme costing £68,000. The school could accommodate 220 pupils following the addition of seven new classrooms.

Newtownards Lions Club was inaugurated at a meeting in the Devonshire Hotel on 16 February, with the 25 foundation members being joined by a further 20 Lions from Bangor, the club sponsoring the formation of the Newtownards group. The first president was Dr Edmund Quiery and the Charter presentation dinner followed on 22 April at the Queen's Hall.

Blind Newtownards fiddler Edward McMullan won four medals and a cup at Ballymena Music Festival in late February. A former member of the Tower Ceili Band, he was self-taught, also being accomplished in the accordion and various other instruments.

Appeal against Council refusal

TEN - STOREY FLATS WOULD "FIT IN"

'Dee project is proposed

DURING a planning appeal by Mr. Thomas Clokey against the refusal by Donaghadee Urban District Council of planning permission for the erection of ten-storey flats at Warren Road, Donaghadee, Mr. G. S. N. Hawthorn, architect, said that a building could be different without being unsympathetic to its environment.

He felt that the development would be a definite advantage and improvement to the amenity of the area and rather than provide an undue dominant it would provide 'life' and interest to the roadscape.

Donaghadee Urban Council refused planning permission for the erection of a block of luxury 10-storey flats at Warren Road, declaring they would be detrimental to the amenities of the area. The developer, Thomas Clokey, appealed against the decision, with his architect declaring that a building could be different without being unsympathetic to its environment. The Ministry of Development sided with the Council and the appeal was rejected.

Newtownards Ratepayers' Association candidate Norman Kennedy won a Scrabo Ward bye-election on 16 March, occasioned by the sudden death of Cllr Hugh Drysdale (NRA) earlier in the year. The only other candidate was Richard Elwood (Labour). Following a 28 per cent turn-out, 470 votes were cast for the eventual winner, with 275 going to the runner-up.

The Northern Ireland Hospitals Authority warned in early April that it might become necessary to close the shop at Newtownards Hospital because it was running at a loss – to the tune of £3/10/0d a week. Responding, Cllr Stanley Woods said the shop was a vital amenity and as such was part and parcel of the hospital. There was full agreement from the North Down Hospital Management Committee that the shop had to remain open.

The Governor of Northern Ireland, Lord Erskine, formally opened the Temple of the Winds at Mount Stewart on 23 April, describing the replica of the Temple of the Winds in Athens as "a jewel in the crown of this magnificent property." It had been extensively restored over a period of some four years after being presented to the National Trust by Lady Mairi Bury.

Singing duo David and Jonathan (alias Roger Greenaway and Roger Cook), appeared at the Comber Ballroom on 14 May, while on the same night Dave Dee, Dozy, Beaky, Mick and Tich topped the bill at the Queen's Hall in Newtownards.

A nationwide seamen's strike, which ran for six weeks between late May and the beginning of July, forced many exporting firms in Newtownards to use air freight to bring their raw materials into Northern Ireland and then to export their finished products.
Fishing boats based in Donaghadee were also being used to bring sugar, fruit and fish, as well as daily newspapers, into the country from Portpatrick in Scotland. Members of the Seamen's Union reacted angrily to this, with some 50 of them forming a picket line at Donaghadee Harbour on 8 June.

Speaking at Stormont on 24 May, Minister of Development Bill Craig said he believed a tunnel between Donaghadee and Float Bay (south of Portpatrick) would, in time, replace existing shipping services to Scotland. As a result, the Government was backing a preliminary examination of the economic aspects of a tunnel link, the assumption being that such a link was technically feasible and the cost would be about £35m.
Mr Craig added that the scheme, when completed, would transform Donaghadee into one of the most important towns in Northern Ireland – possibly in the whole of Ireland.
The undersea tunnel proposal was also endorsed by Prof. Alan A. Wells, from the Faculty of Applied Science at Queen's University, when he addressed the Northern Ireland branch of the Institute of Directors in late June. He described the scheme as "a 23 mile-long concrete worm, 28 feet in diameter and sheathed in a glistening coat of aluminium."

He believed it would be able to cope with 4,000 vehicles a day in each direction, at an estimated cost of £5 per vehicle. He envisaged a two-lane tunnel, with the lanes separated by a central partition. In terms of resolving the issue of ventilation, the vehicles' own air resistance would be sufficient to ensure all harmful fumes were carried out of the tunnel.

At the General Synod of the Non-Subscribing Presbyterian Church, held in Belfast in mid-June, the Rt. Rev. William J. Wharton, minister of First Presbyterian Church in Greyabbey, was unanimously elected to serve as Moderator for a second term.

The 50th anniversary of the Battle of the Somme was recognised at a wreath-laying ceremony on the evening of 1 July at the War Memorial in Court Square, Newtownards. The service was conducted by the Rev. Reggie Chisholm, rector of St. Mark's Parish Church, and the Rev. C. H. McKeown, minister of Regent Street Presbyterian Church. Alderman William Spratt, Mayor of Newtownards, laid the Borough Council's wreath – one of many that evening – escorted by Town Clerk Wyndham Scott.

Belfast company Solar Cinemas Ltd., owners of the Regent Cinema, took over ownership of Newtownards' second picture house, the Ritz, in mid-July. It had previously been owned by ABC. A Solar spokesman said the Ritz name would not be changed and as far as the public were concerned it would be business as usual.

The Borough Council granted permission in late July for the controversial film *Fanny Hill* to be shown to adults in Newtownards. It was screened at the Ritz Cinema from 19-21 September.

Donaghadee Urban District Council voted on 1 August to allow the town's outdoor swimming pool to remain open until 9pm for the remainder of the summer. Complaints had been raised that visitors, arriving at the pool after enjoying "an evening meal and a rest", were finding it was already closed.

Members of Newtownards Young Farmers' Club launched a fundraising campaign aimed at raising £3,000 to enable them to build a new club hall. The first event, a bring and buy sale in mid-September at the home of Mr and Mrs W. S. McKinney, of Ballyreagh Farm, realised £200 towards the target.

Minister of Development Bill Craig visited Comber on 6 October to perform the ceremonial switching-on of the pumps for the Enler River Gravels water scheme. The £100,000 project, the result of four years of discussions and construction work, created a potential yield of 500,000 gallons of water a day, as well as a 30 million gallon storage capacity. As a result it was anticipated that Newtownards householders, the main beneficiaries of the scheme, would no longer suffer the inconvenience of a restricted water supply.

In a Cabinet reshuffle by Prime Minister Terence O'Neill, Ards MP Capt. William Long was appointed Northern Ireland's Minister of Education.

It was announced that Ballygalget Primary School, erected in 1853 and still serving the Parish of St Patrick, would be demolished before the end of 1966, with its pupils moving to a new £23,000 building a few yards away.

JUNIOR OFFICE GIRL
Wanted for General Office Duties.
WAGES ACCORDING TO EXPERIENCE
5 Day Week. Monday till Friday.
— ALSO —
YOUNG LADY
as Pricing Clerk, with knowledge of Typewriting
Apply to :—
R. CHRISTIE & SONS
16 CASTLE STREET, NEWTOWNARDS. Phone 2641

Sir Robin Kinahan, chairman of the NI Abbeyfield Society, performed the official opening ceremony on 12 October for the first Abbeyfield House in Newtownards – located at 8 Victoria Avenue.

Nearly 100 years after the construction of Strean Presbyterian Church in Newtownards, a clock was finally added to the tower on 15 October. The original architect's drawing had included provision for a clock – the installation work was carried out in 1966 by Malcolm McKendry, a member of the congregation, who had also presented the clock to the church.

A number of funeral directors from Northern Ireland, led by William Doggart of Newtownards, helped with the funeral arrangements at Aberfan, in South Wales, following the landslide tragedy on 21 October which had claimed the lives of 116 children and 28 adults.
Mayor William Spratt launched an appeal fund for the bereaved parents of the mining village. When the appeal closed on 16 December the total raised exceeded £950.

Down County Council announced in late October that it hoped work on the Bangor to Newtownards dual-carriageway, bypassing Conlig, would be completed within three years.

Because of the difficulty in obtaining collectors and the widely held view that old people were living in better circumstances, Christmas 1966 marked the last year of the Newtownards Coal and Poor Relief Fund. It had been founded in the 1920s to aid old and poor people in the town. Some 120 people had benefited from the scheme but it required £600 being raised each year to meet its various requirements.

Mr and Mrs Robert Johnston, of The Cottages, Killaughey, Millisle, aged 83 and 84 respectively, celebrated their 60th wedding anniversary on 16 November. The couple had married at Ballycopeland Presbyterian Church on that same day back in 1906.

An exhibition was staged in the Queen's Hall on 30 November by Rothmans of Pall Mall (Northern Ireland) Ltd. The central theme was the first major launch of a new cigarette by the company for a decade – the Crown Filter which cost 4/7d for a packet of 20.

Under the terms of the Strangford Lough Ferry Bill, set to go before Stormont the following year, the county itself (through its local authorities) faced paying a considerable amount towards providing the service, including 10 per cent of acquiring a suitable vessel and the construction of the shore-based facilities, plus 50 per cent of the nett operating costs, as well as one-third of the ongoing maintenance costs of the shore-based facilities.
Newtownards Borough Council reacted angrily to the news, declaring in early December that a bridge would be a more satisfactory solution and insisting the entire cost be met from Central Government funds.

The Rev. T. A. Houston, minister of Portavogie and Cloughey Presbyterian Churches, blesses the new Portavogie-Cloughey lifeboat at the end of January 1966. There were opening remarks by Lt. G. W. Ross, district organising secretary of the RNLI, along with Bible readings by the Rev. H. Cooke.
136-8-2

First Greyabbey Troop Scoutmaster Ivan Morrison is thanked by Mrs S. McAvoy, who presented him with a silver tray to mark his retirement in February 1966. Included are the Revs. Wharton and Ridgway, Miss Ann Pritchard, Mrs Pritchard, Mr J. Caughey and Miss Joan Atcheson. Back: Andrew Robson, W. Donnan and W. Long.
136-74-3

Regent House was placed second in a major countryside competition organised by Shell-Mex and BP, winning £100 worth of photographic equipment and a painting for the school. The prizes were handed over in February 1966 by Mr D. B. Stewart, on behalf of the company.
137-20-3

Entertainers who took part in an Irish concert in Portaferry on St Patrick's Night in March 1966. Included are producer Liam Gilmore and pianist Sean McCarthy.
139-4-2

The Rev. R. J. McCracken (third from left) is pictured with some of the clergy who attended his installation in April 1966 as minister of Millisle Presbyterian Church. Included (from left): Rev. R. H. Gamble, Rev. R. H. G. Gilmore, Rev. C. W. D. Kerr, Rev. J. Lorimer and Rev. J. Murray Moore.
139-78-2

Third Newtownards Company of the Boys' Brigade and Life Boys in their tableaux class, a part of the annual display which was held in the McIlwrath Memorial Hall in April 1966.
140-64-2

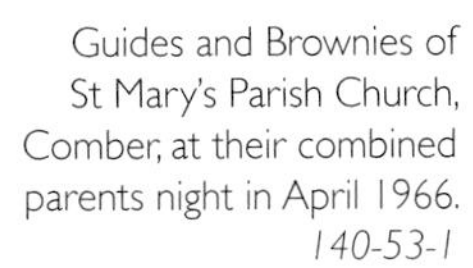

Guides and Brownies of St Mary's Parish Church, Comber, at their combined parents night in April 1966.
140-53-1

Candidates, Juniors and Seniors of the 58th Northern Ireland Company of the Girls' Brigade (First Donaghadee Presbyterian Church) in May 1966.
141-1-1

Members of the First Donaghadee Life Boys team with leader-in-charge Mr Massey in May 1966.
140-65-1

The captain, officers and members of First Carrowdore Girls' Brigade at their annual display in May 1966.
141-53-3

Officers and cadets of First Donaghadee Girls' Brigade with their chaplain, the Rev. J. E. Glenfield, in May 1966.
141-79-1

Members of Killinchy Old York LOL No 1545 with their new banner, which was unfurled in late June 1966 by the Rev. John Girvan.
144-95-2

Members of the ladies committee who provided the refreshments during the Kircubbin Yacht Club regatta in July 1966.
146-94-2

Audrey Dickson, from Ballycloughan, Ballygowan, won the Little Miss Northern Ireland competition at Pickie Pool, Bangor, in August 1966.
146-99-3

This "truly shocking contraption" (to quote from the original caption) was an electronic maze which proved a popular attraction at a fete organised by some Ballydrain children to raise funds for Oxfam in late August 1966. Back (from left): E. McFerran, Paul McFerran, Peter MacArdle, Peter Bathgate, Paul Kelly. Front: Pat McFerran, A. Kelly, Mark Bathgate, Norman Parker and David Kelly.
148-98-1

Members of Portavogie Scarlet Crown RBP No 657 at the Royal Black demonstration in Dromore at the end of August 1966.
148-99-2

Cadets of Christ Church, Carrowdore, during the 'bedtime' finale in September 1966 at their parents night in the Woburn Hall.
149-69-2

Stormont Minister William Craig samples the water after switching on the Enler River Gravels Scheme at Comber in October 1966. Looking on are members of North Down Rural District Council and Newtownards Borough Council.
150-77-1

Local woman Miss Elisabeth Spiers (26), who was commissioned on 30 October 1966 as a missionary to India at a service in First Newtownards Presbyterian Church, is pictured with the participating clergy. From left: Rev. G. McK. Eagleson, Strean Presbyterian Church; Rev. J. H. Davey; Rev. C. W. D. Kerr, Moderator of Presbytery; Rev. A. M. Adams and Rev. D. G. Bailie.
152-31-1

The choir of Victoria Primary School, Newtownards, which won the David Henderson Memorial Cup at Bangor Music Festival for the third year running in November 1966. Included is conductor Miss C. E. McNickle.
153-22-1

Pupils from Londonderry Primary School who received awards in a 'Hazard House' competition organised by the Royal Society for the Protection of Accidents in December 1966. They are: Brian McGimpsey, Ivan Russell, James Weir, Georgina Johnston and Patricia McMahon.
154-11-2

Cast members from *Sinbad The Sailor*, which was presented by children from Second Presbyterian Church, Comber, in December 1966.
154-30-2

Children from Portavogie Primary School who took part in the annual Christmas play in December 1966.
154-99-3

Sport in 1966

in the Chronicle

Newtownards table tennis player George Cardy won his first major open singles title on 8 January – the Ulster County singles in Omagh. He followed in the footsteps of two other Newtownards players, Harry O'Prey and Carroll McBride, who had previously won the same title.

Glenford Ladies defeated Kingsland B 7-2 on 21 March in their concluding fixture in the Bangor and District Table Tennis League to secure the title.

Ards FC Player of the Year was half-back Billy Nixon, who received the trophy on 6 May from *Belfast Telegraph* sports editor Malcolm Brodie.

ARDS PLAYER OF THE YEAR

Billy Nixon is popular choice

Ards Table Tennis Club went out of existence on 6 June, after many years of outstanding success, including winning the Belfast and District Senior League for 15 years in succession.

The *Chronicle,* commenting on the beginning of the 1966-67 soccer season, highlighted Warren Feeney as "one of the promising young players who have joined Ards." His father was former Ards player Jimmy Feeney.

Donaghadee 1st XI lost to Dundrum in the final of the Junior Qualifying Cup (cricket) at Ewarts, Belfast, on 6 August.

Fifteen-year-old Roger Killen, of Milecross Road, Newtownards, won the Titterington Cup at Donaghadee Golf Club in mid-August.

One of Northern Ireland's best known professional golfers, Norman Drew, joined the newly-opened Bradshaw's Brae Golf Driving Range as Professional on 6 October.

Manchester United's assistant manager Jimmy Murphy visited Castlereagh Park on 6 October to cast an eye over Ards forward Ray Mowat, who played in a 3-1 Gold Cup win over Portadown.

Ards Rugby Club launched a major fundraising drive after it was agreed at an extraordinary meeting on 7 November to purchase the club's ground close to the canal from the Londonderry Estate for £1,300. They had been playing at the same location since the 1930s.

Ards II were strongly outclassed by Glentoran II in the Boxing Day Steel and Sons Cup final at Solitude, going down 4-0. The Ards team included Warren Feeney.

The badminton team from St Mary's Parish Church, Comber, won the Church of Ireland League, Second Division, and the North Down Knock-Out Cup in May 1966. Pictured with the Rev. Hamilton Leckey are (back, from left): J. Bennett, R. Watson, A. Gregg, G. Moffett, I. Tate, J. Curtis. Centre: M. Cargo, M. Connor, M. Spratt, Y. Hamilton. Front: G. Hull and J. Watson.
141-50-1

Members of the Carrowdore Presbyterian Church badminton team in June 1966 with the trophies they had won in various competitions, including East Antrim Handicapped, Mixed (runner-up trophy); NBBUI Minor Championships Handicapped, winner of A mixed doubles; and the Belfast and District Presbyterian League, Second Division. Back (from left): R. White, W. Stewart, B. McCully, R. Jordan. Front: R. Jordan, A. McCully, P. Gowdy, F. Burrows and A. Robinson.
141-77-2

Ards Boys Football Club were proclaimed 'team of the year' in late May 1966 after winning the Dunmurry and District League, the Irish Youth Cup and the Barry Cup, as well as finishing runners-up in the Francis Cup. Back (from left): A Crozier, D. Mills, I. Patterson, B. Finlay, D. Davidson, R. McAteer. Middle: D. Morrison (official), S. Evans, H. Huddleston, D. McEvoy, J. Lemon, J. McGurk, J. Patton, E. Hawkins (manager). Front: S. Murdock, R. McKenzie, A. Larmour, D. Arneill (captain), D. Stitt, C. Field and B. Lindsay.
143-9-2

North Down Boys, who beat Bangor Boys in the third round of cricket's Graham Cup in July 1966, are pictured (back, from left): Mr J. Boucher (manager), M. O'Prey, W. Barker, G. Crosbey, A. Maxwell, K. Campbell, G. Dempster, Mr R. Thompson (secretary). Front: D. McCracken, W. Campbell, N. Beck (captain), J. Campbell and D. McVeigh.
145-46-3

The Millisle Junior BB team pictured before playing on 10 December 1966. Back (from left): T. McAuley, D. Hunter, D. Pollock, N. McDowell, G. White, M. Dorrian. Front: L. Haire, R. Haire, W. Warden, D. Colwell and C. Dorrian.
154-34-1

1967

in the Chronicle

James McCormick, of Whitechurch, Ballywalter, and Harold Thomas, of Craiglee Way, Newtownards, were awarded an OBE and a BEM respectively in the New Year Honours List. Mr McCormick was prominent in educational and Young Farmers' Club circles, while Mr Thomas was team leader of guided weapons trials with Short Brothers and Harland at Castlereagh.

Newtownards Borough Council agreed in January to ask the Ancient Monuments Advisory Council to take over and maintain the Old Cross. The move was the result of discussions with both the Londonderry Estate and the National Trust. The Advisory Council subsequently indicated it would accept responsibility.

Eddie McConkey reads one of the many cards he received on his retirement in January 1967.
155-97-3

Donaghadee bread server Eddie McConkey retired in January after 38 years of service in the Ards Peninsula area, during which time he seldom missed a day in delivering bread to the 200 customers who regarded him as a friend. He had lived all his life in Donaghadee.
Mr McConkey's route had taken him from Donaghadee to Ballywalter and on to The Roddens and back via Greyabbey and Carrowdore.

Education Minister William Long announced

on 19 January that Carrowdore would be getting a new primary school and that architects had already been commissioned by the Down County Education Committee.

Twelve-year-old Newtownards girl Maureen Redmond appeared on Ulster Television's teatime *Hello There* programme on 24 January. She sang *The Green Glens Of Antrim* and *Alice Blue Gown.*

At the annual meeting of the Newtownards Horticultural and Horse Jumping Society, held at the beginning of February, it was unanimously agreed that retiring vice-chairman Walter McKinney, of Ballyreagh, be made an honorary life member in appreciation of his work for the Society over many years.

Plans for the demolition of the Ritz Cinema in Newtownards – which was still operating – and the redevelopment of its site for shops and a supermarket were submitted to the Borough Council in February by a Belfast company.

The decision by Newtownards Borough Council to refuse planning permission for the redevelopment of a property at Frances Street as a Chinese restaurant on access grounds led to accusations – which were strongly refuted – of racial discrimination against the local authority. Letter writers to the *Chronicle* argued that such a development would be a boon to that part of the town and, better still, would provide reasonably-priced meals in pleasant surroundings. Approval for the restaurant was subsequently granted, with conditions, by the Ministry of Development and the premises opened for business later in the year.

After almost a year in existence Newtownards Credit Union had a total of 69 members but there was a warning from the directors that constant overhead charges could only be met by further increasing the membership.

Comber typist Eileen Stewart (20) made history in March by becoming the first Northern Ireland woman to pass her PSV test since the Road Traffic Act was amended to include female drivers. Her late father, Hugh, had been a taxi driver in the town and she had ambitions to follow in his footsteps by running a part-time taxi business from her Mill Street home.

Greyabbey farmer Hubert Walker (23), of Tullycavey, won the Burnhouse Award, run by the Young Farmers' Clubs of Ulster in association with Robert Wilson and Sons (Ulster) Ltd. The award enabled him to undertake a nine-month study tour of New Zealand.

An unexploded German bomb from the Second World War was discovered in April on the fifth fairway of Scrabo Golf Club. It was dismantled and removed by the Royal Ordnance Corps Bomb Disposal Unit.

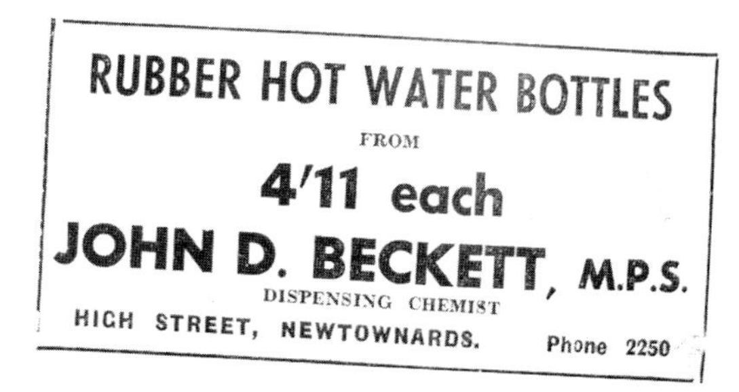

A service to mark the 150th anniversary of the consecration of St Mark's Parish Church, Newtownards, was held on 25 April. Taking charge was the rector, the Rev. Reggie Chisholm, and the special preacher was the Most Rev. Dr. J. McCann, Primate of All Ireland.

There were 19 candidates in all for the 12 seats on Newtownards Borough Council in May's local government elections. Remarkably, three of the seats were not contested as only three candidates had put their names forward in Glen Ward: Georgina Foulis, James White and Alexander Bailie.
Successful candidates in the other wards, following the elections, were as follows: Castle – Norman Crothers, John Beckett, Samuel Gracey; Scrabo – Stanley Woods, William Allen, Thomas Miller; Victoria – Thomas Harkness, Norman Francis and William Morrison.

Twenty-year-old Bill McAvoy, secretary of the Greyabbey Presbyterian Church Youth Club, was one of 20 people from the British Isles chosen to spend a month in the USA as guests of the American Presbyterian Church. The scheme was viewed as a way of encouraging the exchange of ideas and views with other young people.

Castlereagh Park hosted a 'Dusk To Dawn' pop festival headlined by British chart-toppers The Tremeloes, along with other groups and showbands from all over Ireland, on Friday 9 June. At the very time they were in Newtownards The Tremeloes were top of the UK charts with *Silence Is Golden*. The admission charge was 10 shillings and an estimated 7,500 attended.

Almost two weeks later the ministers of nine Protestant churches in Newtownards issued a statement condemning the festival and the actions of young people attending it. The ministers made allegations of disorderliness, drug taking, drinking and immorality – all of which were strongly refuted by promoter Trevor Kane. He issued an open invitation to the ministers and other critics to meet him "in order to ascertain the true facts". Speaking in defence of the festival, the Rev. Albert McElroy, minister of Newtownards Non-Subscribing Presbyterian Church, suggested the statement from the other clergymen "sensationalised" the event and, as a self-confessed "square", he challenged the accuracy of their information. "I don't doubt for one moment that the youngsters let their hair down and that even some of them – a tiny minority – had taken too much drink, or that some others – also a tiny minority – behaved as hooligans, but even they are not wild drug addicts and sex maniacs. I am also persuaded that the vast majority – high-spirited as they were – behaved with seemliness and propriety."

Part of the large crowd that gathered for the Dawn to Dusk pop festival at Castlereagh Park, Newtownards, in June 1967. 165-63-1

Miss Annie Quinton retired from Conlig Primary School after a teaching career that had spanned 44 years, including 12 years as principal. At a farewell evening, held in the school on 30 June and attended by many past and present pupils, Miss Quinton was presented with a television set as a token of the esteem in which she was held.

Miss Agnes Edgar retired from the Newtownards mill of George Walker and Co. Ltd., in early July after being employed there for 62 years. She had joined the company at the age of 12, working one day at the mill and then attending school the next. She was employed as a reeler and also, for many years, assisted in the training of new employees.

Plans were announced for Newtownards Road Courtesy Week (14-19 August), the aim being to press home to drivers and pedestrians alike the need for greater respect on local roads and thus "ease the appalling toll of lives forfeited on our roads."

The Youth and Sports Council for Northern Ireland advised the Ministry of Education to pay a grant towards the proposed new £212,000 swimming pool for Newtownards. It was indicated that the grant would represent 56% of the final bill for the facility.

The decision of Newtownards Borough Council to allow the Ritz Cinema to screen religious films for members of the Ards Presbytery Youth Committee on Sundays later in the year met with a vehement protest from Alderman John Algie, who was also a Presbyterian Church elder. He warned they were setting an undesirable precedent that could lead to the cinema seeking to show commercial films seven days a week.

Newtownards Borough Council agreed on 12 September to move towards supplying gas to local consumers from a new £2m plant then under construction in Belfast. The decision spelt an end, inside two years, to the production of gas in the town – and indeed anywhere in North Down as a similar agreement had been reached by their Bangor counterparts.
The two local Councils subsequently worked together on the laying of pipes to the Clandeboye crossroads, from which point each authority then laid mains to their respective storage containers.

Eleven-year-old Georgina Hale, from Main Street, Carrowdore, appeared on Tommy James' *Toyshop* programme on 18 October, during which she sang and chose a toy for a child in hospital. She was a member of Greyabbey Girls' Choir.

A spokesman for Solar Cinemas announced the Ritz Cinema would be closing on Saturday 4 November. He indicated that with producers making fewer but better films, the company would be concentrating on showing quality films at the Regent, their other cinema in the town.
The last double bill at the Ritz was *Three Coins In A Fountain* (made in 1954, starring Clifton Webb and Dorothy Maguire) and *Legions Of The Nile* (made in 1959, starring Linda Cristal and Ettore Manni).

Newtownards housewife Mrs Richard McKee, of James Street, reported spotting an unidentified flying object over the town on 7 November. Saying it was not like anything she had ever seen before, Mrs McKee described it as "square-shaped, about two foot in size, a golden colour and showing four red lights – one at each corner." The UFO had moved at great speed over her house heading in the Scrabo direction.

Mrs McKee added she had not been scared by the unusual sight but needed to sit down afterwards because she "felt funny and a bit shaky."

The following week other *Chronicle* readers reported they too had seen the UFO, with John Conway, from Bridge Street in Comber, firmly believing it was "a visitor from another world."

And a further unidentified flying object was seen over Newtownards by several local residents on the night of 15 November. One man said it was about 18 inches across, circular in shape, and travelling at a speed of 90-100mph.

Drastic measures were adopted by the Ministry of Agriculture to keep Northern Ireland free from Foot and Mouth Disease following an outbreak on many farms throughout England. Stormont banned horse racing and jumping, dog racing, ploughing matches, rallies, hunting, fishing and the playing of games at any places where there had been livestock.

At a public meeting in Newtownards on 22 November it was decided to set up a Citizens' Advice Bureau in the town. Those in attendance heard the Bureau would have free use of an office, along with a telephone and filing cabinet.

In a post-Christmas advertisement, Orr's Travel Service of High Street in Newtownards offered 15-day holidays by air to Majorca for £37 or 15 days on the Costa Brava for as little as £36. In each case, stressed the company, this was "despite devaluation" (the recent decision by Prime Minister Harold Wilson to devalue sterling against the US dollar by just over 14%).

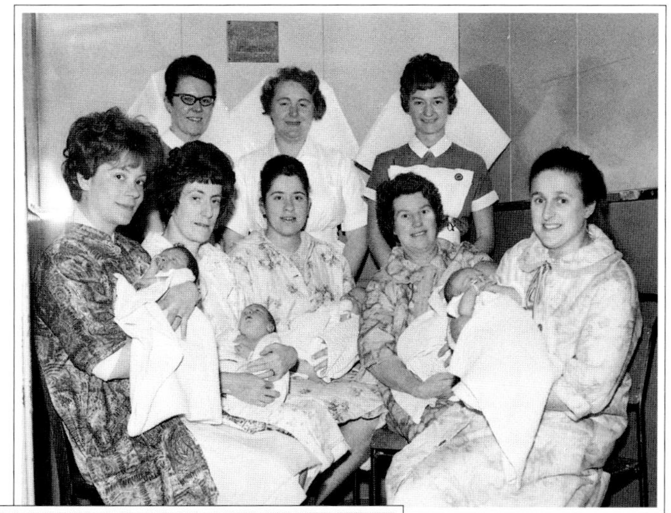

Proud mothers with babies born in Ards Hospital on 1 January 1967 (from left): Mrs Jennifer McMinn, Enler Park East, Ballybeen (baby not named at time of photograph); Mrs T. Wilson, Main Street, Carrowdore, with Samuel: Mrs Ruth Segrott, Shimna Close, Newtownards, with Heather Amanda; Mrs R. Hawkins, Old Priory Close, Newtownards, with Mark, and Mrs S. Jamison, Edith Helen Road, Newtownards, with Scott. Included are Staff Midwives Cully, Drain and Milliken. *155-55-1*

Children enjoy playing on the see-saw in the new children's playground in Portavogie – it was opened in the middle of January 1967. *156-90-2*

Young people who attended a party in January 1967, which was organised by Glastry Presbyterian Church Christian Endeavour. *156-91-1*

Members of the Portavogie Fishermen's Choir at the annual Harvest of the Sea and Sailors' Service in Glastry Presbyterian Church on 22 January 1967. Included are the minister, the Rev. N. M. Heaney, and the Rev. Rupert Gibson, special preacher.
156-89-2

Members of Comber LOL 1037 at a Lodge meeting in early February 1967.
156-29-1

Twenty-year-old Rosemary McConnell, of Killinchy Road, Ballygowan, was elected Northern Ireland Labour Queen in February 1967 at the Northern Ireland Labour Party's first annual dance in Romano's Ballroom, Belfast. She was previously named North Down Labour Princess.
154-36-3

Emily McDowell (18), from Shore Street, Millisle, was placed third in the Miss Young Unionist competition, which was held in Lisburn in February 1967.
158-15-1

A going away party was held in the Devonshire Hotel, Newtownards, in mid-February 1967 for Mr and Mrs David Lee (seated), of Windmill Row, Newtownards, who were moving to Connecticut, USA.
158-44-1

First Donaghadee Boys' Brigade won the Ards Group Squad Drill competition, which was held in First Presbyterian Church Hall, Comber, in February 1967. Back (from left): T. Girvan, F. Tompkins, J. Caldwell, A. Dawes, B. Irwin, N. Adams. Front: R. Elliott, A. Martin, B. Campbell, Staff Sgt. G. Elliott, C. Bradford, N. Donnan and N. Gilmore.
158-62-3

First Comber Boys' Brigade competed in the Ards Group Squad Drill competition at First Presbyterian Church Hall, Comber, in February 1967.
158-59-1

Award winners in a road safety poster competition received their prizes in the Wesley Hall, Donaghadee, in late February 1967.
159-6-1

Second Newtownards BB Junior Section won the Ards Group Figure Marching competition in February 1967, qualifying for the Northern Ireland Area competition later in the year. Back (from left): J. McCormick, B. McCallum, J. McChesney, B. McCutcheon, D. Russell, C. Truman. Seated (from left): J. Smyth, J. Boyce, D. Cairns, J. Gibson (captain), I. Donaldson, S. Boyce, T. Thompson. Front: J. Millar, J. Mills, T. Millar and J. McDonald.
159-92-2

The Lord Bishop of Down and Dromore, Rt. Rev. F. J. Mitchell (fourth from right) dedicated carpeting and personal memorials which had been presented to St Andrew's Parish Church, Ballyhalbert, in March 1967. Included are church officials and some of the people who presented items for dedication. Back (from left): Mr C. J. Armstrong, rector's churchwarden, Mrs Mitchell, Mrs Bell, the Rev. F. W. A. Bell, minister of the church, Mrs R. Johnston, Miss C. Waycott, Mrs V. Gill, Miss M. Thompson and Mr A. Coffey, people's churchwarden. Seated: Mrs S. Todd and Mr A. Perryman.
159-82-1

Newtownards and District Camera Club prizewinners at their annual get-together in April 1967. From left: G. Coulter, T. Robinson, H. Wylie, Mrs D. S. Nash, B. Kirk, T. Killick (chairman), S. Walker and R. Campbell.
161-57-3

Scouts from the Sixth Ards Troop who had gained the Queen's Badge were presented with their Royal Certificates at a ceremony in Carrickfergus in April 1967. From left: Howard Cromie, John Algie, John Hunter and Jim McGovern.
162-32-2

Officers and members of Millisle Boys' Brigade at their annual display in the Old School, Main Street, in April 1967.
162-70-3

Heather Dorrian and Garry Chambers, both pupils at Millisle Primary School, received awards in May 1967 for their entries in the Brooke Bond Tea-sponsored National Schools Handwriting competition.
163-27-1

Members of Ballywalter Girls' Brigade at their annual display in May 1967.
164-7-2

Taken in 1967, this picture shows five friends from Newtownards who had just launched a youth music club in the Young Farmers' Hall at Victoria Avenue. From left: Derek Graham, Derek 'Mad' Beattie, Margaret McKeown, Tommy 'Tucker' McMillan and Jimmy Walsh. The popular venue attracted many local bands, including Sam Mahood and Just Five.
Newtownards Chronicle picture

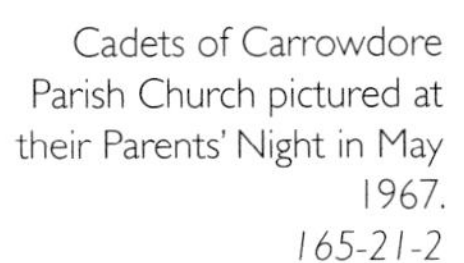

Cadets of Carrowdore Parish Church pictured at their Parents' Night in May 1967.
165-21-2

Two boys from First Donaghadee Sea Scouts (Donaghadee Parish Church), Roy Whitehead (left) and George Barrett, received their Queen's Badges at the Troop's annual display in June 1967. They were congratulated by the Rev. J. C. Swenarton, rector, and Mr J. McComiskey, Scoutmaster.
165-40-1

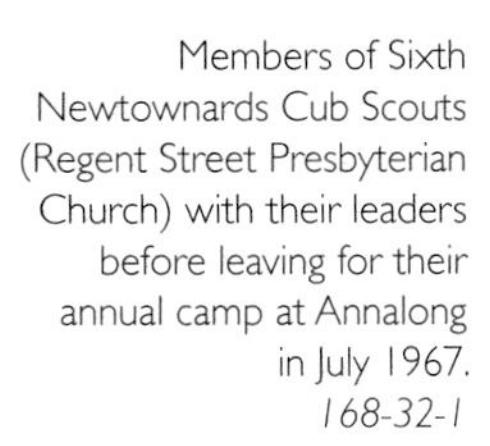

Members of Sixth Newtownards Cub Scouts (Regent Street Presbyterian Church) with their leaders before leaving for their annual camp at Annalong in July 1967.
168-32-1

Rosemary Massey, who was voted 'Perfect Secretary' by Newtownards Chamber of Trade in August 1967, is pictured with *Newtownards Chronicle* pop music correspondent Wilbert Palmer at the Apprentice Boys of Derry Crimson Ball and Beauty Competition in Dundonald, where they were two of the judges, along with ex-Linfield footballer Tommy Dickson.
169-45-1

Five members of Third Newtownards (St Mark's Parish Church) Scouts were presented with their Queen's Badges in October 1967 at a special tea in the Parochial Hall. From left: David McCormick, Kenneth Keag, Alastair Chisholm, Raymond Finlay and Crosbie Cleland.
172-57-1

Pupils from Newtownards Model Primary School plant a tree in the school grounds as part of the Tree Week activities in November 1967.
174-63-3

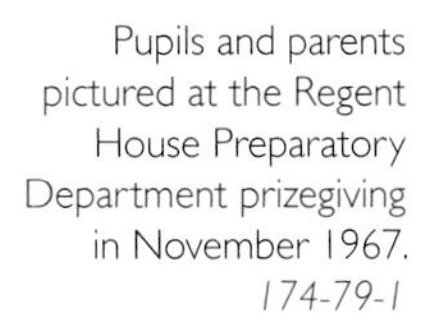

Pupils and parents pictured at the Regent House Preparatory Department prizegiving in November 1967.
174-79-1

Some of the many children who gathered to witness Santa's arrival by air at Ards Airport on 2 December 1967. He was on his way to the Newtownards and District Round Table Christmas bazaar in the Queen's Hall.
175-44-2

Mr A. Edgar, president of Newtownards Lions Club, presented a record player to Mrs Barber, secretary of the local Gateway Club, at St Mary's Parochial Hall in December 1967. Included (centre) is Mrs W. Mawhinney, chairman of the Gateway Club.
175-67-3

Prizewinners from a talent competition held in Greyabbey on 8 December 1967. Included are adjudicator James Johnston, organiser Samuel Keenan, Herbert Keenan and Mr Regan, chairman of the Village Hall Committee. *175-12-1*

The Newtownards Elim Church Sunday School and Thursday Night Children's Hour Christmas party was held on 23 December 1967. Included are Pastor and Mrs Holohan, Sunday School teachers and helpers. *175-92-3*

Edward Gilmore (left) shows the 140lb common skate he landed off Kircubbin in 1967 to 84-year-old Frank Hagan. *168-26-2*

Sport in 1967

in the Chronicle

Whiterock helmsman Eddie Magee, previous winner in 1962 and 1964, sailed his Vixen to victory in the Northern Ireland Flying Fifteen championships at Quoile Yacht Club on 15 July.

Irvine McKay, from Newtownards, and his cousins Heather and Rosanna Patterson, both from Ballygowan, represented Northern Ireland at the European cold water skiing championships in Finland on 29 and 30 July.

Tom Robinson, originally from Balfour Street in Newtownards, returned to his home town at the age of 87. He had been a foundation member of the old Ards Football Club, serving as their first captain back in 1900. He believed he was the last surviving member of the team.
During the First World War Mr Robinson was a member of the 13th Battalion of the Royal Irish Rifles and also served in France with the 8th Battalion of the Rifles.

At the annual meeting of Ards Cricket Club on 15 November chairman Carl Anderson said Ards would be among the strongest junior sides in Ireland and would be challenging for a place in the Senior Qualifying League if it had adequate playing facilities.
However, without a proper ground and pavilion facilities for use during the week, stated Mr Anderson, the club would not be able to rise above its present standing. This was unfortunate, he added, as the club was in a position to do "big things."
During the year the 1st XI won the Junior Qualifying League while the 2nd XI won their section after being promoted to a higher division.

Prizewinners from Portavogie Olympic FC are pictured at the annual dinner and presentation night in early January 1967. Back (from left): W. McMaster, D. Blakely, H. Young, I. Kelly, N. Sharpe, S. McCracken, also J. Thompson and W. Ross (managers). Middle: J. Palmer, G. Shaw, Sammy Pavis (of Linfield FC, who presented the prizes), R. McDowell. Front: R. Gibson, S. McVea (captain), J. Mawhinney and R. Thompson.
155-80-1

The Newtownards Technical College U-14 football team defeated Ballynahinch Tech. 6-5 in the second round of the Northern Ireland Technical Schools' Junior Cup at Londonderry Park in early February 1967.
157-59-1

In advance of the Border Regiment Cup final in February 1967, John Patton (left), captain of Ards Rangers FC, accepts a new football skip from Bobby Scott, representing the ex-members.
158-93-3

The PT team from First Comber Boys' Brigade won the Ards Group Physical Training Shield at the Group competitions in Newtownards in late February 1967. Back (from left): M. Crossen, W. Bennett, C. Lindsay, R. Magowan, T. McComb. Front: J. Campbell, T. McMillan, W. Campbell, W. Barker, C. Magowan and W. McClean.
159-10-2

Second Comber Presbyterian Church Indoor Bowling Club members pictured in April 1967 at their annual prizegiving in the church hall.
161-14-1

Members of the North End A team, winners of the League Cup, the Knock-Out Cup, the Londonderry Cup, the Five-A-Side Cup, the Individual Cup and the Average Cup in the Newtownards Temperance Darts League, pose in early April 1967 with their trophies at the League's annual prizegiving in the Queen's Hall.
160-86-1

Comber Ards Supporters' Club prizewinners at their annual dinner in late April 1967.
163-19-1

Members of the Grove View Star Rifle Club from Carrowdore won the Dixon Shield among other trophies in the Belfast and District Rifle Club competitions. Their presentation night was held in May 1967.
165-20-2

Donaghadee Cricket Club's 1st XI met a team comprising men who had played for the club during the previous 17 years in a friendly at their Northfield ground at the end of July 1967.
168-29-2

Ballycran Camogie team, pictured in July 1967, were winners of both the senior championship and league that season.
170-29-1

The Down Junior Hurling team were beaten by Kerry on Sunday 27 August 1967 in the All Ireland semi-final.
170-27-1

Strean Presbyterian Church Indoor Bowling Club's new season was launched in September 1967 by Mrs Eagleson, wife of the minister, the Rev. G. McK. Eagleson.
171-53-2

Scrabo Rangers defeated Duncrue United 6-4 on 23 September 1967. Back (from left): L. McKillen, D. Murdock, L. Dempster, J. Savage, S. Gamble, R. Malt. Front: B. Doak, R. Brown, D. Hagan, I. Heaney, B. Graham and J. Taggart.
172-1-2

Jean Whitford and Pat Watton, both pupils at Newtownards Further Education College, were chosen in October 1967 to play for the Northern Ireland Schoolgirls netball team in Liverpool later that same month. Included is coach Mrs Anderson.
172-76-2

Mrs H. C. Spence, wife of the chairman of the newly-formed Kircubbin Presbyterian Church Indoor Bowling Club, delivers the first wood in October 1967 to officially open the club. One of the members holds a trophy which was presented to the club by Mrs E. McKendry in memory of her late husband.
173-18-3

The Sporting World in The Ards in the Sixties

Alfie Wright

remembers... Table Tennis

Alfie Wright as an IFA Youth player

Born on 5 April 1946 at Ards Hospital, Alfie Wright was found to have twisted ligaments in both legs. His parents were advised to wait a few years for an operation to rectify the problem, hence at the age of four Alfie faced being in plaster from toe to thigh for 12 months.

At nine his father took Alfie along to Glenford Table Tennis Club and thus began his very successful table tennis career. Soccer, as a very capable goalkeeper, and cricket were important elements to his teenage years and beyond.

My brief in compiling this article on table tennis was to confine it to the Sixties but, in truth, that's quite a difficult task as table tennis in Newtownards enjoyed many fine years going back as far as the 1930s.

Thus, given that limitation, this contribution contains my memories and observations going back to those years following the momentous time when, as a boy of nine, my father taught me how to play the game that became a very important part of my life.

During the years in question, Ards and Glenford were the established table tennis clubs in the town, with Ards being the more senior of the two as Glenford had only opened in the 1950s. Table tennis was also played with enthusiasm at the Blaxnit Social Club, the British Legion and at several of the Ards football supporters' clubs.

The early 1960s was very much a boom time for table tennis, with Ards continuing along its successful path and Glenford emerging to challenge for the position of top club in the town.

Ards had two excellent players in Harry O'Prey and Carroll McBride. Both held many Ulster and Irish titles and were members of the Ulster and Irish teams during the 1950s and 1960s. Carroll was a left-handed player while Harry defended from all angles of the table.

Glenford had many young players coming through –

Glenford in 1955-56

He met his wife Margaret (née Finlay), another very successful table tennis player at Glenford, when they were both 15.

Alfie won several junior and senior table tennis titles throughout Ireland, was an Ulster junior inter-pro team member and captain of the Ulster senior inter-pro team.

His footballing honours included six youth international caps and an amateur international cap.

I'm most fortunate to be able to include myself among that number. Others included George Cardy, Jack Mateer, Clifford Thompson, Jack Cash, Zander Dorrian, David Miskelly, Gary Bowman, Hugh Moore, Billy Scott, Derek Matier, Margaret Finlay, Brenda Armour and Iris Morrison.

Many of those I have named would in time become the winners of Ulster and Irish individual titles and would also play for Ulster and Ireland at junior and senior level.

Glenford had the good fortune to gain the services of Harry O'Prey during this time. Hugh Cardy, founder member and mainstay of the club, invited Harry to the club so the young players could avail of his widely acknowledged skill, knowledge and experience to further their own development. This was to be a turning point in the local game; with Harry there, Glenford came to the fore and gradually overtook the Ards club. The latter had no young members coming through and membership figures were dwindling.

Newtownards hosted the Ulster Open for many years at the Guild Hall attached to First Presbyterian Church in Frances Street. Thanks to the organisational skills of Hugh Cardy, George Lindsay and Billy McCaw, this tournament became one of the most successful in Ireland.

Regrettably, however, the latter half of the 1960s witnessed the demise of both clubs – firstly Ards in June

Alfie Wright

Alfie sharing his 1962 Ulster Open victory with his father (also Alfie)

1966 and then, some years later, Glenford. In both instances this was due to a lack of members.

Looking back to those special times as a player I count myself lucky to have shared more than a few tables with all the people I have mentioned and many others. It was very sad to see table tennis disappearing as a competitive sport in my home town.

People in Ards and district may also remember me from my soccer-playing days. I was one of Earle Hawkins' first signings for Ards Boys. He developed my goalkeeping skills and I was fortunate to be a part of a very successful team, winning league and cup titles in the Dunmurry League, as well as the Irish Youth Cup.

At the age of 17 I signed for Brantwood and played in the 1963 Steel and Sons Cup final, but we lost 2-0 to Larne. I moved to Bangor in December 1966, 10 days before my wedding to Margaret Finlay. My debut against Linfield, on 10 December, proved unsuccessful, although I did save a penalty.

On my wedding day, 17 December, I left Margaret and our guests at the reception and was driven by taxi to Castlereagh Park, where I played against Ards. The game finished 2-2 with Ards scoring an 89th minute equaliser.

After several years at Bangor an offer came from Sligo Rovers and so began another chapter in my sporting career. It meant a 340-mile round trip for home games, as well as trips to Cork, Waterford, Limerick, etc.

During 1977 Ards FC manager Billy Humphries signed me and I helped Ards IIs reach the Steel and Sons Cup final. We lost the game 2-0 to my old team Brantwood. I went on to spend several years in amateur football, winning a Clarence Cup medal with Civil Service before retiring at 42.

Dennis S. Nash

remembers... Junior Amateur Football

One of the main shifts in concentration during the Sixties, certainly as far as junior amateur football was concerned, was the development of the locally-organised competition during the winter months.

The Cardy League had surfaced in the 1950s, starting the trend in Ards Borough, and was still active as the new decade dawned. The idea did falter after its promising start and in 1963 it was wound up. However, the seeds had been planted and in 1966, with Sam Monan at its head, the idea was revived and the Cardy League was re-launched.

It encountered further difficulties in 1968, but by the following year Charlie Murphy re-opened the possibility of the game being organised within the Borough during the winter season. The Cardy League adopted a name change as the decade ended, and thus it was the Conlig and District League which carried the idea forward into the Seventies.

The North Down League, formed in August 1972, would bring the aim of locally-organised competition into regular practice and tournaments like the Co. Down Premier League, and eventually the Down Area Association, would in the future truly establish the trend, but it was during the late Fifties and throughout the Sixties that the concept really matured.

Dennis S. Nash in the 1960s

Dennis Stafford Nash was born at Cardy near Greyabbey on 28 June 1937. He attended Dunover Public Elementary School from 1941 until he moved to Regent House Grammar School in 1948.

In 1955 he entered Stranmillis Teachers Training College and after the three-year course joined the teaching profession in 1958.

Dennis was appointed to Victoria (Newtownards) Primary School that year and served in the East Street establishment until his early retirement in 1996. From 1977 he was Senior Deputy Headmaster at Victoria.

He holds a Bachelor of Arts

Degree (Open University) and a Diploma in Advanced Studies of Education (Queen's University).

One of his many interests has been sport; he won the Chronicle Shield as the outstanding boy athlete at Regent House in 1955, was awarded his Rugby Honours Badge in the same year and later, in 1968, won an Honours Plaque at Ards Rugby Club.

Dennis was honoured in March 2000 when the Rotary Club of Newtownards, in association with Ards Borough Council, presented him with a Millennium Award for Voluntary Service to Sport.

He was a recipient of a Hearts of Ards Award in 2006 and in 2011 won a Community Heroes Award for outstanding contributions to the Ards community.

More recently Dennis was presented with a Lifetime Achievement Award at the 2012 Sports Development Committee's awards ceremony.

To acknowledge 60 years of covering sports in the local press he recently received recognition from the *Newtownards Chronicle*, Ards Borough Council, Newtownards and District Charity Committee, Down Area Football Association, Newtownards and District Primary Schools Association and numerous sporting clubs, businesses and charitable organisations.

Dennis is a published poet and author, a recognised entertainer, a respected quiz master and a much-in-demand after-dinner speaker.

He has been married to Jennie for 50 years, has two sons (Mark and Darren) and two grandsons (Elliot and Alexander).

In the Sixties the summer tournaments were still very much in evidence, with the Lower Ards competition and the Donaghadee tournament probably attracting the greatest attention. Portavogie Rangers emerged in the early 1960s and went on to dominate the summer competition. Indeed they made quite an impact by winning the Lower Ards Summer League Championship an astonishing seven times in the course of the decade!

Portavogie Olympic, the established local side before the Rangers surfaced, actually took the title in 1968, so in fact the Championship flag only left the fishing village twice during the Sixties.

Portavogie's mastery in the context of Peninsula football was really underlined in 1962 when the Lower Ards KO Cup final actually featured both teams from the village. Needless to say, this created quite a stir and a competition renowned for attracting big crowds certainly packed in the spectators that Saturday evening. The Rangers eventually beat the Olympic 3–1 in a game which saw three penalty kicks being awarded!

Back in the Sixties if a knock-out game ended in a draw the procedure in junior amateur football was to replay the fixture. Indeed, that was also the only means employed at that time in the professional game when the scores finished level. (In England the first shoot-out from the penalty mark didn't take place until the 1970 Watney Cup semi-final when Hull City and Manchester United finished all square at Boothferry Park.)

Obviously, fitting in dates for replays was very time consuming but it was the only method in common usage in the Sixties. The 1962 Lower Ards Summer KO Cup competition was particularly plagued by drawn games. The first round game between Portavogie Olympic and Kircubbin United actually needed four games before Portavogie booked their place in the next round. In the semi-final, Portavogie Rangers and Ballyhalbert had to meet no fewer than five times before the Rangers won the right to contest the final!

The Irish Alliance League, the Amateur League and the Minor League provided most of the opportunities for

Ards area teams to compete during the winter. Naturally these competitions also faced the problem of settling results when knock-out games finished without a clear-cut winner.

The Minor League promoted the Gibson Cup as its major knock-out tournament and in 1964, when Ards Borough side Cyril Lord's contested the final against St Malachy's at Wilgar Park, it ended level. The League authorities, clearly worried by the prospect of having to set another date, had come up with a rather unique way to resolve the situation. It was decided to play two periods of extra time – and to count the corner kicks awarded to each team in case the score didn't change. The competition was settled after it was determined that St Malachy's had won more corners following the normal 90 minutes!

Junior football facilities invariably faced heavy criticism at that time. Nevertheless, during the Sixties great strides were made in an effort to improve standards. On 21 May 1960 the first matches were played on new pitches at Londonderry Park, while later in the decade the Dairy Hall playing fields joined the list of facilities made available by the Council to teams within Newtownards.

In 1963 the Ards Olympic club, after completing an extensive programme of work on a site near the airport on the Portaferry Road, opened their own ground which was ruled fit for Minor League games. Further work followed and today, of course, 'The Drome' caters for intermediate football with 1st Bangor OB.

Dennis S. Nash (left), Ards Olympic club manager, presents a farewell gift in 1964 to Olympic centre half David Trolan who was leaving for Canada that week. Looking on are Michael Mayne, John Gunning (team captain) and Bert McClements. *90-90-2*

One of the main highlights of the Sixties involved the arrival of the Newtownards Factory League. A Saturday morning competition in the late 1950s, involving teams from the various Newtownards factories, proved the starting point and in 1960, prompted by the efforts of Hamilton Lawther and Will Arnold, a fully-fledged factory competition began.

The foundation teams were Berkshire, Black's, Crepe Weavers, Ulster Print Works, Cyril Lord's, Kiltonga, Goblin Works and GWB Furnaces. The competition grew and flourished right throughout the decade.

Another huge development in local amateur football during the Sixties was the emergence of Ards Boys. Earle Hawkins was the leading figure behind the creation of a club destined to produce so many players who progressed to Irish League standard.

The side played their first match on 19 March 1960, against Hemsworth Square from Lambeg. They competed in the Belfast Summer Youth League during that first year, with home games being staged initially at Glenford Park and later in Londonderry Park. In their first year in competition the team won the League Championship – with an unbeaten record!

Ards Boys won the Northern Ireland Youth Cup in 1963, while in August 1968 they remained in the glare of the local spotlight by undertaking a tour into Europe, taking in Belgium, Holland and Germany. One of the most memorable matches was against Belgian Division 2 Champions Ourodemberg. That game was played under floodlights at the Ourodemberg Stadium outside Brussels – and Ards Boys won 4-2!

During the decade three teams from the district made their debuts in the Amateur League. Killyleagh YC became members in 1961, while Abbey Villa and Ards Rangers both joined in 1962.

Schools football was constantly in the headlines during the 1960s, with the recently-formed Newtownards and District Primary Schools Association really coming to the forefront. Victoria Primary, in East Street, Newtownards, captured attention by becoming the first school to land a League and Cup double. That was in 1960 and by 1963 they had repeated the feat four times!

On Saturday 15 October 1966, Ards Olympic notched

up a 10-1 victory over Windsor Rec., with Gordon Stewart scoring six goals in the final 15 minutes! It has never been contradicted that Gordon's feat represented the fastest double hat-trick ever recorded in local junior football!

Substitutions were first permitted during matches in England's Football League in the 1965-66 season. During the first two seasons after the law was introduced (in professional football), each side was permitted only one substitution during a game. Moreover, the substitute could only replace an injured player. However, from the 1967-68 season this rule was relaxed to allow tactical substitutions.

In local amateur football one of the first uses of the substitute came on 16 March 1968 in a Cochrane Corry Cup tie at Drome Park between Ards Rangers 2nds and EBNI. Jim Ritchie retired with a pulled muscle and was replaced by team manager Jackie McCallum.

Charity matches have always been an important element of the junior game. Back in 1960 Kenneth Courtney worked on the idea of staging a match to benefit the Ards Mayor's World Refugee Fund. The game, involving a contest between 'Youth' and 'Experience', took place at Castlereagh Park on 19 March that year.

The summer emergence a year later of 'The Fabulous DDs' again prompted the idea of raising funds for charity. That team, made up of local boys with a loose connection to Ards Rugby Club, managed to attract a high standard of guest players to their ranks and the likes of Mick Lynch, Michael O'Connell and Chris Duffy, who had won an FA Cup winner's medal with Charlton Athletic, certainly put their efforts in the sporting spotlight.

In the 1969 Donaghadee Summer League, Newtown Olympic were trailing Seaview 5–1 with the game already 10 minutes into the second half. In those remaining 35 minutes, however, the Olympic netted five times to finish up with a winning 6–5 scoreline. To this day that achievement is often debated as being possibly the greatest comeback ever in local junior football.

Ards Rangers 2nds also laid their claim to the final headlines of the Sixties. Their 12–1 victory in an Amateur League game against Queen's Colts at Drome Park in

Dennis S. Nash

November 1969 certainly rattled the record books. The fact that Brian Mills, returning to action after injury, helped himself to a personal tally of six goals really did push the match into that place earmarked for special reminiscences.

The really big news in local amateur soccer circles involved a decision announced by the Amateur League authorities in late December 1969. Their statement indicated it had been decided to introduce a system of promotion and relegation to Sections 1A and 1B. While the subject of promotion and relegation had often been mooted, it had always been rejected by the Committee on the grounds that such a policy would be undesirable.

However, most of the teams had regularly endorsed the idea so with the new decade dawning there was plenty of eager anticipation for the fresh targets and objectives that lay ahead.

David Coffey

remembers... Rugby

My commission is to focus on local rugby with special reference to the Ards club. Let's start with a short statement on origins.

There is evidence that Newtownards had a rugby club as far back as 1878, though it foundered in the new century. The Donaghadee club started slightly later, in 1885, but like Ards it disappeared for a while. The current Ards club regards itself as having started in 1928. The years after that at Ards were characterised by honest endeavour but, despite some near misses, no trophies were won before the 1960s.

The Ards 1st XV with the Ulster Towns Cup in April 1962. Back (from left): J. Hamilton, D. McDonnell, R. Hodgkiss, G. Hunter, G. Ferguson, R. Bishop, W. Whiteside, J. Dalzell, D. McKee. Seated: G. Kennedy, W. Herron, D. Coffey, R. Haslett (captain), S. Kielty, K. Halliday, E. Gourley. In front: W. Shaw and B. Jordan.
33-19-3

David Coffey played rugby at Regent House School and Ards.

He has a primary degree and PHD from Queen's University, Belfast. Now retired, he taught History at Annadale Grammar School, Belfast, and, as a Senior Lecturer in Guidance and Counselling, at the University of Ulster.

The Dee club, on the other hand, resurrected in 1902, was much more successful, reaching the finals of, and also winning, both the Junior and Towns Cups. In 1957/58, for example, the Dee won the Junior Cup and were beaten only narrowly in the final of the Towns Cup.

The 1960s, however, ushered in a different story. While

Married to Barbara (née Cole), he has two daughters, Sara and Lisa, and two grandsons, Joseph and Oliver. He continues to live in Newtownards.

the Dee languished to an extent, Ards made steady progress on and off the field of play. The breakthrough for Ards occurred in the 1960/61 season, with the first ever visit, and a narrow defeat, by an Ulster Branch President's team in early season. As if in instant response to Dudley Higgins' encouragement, Ards won the Towns Cup for the first time in the following season, 1961/62. The route to the final included a victory against Bangor, another local team on the rise.

Bobby Haslett, skipper of Ards RFC 1st XV, holds aloft the Ulster Towns Cup as jubilant teammates join the celebrations. They won the trophy for the first time in their history by defeating Dungannon in the final at Ravenhill in April 1962.
33-20-1

As it happened, and this is where my story really takes off, I played at fullback in both the President's game (as captain) and in the Towns Cup campaign. Those who accompanied me in both advances comprised Billy Shaw, Bobby Bishop, John Dalzell, Eric Gourley, Sam Kielty, Ken Halliday, Gordon Kennedy, Bert Jordan and Bobby Haslett (who captained the Towns Cup team). The 'extras' in 1962 were Billy Herron, Wilgar Whiteside, Raymond Hodgkiss, George Ferguson and George Hunter.

Those who were around at that time – and survive – will never forget Bobby Haslett's cross kick from the right wing which the young Bert Jordan gathered to score at the posts, leaving vice-captain Billy Shaw with an easy conversion (5-0), or Eric Gourley's breakaway try against the wind in the second half (8-0), or Dungannon's nail-biting response, an unconverted try (8-3).

The *News Letter* report captured the scene vividly: "With only five minutes remaining the excitement was intense as Dungannon pounded away at the Ards line. But over-eagerness linked to solid tackling and fine covering denied them a score."

In the same season Andy Moore's 'Wee threes' finished joint winners of their section of the Fourth Division, also for the first time. On and off this team included such other luminaries as 'Jazz' Millin, 'Gandhi' McMorran, Billy Wallace, Rex Cavan, Sam Orme and Tom McCullough. Many a novice was proud to start an often illustrious career on that ensemble.

The Ards II rugby team, challenging for league honours in late February 1963, pictured before defeating Instonians IIIs 9-0 on 16 February 1963. *56-42-3*

Apart from those cited, there were other great characters and clubmen in local rugby in the 1960s. At Ards we had also the rangy Will Sloan, the promising Denis and Barry Calvert, the tenacious Billy Dickson, David Heron, our first official coach, and the time-honoured John P Hamilton, among others.

The Dee had the long-standing Jimmy Donaldson, the perennial Bob Foster, the formidable Trevor Sailes and Jim Anderson, the effervescent Jack McKeag, the gnomish Ken Lennox, Jack Simpson, a touch judge to watch, Billy Kirk and a host of others scarcely less prominent. Many of us had learned our rugby together at Regent House but became increasingly partisan as we grew older.

Donaghadee Rugby Club's 1st XV who lost 6-3 after extra time to Ards in the Junior Cup on 29 October 1961. Back (from left): J. Hamilton, W. Love, W. Martin, G Taggart, L. Hall, R. McMullan, D. Patton, W. McConkey, T. Sailes. Front: W. Boomer, B. Maxwell, W. Strain, K. Lennox, J. Davidson, J. Hopday. *76-2-21*

We all avidly scrutinised R.C. (Bob) Stuart's 'Judex' column each Wednesday in the *Northern Whig* in the hope of getting a mention from that great Dee man. I treasure an excerpt from his column on 23 March 1960: "Coffey was in grand form for the winners at fullback." Yes, we beat Coleraine that unforgettable day in the Towns Cup –

Members of Ards Rugby Club pictured at a dinner held in late April 1965 to celebrate Ards winning the second division of the Junior League. *115-16-1*

and I remember it well.

Ards never really looked back from the initial Towns Cup triumph. In 1965/66 my brother Ivan's 1st XV won promotion to the premier Ulster Junior League for the first time. In the following season, 1966/67, four league teams and a fifth side playing 'friendlies' were fielded. In 1968/69 Brian Hutchinson's 2nd XV won the Forster Cup and repeated the feat in the following season. For veteran Billy Shaw it was a third appearance on a winning Ards team at Ravenhill.

During the Sixties the Dee began to fall under the shadow of their neighbours (particularly Bangor). Ards on the other hand continued to grow in strength. Win or lose, Ardsmen always displayed a whimsical, self-deprecating sense of humour. A glossary attached to a short history of events at the time contained the following references, among other gems:

The Oul' Hut – Our changing room, viewing area, pavilion and social club.

The Dev. – A hostelry much frequented by Ardsmen of the rougher sort.

Cafolla's – A coffee house patronised by Ardsmen of gentler type and starting place for away games.

Regent – Another educational establishment of some local significance, teaching basic skills in rugby and other disciplines.

David Coffey

Put that man onside, Ards – A subtle and polite hint to a referee that an opponent may be offside.

Ardsman – The definitive Ardsman has always defied description. He exists – ask any Dee man or Bangorian.

That'll do us, Ards – This does not mean that Ards have scored enough tries for one day. Refers instead to any kick to touch by an opponent, either good or bad, with the aim of upsetting him.

Jim Hayes

remembers... The Ballydrain Harriers

Being born and brought up in Killinchy, it wasn't long before the name Ballydrain Harriers was embedded in my mind. With my cousin John Hayes, his friends John Reid and Joe Cromie and others we knew running for the club, my father would take me to watch the cross-country events in the mid 1950s.

The 1958/59/60 seasons were particularly exciting times in the greater Ballydrain area, although the club minutes and reports record many outstanding individual and team performances before this period. It would have been the fact that I was to witness the events first hand that would make them so real – even now.

Led by Jim Kenmore and Tom Cromie, who had both been youth champions, the squad of 10 or more (six were required for a team) scored many victories, culminating in an All Ireland Junior Championship victory in 1959. As well as taking the individual honours, Jim Kenmore was also crowned Northern Ireland Senior Champion that year and again in 1960.

By 1962 Ballydrain was entering a period of decline as this team had broken up, although Jim Kenmore was still running when club member George Geddis took me down for the first time (as a 16-year-old) in 1963. My first serious races though were in fact with the Boys' Brigade, having qualified for the Northern Ireland District

Jim Hayes and his wife Ethnie

For almost 26 years home for Jim Hayes was Balloo and Craigrusky, near Killinchy.

Primary education at Killinchy and Ardmillan schools was followed by spells at Comber Intermediate then Comber and Newtownards Techs.

After school Jim was accepted for an apprenticeship at the Sirocco Works in Belfast, but a last minute change of heart saw him follow his father into joinery, the lure of working in a country environment proving too strong.

In 1972 Jim married Ethnie and set up home in Comber, working with his father – Hamilton – until his retirement in 1983. Jim took over the business at this point

Officials and prizewinners who attended the Ballydrain Harriers' presentation night and dance in the Andrews Hall, Comber, in April 1963. *61-14-1*

and at one stage had three employees, doing all types of building work. In the lead-up to his own retirement in 2012, he was lucky enough to wind down gradually, working alone for a few years.

Jim's athletic career only took off in the 1970s with, amongst other achievements, international cross-country trips to Spain and Morocco. Mountain running became popular in Northern Ireland in the same decade and Jim notched up four wins in the Slieve Donard Race between 1974 and 1981.

He was a founder member of the NI Mountain Runners' Association, in 1979, and won the first six Championships, as well as two All Ireland titles.

After turning 40, Jim became NI Masters cross-country champion in 1989 and, with mountain running having become international in the 1980s, a highlight was the World Trophy event in Switzerland in 1991.

Championships in 1964. The race was held at what is now the site of Newtownbreda High School. Being inexperienced and unaware of the opposition, I found myself pacing (as I would find out later) two very good club runners in the race for second place. Inevitably I would finish fourth.

It was around this time that Matt Wilson became the leading Ballydrain runner, having joined the club as an 18-year-old in 1960. Matt's first event was the McConnell Shield junior race in November of that year, when he finished in a very creditable fifth position. He concluded the season by winning the Whitehead Novice road race the following Easter Monday, leading the team to victory. Unfortunately, after the summer break most of this winning team lost interest and it was left to Matt to plough a lonely furrow until the middle of the decade, when a unique squad of teenagers appeared on the scene.

Nowadays, on studying the Athletics NI fixture list it is hard to believe that up until the early 1980s races were promoted by either the clubs or, in the case of championships, by the NIAAAs, as it was then. It would be unheard of to have more than one race meeting on any particular Saturday – quite often every two weeks. In the free weeks clubs would sometimes have combined runs, when they would invite other clubs to sample their training routes.

In the case of Ballydrain these runs would be an eye-opener for the Belfast clubs. In particular, they would involve running on roads, laneways, fields, crossing ditches and hedges and, if the tide was out, negotiating a stretch of the Strangford Lough shoreline. These trails would also be used on the other free Saturdays by the Harriers themselves and by mid-winter could be extended to 15 miles. Indeed, the later success of this squad of runners can be attributed in no small way to these runs.

Quite often the runs would be all-out races with the result that I, for one, would be inflicted with serious cramp at 'the pictures' on the Saturday night. One particular incident I am reminded of from such runs round the country occurred when we headed up a lane that had just been freshly concreted. Although most of us saw it in time, one member – who shall remain nameless – ran half a dozen steps in before realising his predicament. The excuse was he was running faster than the rest. A hasty repair job was done later before the damage was spotted and the concrete set.

Nowadays Jim just cycles and runs to keep fit, while he and Ethnie enjoy travel, walking and social dancing.

Following a dip in fortunes at the Ballydrain Harriers in recent years, Jim can happily confirm the club is back on an upward trend since moving its base to Comber.

I am also reminded of a prank Bobby Simpson played on younger and not so young members who would have been quicker than himself by then. Bobby had been a member of the successful 1959 team and was of great encouragement to all the newcomers. However, on one particular eight-mile road run he knew a shortcut – at around six miles and in the dark, when we were certain he was behind, we would suddenly find him in front again. Another memory from those days was the fact that if you saw someone out running it was pretty certain they would have been a club runner.

Back in 1930 a new school was built at Ballydrain, leaving the Old School vacant, so when the Harriers were formed in 1932 the owners, Killinchy Presbyterian Church, allowed the club the use of the old premises. Throughout the next 33 years changing facilities were fairly basic, with really only a roof over our head and no showers. Stories are told of washing in the river, progressing to a tin bath in front of the open fire or just a towel rub down, which I experienced from trainers Wilson Lowry, John Bathgate or Tom Cromie senior.

The Old School at Ballydrain (the picture was taken after renovations in 1986)

Another function these men would undertake was to massage aching calf muscles. Before specialised running shoes were developed in the late 1960s, lack of cushioning in the old gutty-type slippers was a major hazard of too much road running, coupled with only training twice or three times a week. By then, however, the new generation of runners were reading and learning of the methods adopted by the leading British athletes and it soon became the norm to run at least six times a week. This resulted in more flexible calf muscles, which astounded the trainers and left one less chore for them to perform. Things changed for the better in September 1966, when showers were installed, heralding a new era and coinciding with the arrival of the aforementioned new young blood.

Members pictured in September 1966 at the opening of the first showers at the club, with Mr W. J. Faulkner (seated, centre), founder member and long time president of the Ballydrain Harriers

Results started to improve and Matt Wilson now had a team around him; in fact in November of that year the team finished second in the opening junior cross-country race of the season, the McConnell Shield, at Ballyclare and were led home by individual winner Ian Morrison. The rules of this event prevented previous individual or team winners from taking part again so 12 months later it was quite a feat when Matt Wilson, Eddie Smith and 17-year-old Tom Price filled the first three places and led the team to overall victory. The 1967-68 season saw the team also take all the junior honours, culminating with the Northern Ireland Junior Championship, including the individual champion in Ian Morrison.

The winners of the West Down Cup in 1968 (from left): Ian Morrison, Tom Price, Eddie Smith, Matt Wilson, John McNeilly and Jim Hayes

A popular event throughout the 1960s was the Lagan Valley relay, sponsored by the *Ireland's Saturday Night* (the former *Belfast Telegraph* sports paper for all those young people out there). This race started at the Albert Clock in

Belfast and passed through Dunmurry, Lisburn and Lurgan, then on to Portadown and back via Banbridge, Dromore and Hillsborough, finishing in Ormeau Park after 12 stages. The top Dublin teams were regular entrants, along with the leading Northern clubs. It would seem impossible to run these roads and through these towns today.

The 1968 race was memorable for Ballydrain but for the wrong reason. While challenging for a top-four place on entering Portadown, Trevor White was sent in the wrong direction by a police officer, who knew nothing about the race (he was there to look after the Mayor's Parade, which was taking place at the same time). As it happened I was the one following by car. Having located Trevor, I bundled him into the vehicle and in a panic took him back along the route ahead of the runner he had been in front of, rather than to the point where the mistake was made. Disqualification was the penalty.

Ian Morrison (265) and Eddie Smith (266) were first and second in the 1968 Northern Ireland Junior Cross-Country Championships. Included is the club mascot of that time.

Another source of inspiration at Ballydrain for many years was Mr W. J. Faulkner, a founder member and long time president of the club. Mr Faulkner was uncle to Brian Faulkner, later Prime Minister of Northern Ireland, and had been headmaster of both the old and new schools at Ballydrain.

He was also involved in the earlier Ballydrain Motorcycle and Athletic Club in the 1920s and took a keen interest in the Harriers, right up to his death in 1974, aged 91.

With the popularity of marathon running today, it may be hard to imagine that in the 1960s through to 1980 only a handful of people ran marathons in Northern Ireland. There was never any tradition of long-distance road running at Ballydrain anyway, although Bobby Simpson did run the distance in the mid-1960s. It was in April 1969 that I decided to prepare for that June's Northern Ireland Championships and, along with no more that 10 others, I set off along the Antrim Road to Dunadry and back, finishing fourth in 2hrs 44mins and very satisfied with that first attempt. Talking to one of Ballydrain's greatest runners, Johnny Marshall, just a few months before he

Members of Ballydrain Harriers at their annual general meeting in the club headquarters, Ballydrain Old School, in September 1968. Included is club president Mr W. J. Faulkner (seated, centre), *191-30-2*

died, he admitted his biggest regret was never getting the opportunity to run the marathon distance.

In the previous decade both Adam Brown (1958) and Jim Kenmore (1959) had appeared in All Ireland cross-country teams, but it was not until 1968 that the Ballydrain club once again had international runners. By then Northern Ireland and the Republic had separate teams and that year saw both Matt Wilson and Ian Morrison being selected to represent the former at the International Championships in Tunisia. The following year three runners were selected to run, this time in Glasgow, namely Ian Morrison in the senior race and Crossgar brothers Tom and Denis Price in the junior event. Being so close to home and the fact that team mates were running, I joined a party of supporters and travelled to Clydebank, on the outskirts of Glasgow. The experience and motivation gained from spectating that day was to lay the foundation for everything I would achieve in the years to come.

Surviving members of Ballydrain Harriers in August 2012 – Sam McMinn, John McKeag, Fred Strickland, Trevor White, Jim Hayes and Raymond Brown

The decade would end disappointingly for Matt Wilson and the club in general, when he broke his leg in the Christmas morning race at Ballydrain. The successful junior team was about to challenge for senior honours, but fortunately every one stayed together and the targets were achieved early in the 1970s – thankfully with Matt back in the fold.

Billy McCully

remembers... Showjumping

Two-year-old Billy McCully attending his first show in Ballywalter with his father back in 1931

The only thing I ever wanted to do was work with horses. When I was a boy my father said I was no good at riding but in time I proved him wrong. There's not a showjumping competition in Ireland I didn't win and it was in the Sixties that I reached the peak of my success.

My father Hugh McCully and my grandfather – also Billy McCully – were both great horsemen and I inherited their love of all things equestrian.

After leaving school in 1943 I started taking part in gymkhanas. It was at Ballywalter Show that I met Herbert Forbes, a builder from Belfast, who had three very good showjumpers but no jockey. The day the Second World War ended in 1945 there was a show in Magherafelt and I won three competitions there for him.

There had been no racing or showjumping during the war but afterwards all the main shows resumed, such as Balmoral, Ballymena and Newtownards, as well as events in all the main towns around Northern Ireland. At that

William (Billy) McCully was born in Carrowdore on 29 June 1929. Parents Hugh and Hannah (née McKeag) had another son, Brian, who was born in 1931, and a daughter, Anne, born in 1936.

The family moved for a few years to Aghadowey, County Londonderry, where Hugh McCully worked for one of the leading showjumping horse owners in

Ireland before returning to their home village just before the Second World War.

Billy still lives in Carrowdore with second wife Margaret; the couple were married in September 1988.

Billy's daughter Lucinda lives nearby with husband Wallace McKee and children Simon, Adam, Ben and Rebecca. Son Paddy lives in America with his wife Sarah and children Liam and Hannah.

Though he admits he was never a good player himself, Billy is a past chairman and current president of Ards Football Club. He was chairman during the club's glory years, including when the team won four major trophies in the '73/74 season under player-manager and Northern Ireland international Billy Humphries – the Irish Cup, Ulster Cup, Gold Cup and Blaxnit Cup.

Billy is also a keen follower of Abbey Villa FC in Millisle and regularly attends their home matches at Adams Park.

time showjumping was flourishing and all the shows were very well attended. They started on Easter Monday and finished at Ballinasloe on the first Monday in October. Horses and riders rested all winter then came back afresh in the Spring. Dublin's Spring Show was always held in the first week of May with the Horse Show in the first week of August; both were very big occasions.

I left home at 15 and moved to Dublin to ride for builder Dick Collen after a chance encounter at the Balmoral Show when he had no rider. There were no horseboxes in those days and I remember coming back from a show and getting off a train with the horse at Malahide at one or two in the morning. Dick was an absolute gentleman and met us at the station with a hurricane lamp. We then walked the four or five miles home.

Tiredness was always the last thing on my mind; I was just so enthusiastic about riding. Sometimes I would be up at 3am to get the horse fed, groomed and ready to set off for a show. None of my horses ever missed their midday meal, no matter where they were.

A few years later I went to work for the Garland family who ran a drinks company in Newry. I took charge of Mrs Garland's four-horse jumping team and they were really good horses. I could have won up to £2,800 per year by showjumping in the 1940s.

Billy McCully rides *Ballyblack* at Ballymena in 1950. *Picture by J. F. Connor, Belfast*

I also rode horses for a parish priest who lived in County Roscommon. His housekeeper was so old she couldn't manage the stairs so we lived off tinned food. She used to fling the tins out the back door and I remember building a jump with all those empty cans. Somehow I always managed to have the worst digs in Ireland!

I well remember the Horse of the Year Show at Haringey in London in 1956, when I won the *Daily Telegraph*

Cup on November's Eve, a horse I'd bought for the Garlands. That was an embarrassing show – I fell off in front of the Queen and was knocked out cold. The paramedics carried me off on a stretcher and some of the spectators thought I'd broken my neck. I woke up in a dressing room and the Queen sent an emissary round to see how I was!

Billy McCully is congratulated by the head of the French Army team after winning on *Ballyblack* at Dublin Show in 1951. There was a military jumping section each year at the Show. *Picture by J. F. Connor, Belfast*

There were plenty of injuries over the years. When I think about it, there's hardly a hospital in the north or south I haven't been in with a broken bone! But I count myself very lucky – nearly all the guys I rode with back then are either dead or are crippled with arthritis.

Eventually I went freelance and competed at shows for anyone needing a rider. By the mid-1950s I'd returned to Carrowdore where I had a yard and kept horses for different people. An English rider called Clare Jenkinson came to work for me. One thing led to another and we got married in 1955 and had two children, Patrick and Lucinda, though neither has any interest in horses.

We bought our own place just outside Carrowdore and started dealing in horses. I paid £250 for one of the first horses I bought. He won me £500-£600 in prize money and I sold him for £1,500. That started the ball rolling. I was lucky enough to buy some good horses – and some really bad ones too!

Billy McCully rides *Sunbeam* at Dublin Show in 1955. *Irish Times* picture

There are three types of horse, good, bad and pathetic, and I had them all. It's difficult to tell if a horse is going to be good as there's a heck of a lot of luck involved. I should say luck and training but a horse has to be honest. The good ones would want to please you but the pathetic ones are working against you all the time. They will stop and dump you. Let's just say I've had more bad ones than good ones!

Commander, ridden by Billy McCully, won the open jumping section at Tubbercurry Show in 1955

The biggest price I ever paid for a horse was £25,000 – and he wasn't worth tuppence. I sold him for £13,000 to someone in Italy. That was very painful but I was never so glad to see a horse heading out of the yard in all my life! He had great ability but was very dishonest. You'd be at a small show where there was no prize money and he'd jump his guts out but then you'd take him to a show with big prize money and he'd stop at every last fence and the jockey would fall off. He was the most annoying bugger I ever owned!

My first wife Clare was very good with horses. She rode the ones I didn't like and was always able to win with them, whereas I couldn't have won a penny on them.

Often, if a horse didn't make it as a showjumper, I would get rid of him as a hunter. Hunts in England were always looking for good mounts and we also had a number more in County Down – for example, the North Down Harriers, County Down Staghounds, Newry Harriers and Iveagh Harriers. Indeed, I was joint master of the East Down Foxhounds, based in Seaforde, for several years during the Sixties. It was always good craic out on the hunting field and great craic in the pub afterwards, though we never caught too many foxes.

Over the years I've been to lots of horse fairs all over Ireland. I remember one time going to a fair in Waterford with £250 and coming back with five horses. The best fairs were usually in Ballinasloe and Cork, while there would always be plenty of foreign buyers at the August show in Dublin, where 1,000-1,200 horses were sold.

Droves of horses would have been heading for the docks to be shipped all over the world. Horses were and still are big business in Ireland. The last really good horse I had, I got £50,000 for it. These days, though, some of the best ones sell for half a million.

Hunting with the East Down Foxhounds in 1963

The final big showjumping competition I took part in was the RDS Horse Show in August 1969. As I was getting older, hitting the ground was also getting harder so I thought I'd quit while I was ahead. By that time I'd done it all and seen it all and it could be tiresome. I was lucky to ride good horses and good horses make good horsemen. I would say success is 90 per cent down to the horse. A rider can make a mistake but a good horse can rectify it for you.

I can remember riding some bad horses for some horrible owners who would say you were a terrible rider. The rider always got the blame!

Eventually I went into property development in a small way and more recently I ventured into the world of racing and bought two racehorses. By the time I'd paid the expensive training fees, jockey fees and entry fees, I was nearly out on the street. I finally caught myself on and got rid of them!

I don't keep any horses now and I certainly don't ride. A fall at my age would kill me but I do still take an interest in the results, read the horsey books and enjoy watching it on TV. But it's all changed so much. It's a tragedy that showjumping, as I see it, has been ruined in Northern Ireland. All the local shows are fading away and most are held in equestrian centres, which can be very boring.

When I started it was a sport, but then money got involved and changed it all. In my competition days they just kept putting the fences higher. I set the high jump record

Billy won his last competitive event, the Novice Championship, riding *Silk Cut* at Dublin Show in 1969. *Picture by J. F. Connor, Belfast*

at Ballsbridge in 1952 when I cleared 6ft 3ins on Ballyblack, another of the Garland horses. There were some great characters riding back then. There was little rivalry and we would have helped each other if we could.

If I had it all to do over again, I would change a few things – but not too many. I'd maybe try to have better horses!

Chris Duff

remembers... Hurling in the Upper Ards

Hurling, that most ancient of Irish Games and often referred to as 'Our National Game', has been played in the Upper Ards for over 100 years. The origins of hurling can be traced back to the late 19th Century when Shinty (locally known as Shinny) was played and which was most likely introduced to the area by our Ulster-Scots ancestors.

Around 1900 the first hurling club in Portaferry, Carraig Ulaidh (translation: Rock of Ulster), was formed but it wasn't until 1912, when Eamon Purcell, a potato inspector from Tipperary, arrived, that hurling was reorganised and began to flourish.

Playing the game was seen as a form of recreation and enjoyment for young able men in those summer days and evenings when not much else was on offer. Local leagues were organised with teams mostly being made up of young men from the various townlands around Portaferry. The teams were given such names as Eire Ogs, O'Rahilly's, Kevin Barry's and, of course, Carraig Ulaidh. They were also joined by a team from Kilclief from the opposite side of the Loughshore, straight across from Ballyquintin Point.

Even though Purcell returned to the South in 1917, the fruits of his work were realised in 1920 when Carraig Ulaidh won the County Championship for the first time.

Chris Duff

Born and reared in Portaferry, Christopher (Chris) Duff took a keen interest in hurling from an early age.

All his school friends played the sport, whether on the street, on the beach or on one of the local pitches. It was all good fun so it was hardly surprising when, at the age of 10, Chris found himself competing in local hurling leagues organised by the Portaferry club.

Three years later he represented Portaferry for the first time, going on to play in all grades in a career that spanned the next three decades. He recalls the feeling of great pride when he pulled on the club jersey for the first time as a very young boy, saying it will never be surpassed nor be forgotten.

Chris had the distinction of captaining different club teams to County Championship titles throughout his hurling career and he was also lucky enough to represent his County and Province over a number of years. Even today he is still involved in coaching with the Portaferry club.

He is a keen follower of all sports, finding it to be a great leveller and a good way to make friends, create comradeships and learn how to accept defeats and enjoy the victories.

In a world of computer technology, Chris also

In 1927 they entered the South Antrim League and two years later did the double by winning both the Antrim League and the County Down Championship.

In 1939 two new clubs were formed with the help of Carraig Ulaidh – St Joseph's, Ballycran (Kircubbin and surrounding area) and John Mitchell's, Ballygalget (rural hinterland sandwiched between Kircubbin and Portaferry). This gave a new impetus to the game and hurling went from strength to strength.

The 1940s, however, proved difficult years but the arrival of Fr George Watson (a native of Slans, Cloughey) as PP to Portaferry in 1946 sparked off the hurling revival that has kept the game going to this day. Carraig Ulaidh and Kevin Barry's had amalgamated and were renamed St Patrick's GAC, Portaferry. Plans were also drawn up to build a new pitch in Portaferry and, with voluntary labour and financial support from Fr George Watson's own personal resources, it was opened in 1950.

This was a huge project to undertake but at last there was a proper playing facility in the area on which to play our national game. For a number of years Ballygalget also had use of the pitch as a suitable field was not always available to them. Prior to this, matches were played in fields at various venues throughout the Upper Ards such as The Brickyard, Ballytrustan and Tullycarnon around Portaferry, the Hen Run at Rubane House which was used by Ballycran, while Ballygalget, through the generosity of a local farmer, played in a field across the lane from their present facilities.

Eamon Purcell

The Hen Run was aptly named as it was slightly shorter than other pitches and the ball could be pucked from one end to the other by such gifted players as Walter Moreland (Portaferry), Hugo O'Prey (Ballycran) and Hugh Dorrian (Ballygalget). Defence was quickly turned into attack with a deft stroke of the ball.

Ballycran, with foresight and motivation, opened McKenna Park in 1966, while Ballygalget opened their own pitch four years later. All three clubs now had first-class facilities.

Fr George Watson

As the competitive spirit between the Upper Ards clubs

intensified, the momentous decision was taken to put the local trio into the Antrim Leagues. This had a profound influence on all who were involved and there is no doubt it stabilised hurling in the area, giving the clubs a new incentive and creating the momentum to develop the sport further.

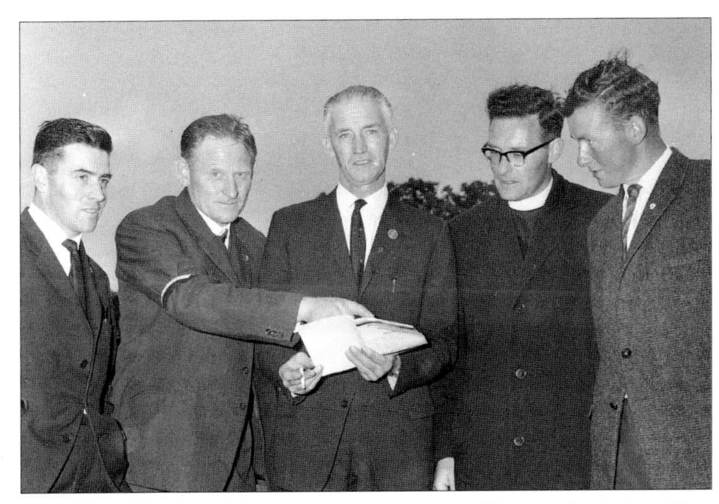

Alf Murray (centre), president of the Gaelic Athletic Association, discusses the programme with Ballycran GAC officials before he officially opened the club's new ground, McKenna Park, in late June 1966. Included are (from left): Gerard McMullan, assistant secretary; David Bell, chairman; Rev. S. Connolly, vice-chairman, and James McNamara, treasurer. *145-2-2*

The Sixties proved to be one of the most exciting decades for hurling in County Down. Ballycran won titles in 1960 and 1961, beating Portaferry on both occasions. Unfortunately the 1962 final between Ballycran and Ballygalget was abandoned due to an altercation between players and was never rescheduled.

In 1963 Portaferry, under the new name of St Patrick's, won their first County title. The final had been fixed for 25 August but the game ended in a draw. Both teams stood together afterwards for a joint photograph; it has been said this was a gesture to show, following the previous year's debacle, that they could take part competitively, with the players remaining good friends at the end.

The final was replayed on 6 October in atrocious conditions, with Portaferry coming out on top by a single point. The pitch carried surface water in many places, with the constant rain and sleet leaving players both wet and cold and unable to play to their full capability.

The youngest Portaferry player that day, 16-year-old Paud Braniff at corner forward, remembers the game particularly for the number of times the opposing defence "put me face down in the mucky pitch." No health and safety in those days!

Portaferry went on to win further County titles in 1965, 1968 and 1969. Ballygalget secured titles in 1964 and

contends there is a growing fear that children are missing out on sporting activities. He says it is imperative that those who played any sport should remain involved after their playing days to encourage the youth and, for that matter, anyone of any age to take part.

The St Patrick's (Portaferry) and Ballygalget teams in the 1963 Senior Championship final

1966, with Ballycran claiming the honours in 1967. No team achieved total dominance, with only the puck of a ball deciding the outcome on many occasions.

With under-age competitions still being played, in 1965 the County Down Vocational Schools team (for those aged under 17), comprising entirely Ards players, was narrowly defeated by Tipperary in the All Ireland Final. Such was their disappointment at losing the game that a rematch was organised in Portaferry, where Down successfully turned the tables on their Tipperary counterparts.

There was a real buzz around the Ards in the Sixties, with matches eagerly awaited and discussed in pubs and clubs and players gathering in groups to discuss the pros and cons of how they had played in their latest game. It was all good fun and, thankfully, people's minds were diverted from other issues happening in our country.

Whilst the Down Gaelic footballers were securing their first two All Ireland titles in 1960 and 1961 – becoming the first Northern county to carry the much coveted Sam Maguire Cup across the border – the hurlers were plotting their own successful course. With competition intense between the three clubs and their inclusion in the Antrim Leagues beginning to pay off, the standard of play and the level of interest in the sport had increased significantly.

As a result, the County Senior hurling team was beginning to show much improvement in the National Leagues

Portaferry Sen. Hurling 1968. Back (from left): Harry Savage, Alex Sweeney, Vincent Mason, Patrick Byers, Martin Coleman, Charlie McMullen, Paud Braniff, Gerard Lennon, Walter Moreland, Gerrard Lennon, Michael Mageean, Gerard Byers, Sean Smith, Harold Ritchie (chairman). Front: Aideen Faloona, Brian McNally, Bernard Mason, Tommy Mason, Sean McCallum, Chris Duff (captain), Fr. Morgan PP, Patsy Ritchie, Paddy Curran, Sean Ritchie, John Dumigan, Sean Savage, Eugene Faloona. Seated: Alexis Magee, Benedict Mathews, Aiden Smyth, Stephen White.

and All Ireland Championships. The County Board saw the potential in this and approached Dubliner Des Ferguson, a very gifted player in both hurling and football, to coach the team. Under his guidance and enthusiasm the final break-through occurred in 1964 when Down won the Junior All Ireland title. This too was a first for any Northern county. They then beat London in Ruislip in a thrilling final to win the title outright.

Ballycran Senior Hurling: Back (from left). : Gerry Fagan, Liam McCarthy, Davy Bell, Terry Bell, Hugo O'Prey, Maurice Gilmore, Frank Gilmore, Fr. Sean Connolly, Noel Gilmore. Front row: Pat Mallon, Kevin Bell, Brian Caughey, David Gilmore, George Gilmore, John Mallon, Maurice Caughey, Eamonn Gilmore.

Such were the celebrations that as the plane carrying the players travelled over Strangford Lough on its way to Aldergrove, bonfires were lit all around the county, with the biggest ones, of course, being in the Ards Peninsula. As the team travelled from Newtownards they were met by a cavalcade of cars some say was up to four miles long. This was a tremendous achievement for the three local clubs as most other counties in Ireland could boast much greater numbers of hurlers to call upon. The sole exception was John McGivern, from Newry, at left full forward.

The Portaferry hurling team which beat Kilclief at Portaferry on 30 July 1961. 21-2-15

Just like any sport, hurling has brought

The All Ireland winning team in 1964. Back (from left): Aidan Faloona, John Coulter, Willie Coulter, Seamus Fitzgerald, Frank Gilmore, David Gilmore, Hugh Sloan, Eugene Faloona, Eddie McGrattan, Paddy Braniff, Hugo O'Prey.
Front: Aloysius Hinds, Hugh Dorrian, John McGivern, Paud Braniff, Charlie McMullan (capt), Willie Smyth, Sean Savage, Pat McGrattan, Pat Mallon, Danny Crawford.

about many friendships and created numerous characters the length and breadth of our tiny island. It generates a whole family of people – players, referees, coaches, administrators and, of course, the spectators who show their keen knowledge of the game during a match. Little wonder they are often referred to as the 'Hurlers on the Ditch'.

Then, as now, every club had its own Mr Motivator and Ballycran were lucky to have such men as Davy Bell, affectionately known as 'Mr Ballycran', and Jim McNamara, who still acts as club treasurer. Ballygalget had John 'Boon' McGrattan (a founder member), Paddy 'Marshall' McGrattan, William Johnson and Benny Crawford, who served as chairman from 1963 to 1982. Portaferry had Walter Moreland, a most gifted player who went on to be an administrator, along with such men as Willie Keating, Harold Ritchie and others too numerous to mention.

Such was the intensity of games in the Sixties that spectators travelled from as far away as North Antrim to witness the Senior Final. Much closer to home, there were also those from different persuasions who had sufficient interest in the sport to pass through the turnstiles and enjoy the excitement and the craic. There was always a great sense of occasion on Final Day, with the two teams parading around the pitch behind a band and the spectators afforded ample opportunity to voice their very definite opinions (which most times were perhaps best ignored!).

So many characters have their deserved place in the game's folklore. For example, one of our most gifted players of that era, Eugene Faloona from Portaferry, caught the ferryboat with the rest of his team and cycled from Strangford to Downpatrick to play a major role in the 1965 final between Portaferry and Ballygalget. He then cycled back to Strangford after the match to catch the ferry home!

On the same day two stalwart Ballygalget supporters, it has been said, decided the celebratory bottle of whiskey would be best drunk at half time as they reckoned the match was lost by that stage. Their names are best not mentioned but they continued to give much loyal service to their club over the next few decades and there were many subsequent opportunities to actually enjoy that celebratory drink.

Another stalwart was Hugh Sloan, who played for Portaferry and was affectionately known as Sam after Sam Bartram, a well known Charlton Athletic goalkeeper in years gone by. Those with good memories will recall Eugene and Sam frequently headed off for Dublin on the latter's motorbike to go to the cinema in O'Connell Street and then returned the same night. They thought nothing of it, considering it was all good fun.

Yes, the Sixties were heady, exciting days when this skilful game was enjoyed by so many.

Davy Bell

Benny Crawford

Walter Moreland

Billy Humphries

remembers... Ards FC

Billy Humphries at Leeds United

Billy Humphries, whose name is synonymous with Ards FC, was born in Donegall Avenue, Belfast, in the shadow of Windsor Park. Thus his early allegiance was to local team Linfield.

He was the fourth son of James and Margaret Humphries, a younger sister completing the family – Alex, Samuel, Ronald, Billy and Beth.

Due to their parents' influence they participated in all the usual activities at St

Coming into the Sixties my boyhood dreams were becoming a reality. Ards had recently become Irish League champions for the first time (and, as it turned out, the only time in their history). I was meeting on and off the pitch with players I had idolised and only dreamt of playing against. Such legends as Peter Doherty, Danny Blanchflower, Stanley Matthews, Bobby Charlton, Harry Gregg, John Charles and Ivor Allchurch all spring readily to mind.

I had joined Ards for a second spell, returning to the club from Leeds United. Despite playing regularly for the first XI in the English First Division, I had never really settled in Yorkshire. In the team were players of the stature of Don Revie (a future England manager), Jack Charlton (a future World Cup winner) and our own Wilbur Cush, who represented Northern Ireland on many occasions.

My return to Ards was on 26 November 1959, the manager at that time being Len Graham, a former Northern Ireland international. He was in the early stages of his managerial career and was developing a young team. We were moderately successful during the season, which ended with the team reaching the Irish Cup final at the Oval on 30 April 1960. We were up against a strong and experienced Linfield side led by 'Wor Jackie' Milburn, of Newcastle United and England fame; they proved the better side and won convincingly, 5-1.

Shortly afterwards, Len Graham, who had done a relatively good job in a short space of time, was sacked and the club started looking for his replacement. At the start of the next season Tommy Ewing, who had the experience of playing in Scotland and England, was appointed the new manager. He had a cultured left foot, was an expert header of the ball and his name appeared regularly on score sheets.

One of his earliest and most significant signings was Mick Lynch from Dublin. He proved a considerable influence on our style of attacking and entertaining football, which attracted large crowds to Castlereagh Park. Mick is remembered with affection for his contribution to the club – his exploits were legendary. During that time I formed a marvellous partnership with him and thoroughly enjoyed the experience.

Tommy Ewing, Ralph McGuicken, Billy Humphries, Mick Lynch and Tommy Moffatt at a function organised by the North End Ards Supporters' Club

Mick scored 84 goals in 95 games, which one can say was truly phenomenal. Of course, there were other fine players during that period, among them Tommy Moffatt, Dessie Hunter, Jimmy Lowe and, of course, Northern Ireland international Tommy Forde. The season ended in disappointment after all our entertaining football. While it brought us close to Irish League success, we finished with no silverware.

The 1961-62 season began with Ards still playing with great flair and imagination and still pulling in the crowds.

Simon's Church of Ireland, being regular attenders at Sunday School and at church services. Billy and Ronald were also members of the Church Lads' Brigade, with Billy attaining the rank of sergeant.

He attended St Simon's Public Elementary School, moving on to Fane Street Primary School (off the Lisburn Road). After passing the Qualifying Examination he was accepted into Annadale Grammar School. There he participated in most school activities and was, in time, a member of both the 1st XV rugby and 1st XI cricket teams.

After Junior Certificate he left school, his first job in a varied career being in the purchasing office of the Belfast Corporation Transport Department. Simultaneously he attended further education classes at Belfast College of Technology, completing a course with the British Institute of Management and obtaining a certificate in Personnel Management.

During Billy's move to Leeds United, he married childhood sweetheart June and they had two children, Julie and Martin. The couple now have five grandchildren – Victoria, Charlotte, Gavin, Robbie and little Lucy.

After returning from a professional career in English football, Billy joined Black & Co. (Blaxnit socks) as a personnel officer and enjoyed eight happy years there. After the company went into liquidation and was taken over by Berkshire International he was offered and accepted the position of manager of their wages department.

A year further on, Billy purchased a newsagent/confectionery at Old Cross (junction of Greenwell Street and Castle Street) in Newtownards. He continued that successful and enjoyable occupation for another decade before selling the business.

He took up employment for the next nine years as a residential child care assistant at the Rathgael Training Centre, eventually retiring in 2000.

Billy and June now live in Bangor where he enjoys swimming and walking. He also meets up on a regular, albeit informal basis with old friends in Newtownards.

Billy Humphries when he played for Coventry City

I was maintaining my good form and thus feeling relaxed, confident and happy at my football home. I was gaining recognition with appearances against the Scottish League and the Football League at Ibrox Park and Windsor Park respectively. Some weeks later I was called into the Northern Ireland squad as a standby for Billy Bingham who was doubtful for the Home International game against England at Wembley. However, Billy reported fit and I sat on the bench watching the Irish get a satisfactory 1-1 draw.

At this stage Ards were competing strongly with Linfield at the top of the league and I was again selected for the Irish League against a semi-professional Italian side, which we won comfortably, 6-2. This was followed by a 3-1 victory over the League of Ireland.

One game which lingers long in the memories of players and fans alike took place in November 1962 at the Oval, witnessed by unbelieving supporters of both Ards and Glentoran. The game was only four minutes old when Ards went into the lead with a goal from Tommy Ewing, but this was quickly cancelled out when striker Trevor Thompson equalised for the Glens. It appeared from those early exchanges that this would be a closely contested game. Mick Lynch though had other ideas about the outcome. He was rampant all over the pitch, his robust style causing big problems for the Glentoran defence, and this allowed me to assist him with his resulting goal spree. Adding to our early first goal, Mick finished with a personal total of five goals and I helped myself to three more. Glentoran ended the game in total disarray, suffering a record 9-1 defeat. The *Ireland's Saturday Night* sports page carried the headline 'Glens take a Lynching from Ards'.

During the latter part of the 1961-62 season my form was apparently attracting attention from English League clubs. I was not aware of this information and a move back to English football was not a priority for me. It all came out into the open when I was approached by Coventry City manager Jimmy Hill with an offer to join the Midlands club, then in the Third Division. The meeting was short and sweet as I told him I was not interested in leaving

Ards. JH accepted my reasons and life for me continued as normal.

At the beginning of April I made my Northern Ireland international debut against Wales – gaining the first of 14 caps. The match had been scheduled for Swansea but due to a smallpox epidemic in the area it was transferred to Ninian Park, Cardiff. It was a proud moment for myself and would have great significance on my future career. My form that evening was good enough for Jimmy Hill, accompanied by his chairman Derrick Robins, to seek a further meeting in a Cardiff hotel, which lasted into the early hours of the morning. The outcome was my acceptance of an invitation to visit Coventry over the approaching Easter weekend.

My wife June and I enjoyed a marvellous few days in Coventry, entertained by JH and his wife Heather. The weather was fabulous and we enjoyed the sights of Leamington Spa, Warwick and Stratford-Upon-Avon before attending the Coventry v. Bristol City game. Our transport to the game was via the chairman's Rolls Royce! After such lavish treatment it was difficult to say 'no' to joining the club. We travelled home on the Monday and I turned out for my last game for Ards against Linfield the following evening. We lost and our chance of league success evaporated. Two thrilling seasons had gone without any trophies.

Any misgivings I might have had about moving back to English football were quickly dispelled. It was a move I never regretted and one which represented a huge extension of my soccer education. Thanks to Jimmy Hill's management skills, it proved the greatest period in the long history of Coventry City and I was privileged to play my part. During the 1962-63 season I was named 'Midlands Player of the Year', we reached the quarter-finals of the FA Cup, only to lose to eventual winners Manchester United, and we narrowly missed promotion to the Second Division. That was rectified the following season when we became Third Division champions. Coventry were well on the way to gaining promotion to the First Division when I left to join Swansea Town. It was while playing for that

The Ards FC team with the Irish Cup in May 1969. Back (from left): Eastham, Bell, Nixon, Crothers, Kydd, Stewart, Johnston, Shields. Front: Cochrane, Sands, Humphries, McAvoy and McCoy.

club during the 1965-66 season that I won a Welsh Cup medal and I also had the honour the following year of playing in the UEFA Cup Winners' Cup.

When I bade farewell to Ards back in 1962 I had promised then chairman Harold Black that if or when I came back to Ireland I would happily return to Ards if they so desired my services. In 1968 I did indeed return, signing for a third spell with the club.

George Eastham was back as manager and after his previous success, when Ards won the Gold Cup and League Championship, expectation for future success was rejuvenated. There was a good nucleus of experienced players with the potential to win trophies. Billy Nixon, Sammy Kydd, Billy McAvoy, George Crothers, Don Johnston and Ray Mowat had already given great service to the club.

While the early season proved uneventful the team was starting to blend. Our performances became more and more encouraging and the signs were clear that Ards were once again emerging as a major force. The first round Irish Cup tie away to Portadown was in doubt due to a snow-covered pitch but on a wintry day in February we ran out 1-0 winners. In the second round we had a home tie against Crusaders and once again gained a convincing 4-1 result in our favour. The semi-final against Coleraine represented a more difficult hurdle but our resolution remained steadfast and a 1-0 win put us into the final.

Billy Humphries when he was personnel officer with Blaxnit in Newtownards

There was an air of excitement around the town and district on Cup Final day, with all roads leading to Windsor Park. On a bright, blustery Saturday in mid-April the big game against Distillery failed to live up to expectations, ending in a 0-0 stalemate. This was mainly due to those windy conditions and the bone-hard uneven state of the playing surface.

However, the following Wednesday, 23 April 1969, proved a red letter day for Ards. A thrilling encounter watched by 15,000 spectators went to extra-time before the game was settled. While fortunes had ebbed and flowed for both sides, Billy McAvoy became the hero for Ards after he scored four goals on our way to a famous 4-2 victory. The team returned to Newtownards with the cup and this led to more celebrations into the wee small hours.

A week later the team travelled by aeroplane to Limerick for a first round tie in the Blaxnit All Ireland Cup but we lost a close game 2-1. Regardless of that result, an Irish Cup victory parade around Newtownards was organised and was well received, ending in the town square where a large crowd had gathered to salute our players. Ards were back on the soccer map after a long absence.

The final months of 1969 heralded the European Cup Winners' Cup draw and our participation in the tournament. Our opponents turned out to be the famous Italian side AS Roma. Unfortunately, due to the Troubles in Northern Ireland and the resulting security situation, the game was played at the Oval and attracted a much reduced attendance of 3,000. It was an evenly fought encounter, with Ards perhaps unlucky not to secure a victory, the game finishing in a 0-0 draw. The return fixture at the Olympic Stadium in Rome, before a crowd of 19,000, ended in a 3-1 defeat for us. It was a great experience for the players who gave a battling performance and emerged with great credit.

Sometime later in the season Ards terminated George Eastham's contract and I was offered the player/ manager position. After a few weeks' deliberation I accepted the club's offer. Before the season ended we appeared in another

Billy Humphries today

final, with the County Antrim Shield in our sights. Along the way we defeated Linfield 3-1 at Windsor Park, joining old rivals Bangor in the decider. The final was played at Solitude and turned into something of a marathon. The teams could not be separated after three games and it took a fourth to break the deadlock, with Bangor recording a 3-2 victory.

My first final as a manager had ended in disappointment but as it turned out further exciting times lay ahead for Ards. I could mention 1974 when I had the honour of guiding Ards to a four-trophy season, winning the Ulster and Gold Cups, the Irish Cup and the All Ireland Blaxnit Cup, but that, as they say, is another story for another day.

1968

in the Chronicle

The Very Rev. Leo McKeown, Parish Priest of Newtownards, reached his golden jubilee in the priesthood at the beginning of January. The committee of the St Vincent de Paul Society in Newtownards invited senior members of the parish – which included Comber and Donaghadee – to a dinner and social evening in the school hall at Ann Street. Fr McKeown had been in Newtownards since 1949.

Ards Borough Council approved tenders in early January for the construction of the town's new swimming pool at William Street. The green light was subsequently given by the Ministry of Education and it was hoped work on the £225,000 facility – comprising a main pool and learner pool – would begin in early Spring and be completed within two years.

The Rev. James S. Woods was installed as minister of Portaferry Presbyterian Church on 4 January – he was only the 12th to be appointed to the position since 1642 (the first was the Rev. John Drysdale and the most recent was the Rev. James Lorimer, who had served from 1939).

to Let on Lease

THE RITZ CINEMA

FRANCES STREET

NEWTOWNARDS

Occupying a first-class position, the site has a frontage 55 ft. 6 ins., with a return frontage to Meetinghouse Lane 125 ft. Total area of building 7,500 sq. ft. or thereabout.

The Cinema business has now been transferred to the Rege Cinema, and the Premises are available forthwith. User will restricted as far as Entertainment generally is concerned.

Inspection by arrangement with the Agents.

OK&M Osborne King & Megran

AUCTIONEERS & ESTATE AGENTS

14 MONTGOMERY STREET, BELFAST, 1. Telephone 202

18 CASTLE STREET, LISBURN. Telephone 3782.

The Ritz Cinema was placed on the market in mid-January, providing a 7,500 sq.ft. building for sale or lease in a prominent site. Planning permission was subsequently granted for a change of use to a furniture salesroom.

Donaghadee native William Gilliland was appointed general secretary of the Ulster Farmers' Union, having previously been employed by the Ministry of Agriculture. He had seen active service during the Second World War as a bomber pilot. He was shot down over Italy in January 1944 and remained a prisoner-of-war until the end of hostilities.

The cover price of the *Newtownards Chronicle* rose from 6d to 8d on 7 March; blame for the increase was placed on spiralling production costs.

It was announced in late February that the new ferry service between Portaferry and Strangford was expected to begin operations in the summer of 1969. Stormont MPs were advised that because of the tides in Strangford Lough it was necessary to have a ferry specially constructed (no suitable vessel being readily available).

It was announced that 40 men employed in the tool room of the Hawlmark factory of Short Brothers and Harland at Crawfordsburn Road, Newtownards, would be made redundant at the end of April, with more possibly to follow. The news came as a shock as the factory had been particularly busy thanks to production work on a number of aircraft, including Shorts' own Skyvan.

The assassination of Dr Martin Luther King had an impact as far away as Newtownards. The town's soccer team had hoped to undertake a short USA tour during the summer but in the aftermath of Dr King's murder many baseball games were postponed and then re-scheduled, having a knock-on effect on soccer. As a result it proved impossible to provide a tour schedule to suit the dates when Ards FC would have been available.

Twenty-year-old Valerie Lemon, from Ballywalter, was chosen as the new County Down Dairy Princess at a Young Farmers' Club dance in Rathfriland on 8 May. She went on to win the title of Ulster Dairy Queen in late June. The following year saw her being crowned a Holiday Princess at Butlin's in Ayr.

The Ards Tourist Development Association expressed an interest in identifying a suitable Ards Peninsula berth for the gun-running ship *Mountjoy II* – also known

as the *Clyde Valley* – which had played an important role in the anti-Home Rule campaign.
Built in Belfast in 1886, the vessel beat a British blockade in April 1914 and landed a 300-ton cargo of guns and ammunition at Larne after trying unsuccessfully to unload in the Bangor-Ballywalter area.
The *Clyde Valley* had been trading along the Canadian coast during the late 1960s; it was hoped to sail her from her berth in Nova Scotia to Northern Ireland that July.

Millisle County Primary School's £36,000 extension was officially opened on 16 May by Education Minister William Long. It helped the school to cope with an enrolment totalling some 200 pupils.

Newtownards' new health centre, only the fourth of its kind in Northern Ireland, opened its doors on 5 June. All the town's medical practitioners were now under the one roof and patients could only see their own doctors by making an appointment. Head of administration was Miss Norma Lewis.

The Small Faces were named as the headline act in mid-June for the second 'Dusk to Dawn' festival at Castlereagh Park on 28 June. Support bands were The Mystics, The Cousins, Crying Soul, and Sam Mahood and The Soul Foundation. Promoter Trevor Kane, while describing it as "very successful", doubted if there would be a third one in 1969.
During the performance by the Small Faces a concrete wall in front of the stage – deemed suitable as a crush barrier – collapsed, with several young women sustaining slight injuries. In addition, a number of people tried to climb over the fences to gain free admission despite the presence of 150 stewards.
The attendance was slightly lower, explained Mr Kane, partly because the first one had a certain "novelty value" and also because it had been necessary to increase the entrance charge to 15/- "to come out on the right side, which I think we did."

A section of the crowd at the Small Faces concert held in Castlereagh Park on 28 June 1968. *187-23-2*

Mr Kane said he favoured the King's Hall, with its 12,000 capacity, as the likeliest

venue for a future pop festival. The previous year's headline act, The Tremeloes, appeared at the New Locarno, Portaferry, on 12 July. The Herd appeared at the same venue on 2 August.

A new £45,000 oratory in the centre of Portaferry was blessed and dedicated to St Cooey on 29 June by the Bishop of Down and Connor, the Most Rev. Dr. William Philbin, who later presided at Solemn High Mass.

James Gray retired in early July after a career in Walker's Mill that had spanned almost 50 years, including 14 years as manager. Aged 16, he had commenced work for the company in the winding and warping department.

Prince Philip paid a short and largely private visit to the Ards area on 16 July. The single public function he undertook was to officially open a new car park and nature hide at Island Reagh. As patron of the World Wildlife Fund, the main purpose of his visit was to view the National Trust's Strangford Lough wildlife scheme.

Irish firm Verolme Cork Dockyard Ltd. was awarded the £100,000-plus contract in late July to build a roll-on roll-off ferry for Down County Council to operate between Portaferry and Strangford. The ferry would hold 150 passengers as well as cars and other vehicles.

Work began in early August on the construction of a new tufted carpet factory on the Comber Road, Newtownards, for Northern Ireland Carpets Ltd. It was hoped production would begin by November.

Education Minister William Long officially opened a new sports pavilion at Cloughey in mid-August. Provided by East Down Rural District Council, its chairman, William McCutcheon, said it was their aim to provide a similar football pitch in every village under the authority's control.

It was announced that 70 new houses would be built on a site between Greyabbey Road and Well Road in Ballywalter – widely recognised as one of the most popular seaside destinations in the Ards Peninsula area.

Ards Borough Council and local businesses were united in their opposition to the new two-tier postal service, introduced in September, with stamp prices of 4d and 5d (the latter being for the 'express' service).
A spokesman for the Ulster Print Works in Newtownards described the 5d stamp as "blackmail", while Cllr Stanley Woods said he could see no reason why the local authority needed to use the more expensive stamps when sending out its circulars.

Newtownards residents were preparing for the installation of the town's first traffic lights – at the junction of Regent Street, Church Street, Frederick Street and William Street. There was still, however, no sign of the town's one-way traffic system being implemented.

Little Petrel, a former lightship with Irish Lights, was towed into Strangford Lough on 14 September to become the floating headquarters of the Down Cruising Club at Ballydorn Bay before the end of the year.

Newtownards Chamber of Trade agreed to consider earlier closing times on Mondays, Tuesdays and Wednesdays – the suggestion was 5.30pm – to allow staff from country areas to catch the most convenient bus services when heading for home.

North Down MP George Currie, following a visit to the Finnish town of Kemi in October, suggested it would be an ideal "twin" for Newtownards because there were numerous similarities between the two places. It was agreed that in the first instance Newtownards Borough Council should write to its Kemi counterpart.

Mr G. R. Lyttle, principal of Movilla Secondary Intermediate School, retired at the end of October, having been a member of the original staff when the school opened in 1932 and headmaster since 1945. He was a grandson of noted author W. G. Lyttle (*Betsy Gray, Smugglers of Strangford Lough, Sons of the Sod,* etc.).

The Ministry of Health and Social Services invited the public to purchase pre-payment 'season tickets' for their National Health prescription charges – £1-10-0d for six months and £2-15-0d for a year.

An agreement was reached in mid-November for the sale – at an undisclosed sum – of Berkshire International to the American firm Vanity Fair Mills Inc., of Reading, Pennsylvania.
Berkshire, with its factory in Newtownards, was already in American ownership and it was not expected the sale would involve any changes in management or personnel.

The Ministry of Development advised North Down Rural Council that work on the proposed extension of the dual carriageway from Quarry Corner (Dundonald) to Newtownards would begin in 1969.

On 2 December members of Donaghadee Urban District Council adopted, by five votes to one, a report recommending the fluoridation of the local water supply be permitted – so long as an indemnity was provided by the Ministry of Development.

Plans for a hotel complex at Regent Street, Newtownards, on the site of the former Londonderry School, were approved in principle by the Borough Council in early December.

During a week of political turmoil in Northern Ireland, Prime Minister Terence O'Neill sacked Minister of Home Affairs Bill Craig on 10 December and appointed Ards MP William Long to replace him on an interim basis, while retaining his position as Education Minister. Following a Cabinet reshuffle a week later the appointment was confirmed but Capt. Long relinquished the Education post.

Greyabbey boy Ivan McKeown took part in the 16 December edition of the popular *Teatime With Tommy* programme on Ulster Television.

The Oceanic ladies' darts team beat the men of Oceanic 6-4 in a friendly match in mid-January 1968. Back (includes from left): Mrs M. McDowell, Mrs R. Carr, Mrs M. Lindsay, Mrs M. McCullough, Mrs B. McMasters, Miss G. Robinson. Front: Mrs E. Robinson, Mrs E. Ward, Mrs J. Lightbody (captain), Mrs E. Walker and Mrs M. Lyttle.
177-68-3

Youngsters from Newtownards and district enjoyed themselves at the Berkshire factory's children's party, which was organised by the Workers' Welfare Committee and held in the Queen's Hall in January 1968.
177-58-1

Mr and Mrs James Beggs, of Ballyfrench, Ballyhalbert, travelled to the Crawfordsburn Inn on 18 January 1968 to celebrate their golden wedding anniversary. Included are (back, from left): William Beggs, Hugh Beggs, Essie Halfacre, Sally Young, John Beggs, Samuel Beggs. Front: Mrs Barron, Mr and Mrs Beggs, and Mrs Bailey. The couple had eight children and 15 grandchildren.
177-86-2

The 74th Killinchy Girls' Brigade PT team won first place in the Associate PT competitions, which were held in Ballynahinch at the end of January 1968. Back (from left): L. Montgomery, L. Lowry, S. Jellie, E. Ritchie, M. Gibson, A. Morrison. Front: T. Lowry, J. Turley J. McKnight (captain) and Lynn Dally.
178-25-2

Six-year-old Thomas Curran, of The Rock, Portaferry, received a pleasant surprise on 9 February 1968 when he learned he had won £50 on the Premium Bonds, courtesy of his £2 holding. He shows the cheque to his brother John.
179-37-2

Children from the Newtownards Salvation Army Corps who attended the annual Sunday School party in February 1968. Included are Captain J. Dangerfield (seated, left), who presented the prizes, and Cadet Orderly R. Thomlinson, along with officers Lieutenant and Mrs Dodds and Sunday School teachers.
178-45-1

The Explorers team attached to Second Comber Girls' Brigade won the Area Cup in the Strangford and Mourne area PE competitions, which were held in February 1968. Included with Miss Joan Coey (left) and Mrs I. Harris are (from left): A. Dobson, S. Cooke, A. Cooke, J. Harris, P. Brown, H. Blackstock, E. Wilson and S. Dugan. *179-9-2*

The large number of boys and girls who attended the Sunday School social event at Carrowdore Presbyterian Church in the middle of February 1968. *178-100-1*

Second Comber Guild Players performed *Cat On The Fiddle*, a comedy by John Dole, in the church hall in February 1968. Back (from left); Susan Smyth, Erskine Willis, Bertie Harris, William McLaughlin, Lorraine Bailie, Adrian Thompson, Eileen Gibb. Front: Jean Pinkney, Desmond McCullough, Lynda Magill and John Smith. *179-46-2*

Mr and Mrs William McDonald, of 3 Windmill Row, Newtownards, celebrated their golden wedding anniversary on 1 March 1968. They were married by the Rev. Whatham in St Mark's Parish Church, Newtownards, and had a family of eight, as well as 22 grandchildren and two great grandchildren.
180-40-2

Members of 195th Girls' Brigade NI, attached to Carrowdore Presbyterian Church, were presented with their Duke of Edinburgh Gold Awards by Prince Philip in early March 1968. From left: Sandra Brown, Edna Garrett, Denise Wilson and Beryl Lavery.
180-76-1

Some of the children and parents who attended a children's party that marked the closure of Killaughey School, Millisle, in late March 1968.
181-43-1

Mrs J. Platt (right), wife of the chairman of the First Newtownards Presbyterian Church Indoor Bowling Club, presents ladies singles winner Kay Sloane with the Elsie Orr Cup in April 1968. Included is club secretary Ken Sloane.
182-39-2

Members of the newly-formed Millisle Junior LOL No. 193 took part in their first parade when they attended the junior demonstration in Newtownards on Easter Tuesday (16 April) 1968. Included (back, right) is Mr George Phillips (superintendent).
182-99-2

Five members of First Comber Boys' Brigade received their Queen's Badges at the Company's annual inspection and display in April 1968. Their mothers are (from left): Mrs R. L. Barker, Mrs W. Campbell, Mrs R. Crosby, Mrs R. McVeigh and Mrs J. Magowan. The boys are (from left): L/C W. Barker, L/C W. Campbell, L/C G. Crosby, L/C D. McVeigh and L/C C. Magowan.
182-60-2

Brownies of St. Mary's Parish Church, Comber, in the church hall before their annual display in April 1968. *183-52-1*

Mr and Mrs R. Wilson are pictured at a function to mark their retirement as principal and assistant at Kirkistown Primary School in June 1968. Included is past pupil Mr R. McMurray, who presented a stereogram to the popular couple. *187-19-1*

Mayor Norman G. Francis, accompanied by Divisional Officer G. Morrison, inspects firemen prior to a fire-fighting display in Conway Square – part of the town's Civic Week programme at the end of June 1968. *186-84-3*

Savings group secretary Mr R. Wilson (left) is pictured with pupils of Portaferry Primary School after he received his 10-year service badge in June 1968. The pupils are holding a certificate marking 25 years of saving at the school. Included is principal Mr D. Vaughan.
187-7-2

Pupils of Ballystockart Primary School took part in a fancy dress parade as part of the school sports day in June 1968.
186-65-1

Residents of Thomas Street in Newtownards with a backdrop of the bunting erected for the Twelfth celebrations in July 1968.
187-53-1

Members of Comber Old Standard LOL No. 567 with their new banner which was unfurled by Mr Jack Scott (centre) on the morning of the Twelfth demonstration in Downpatrick on 12 July 1968.
188-5-3

Members and juniors of First Carrowdore Boys' Brigade who attended a service in late September 1968 for the dedication of their colours.
192-21-1

Eighteen-year-old Joan Hamilton, from South Green, Newtownards, with the Duke of Edinburgh Gold Award certificate she received from Prince Philip at Buckingham Palace in October 1968.
192-42-3

Mr and Mrs John Doggart, of North Street, Newtownards, celebrated their golden wedding anniversary in October 1968. They were married by the Rev. L. V. Upritchard in St. Mary's Parish Church on 30 October 1918.
194-11-3

Young members of Peter Tomelty's dancing class from Portaferry took part in a concert in October 1968 to raise money for the St Cooey's Organ Fund.
194-12-2

Older members of Peter Tomelty's dancing class took part in a concert in October 1968 to raise money for the St Cooey's Organ Fund.
194-13-1

These six members of Sixth Newtownards Sea Scouts were the first from the district to go forward as a Troop for the coveted Life Saving Award in November 1968. Back (from left): Roy Savage, Maurice Boyle, David Mills. Front: Terry Crockard, Alan Wallace and Gary Mills. *195-9-1*

Prizewinners and officials at Donaghadee Racing Pigeon Club's annual dinner in November 1968. *194-78-1*

Members of the James Carroll Memorial Junior Accordion Band who, on only their second attempt, won the NIBA Senior Accordion Championship at the Ulster Hall in November 1968. Conductor Mr J. Filson is seated (centre). *195-76-2*

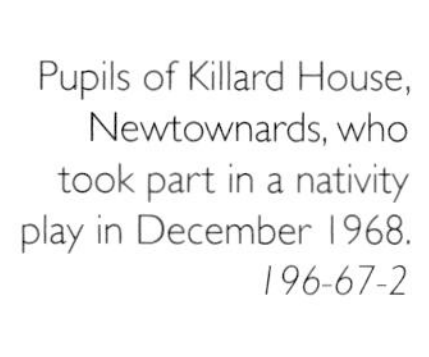

Pupils of Killard House, Newtownards, who took part in a nativity play in December 1968.
196-67-2

Children from Newtownards Nursery School at their Christmas party in December 1968.
196-74-2

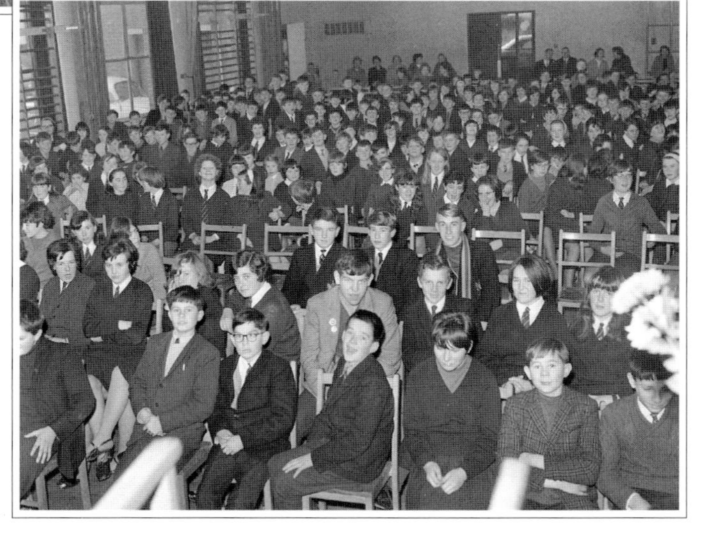

Pupils of St Columba's Secondary School, Portaferry, at their annual prize distribution in December 1968.
197-39-3

Sport in 1968

in the Chronicle

Following an extraordinary meeting of members of Ards FC it was confirmed that the club would be registered as a limited company with supporters, as well as the general public, being encouraged to buy shares.

Denis Campbell and Grant Foster, both 15 and both in their final year at Movilla Secondary School, became the first soccer players from the school to be selected to represent Northern Ireland. Outside-right Grant and centre-forward Denis played against the Republic of Ireland in a schoolboys international on 9 February. Northern Ireland won the annual encounter 4-0, with Campbell scoring twice and Foster once.

The Movilla Secondary School U-16 team became County netball champions in late February after defeating their Rathfriland counterparts by 19-13. This victory took them to the Northern Ireland quarter-finals, where they defeated Girls Model by 12-10.

Ards player Billy McAvoy was presented with a watch by the club's directors in recognition of the under-23 international cap he received for playing for Northern Ireland against Wales on 13 March. He was the first Ards player to attain this level.

Donaghadee Rugby Club successfully completed negotiations in late April for a six-acre field at Hoggstown for their new ground. Speaking at the annual general meeting, chairman Mr J. Donaldson, in justifying the decision to move, said it was a major achievement for a club in a small town with no 'grammar school feed' to sustain four teams.

North End Ards Supporters Club president Hastings Maguinness hit out at changes to the substitution rule during the 1967/68 season which allowed players to be replaced for tactical reasons rather than because of injuries. Speaking at the annual meeting in early May, Mr Maguinness said it was not good for player moral or for the game itself.
A player, he said, was left under the shadow of worry during a game as to whether or not he was going to be taken off at any time. He felt each player should be on the field for the full 90 minutes.

1st Comber Cub Scouts won the Fellowship Shield in soccer following a thrilling encounter with their 1st Donaghadee counterparts at the end of June. Despite being two goals down at half-time, 1st Comber stormed back to win 5-2.

Donaghadee man Fergus McConkey won the Bangor open bowls tournament at Ward Park on 13 July, defeating Tom O'Neill from Shaftesbury by 21-13.

Billy Humphries rejoined Ards FC at the beginning of the 1968/69 season – it was his third spell with the club. Pre-season friendlies against Sheffield Wednesday and Portsmouth ended with a 2-1 defeat and a 2-2 draw respectively. In the latter the Ards side was augmented by England international George Eastham (son of the Ards manager), who was captain for the occasion.

Humphries to join Ards

THE Irish international right winger Billy Humphries has given his promise to Ards that he will sign for them when his contract with Swansea Town expires next month.
Humphries will thus be having his third spell with Ards having in the first instance been transferred to Leeds United. He returned to Castlereagh Park and was then transferred to Coventry City in 1962. Three years later he moved from Coventry to Swansea who are now giving him his release. He is a qualified F.A. coach.

The Down Minor Hurling team – the majority of whose players hailed from the Ards Peninsula – were crowned All Ireland champions for the third time in five years, following a 6-5 to 5-3 win over Kildare on 8 September.

The Down Camogie team, with a sprinkling of Ballygalget and Ballycran players in its ranks, were the first winners of the All Ireland Junior Camogie final, defeating Cork by 2-3 to 1-1 in Dublin.

Ards RFC reached the semi-final of the Towns Cup on 30 November after notching up their biggest score ever – they defeated Strabane by 53-11. Derrick Nash contributed 26 points through penalties and conversions. Three weeks later they were in the Easter Monday 1969 final against Bangor after beating Omagh 8-6. The semi-final win was the team's 16th consecutive win in all competitions.

Regent House 1st XV were defeated by Belfast Royal Academy in the semi-final of the Schools Cup in early March 1968.
180-31-1

Charlie Henderson is presented with a wrist watch by president Norman Boal on behalf of the members of Ards Cycling Club as a token of gratitude for the work he had done for cycling over the previous three decades. Included are Mrs Henderson, who presented the prizes, Mr M. Agnew, treasurer, Mr I. Bell, secretary, and Mr J. Murray, chairman.
181-94-1

Despite playing all their games away from home the Celtic Supporters' Schoolboys team in Portaferry were still undefeated in the Ards Schoolboy League when this picture was taken in early July 1968. Back (from left): N. McMullan, T. Tweedie, P. Convery, L. Adler, R. McManus, B. Ellison, H. Conlon, E. Kelly, L. McMullan. Front: T. Savage, W. McNally, M. McMullan, J. Convery, M. Monan, P. Smyth and J. Curran.
187-41-2

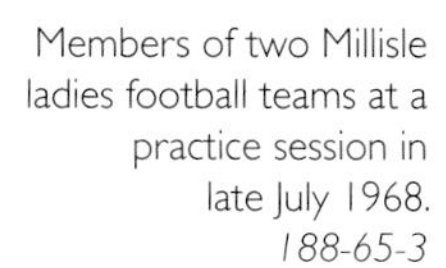

Members of two Millisle ladies football teams at a practice session in late July 1968.
188-65-3

Ballygalget won the County Down Senior Camogie Championship in August 1968, their success coming after they defeated Ballycran in a replay. Back (from left): Anita Hinds, Bernie Braniff, Margaret Dynes, Eileen Coulter, Ann McGrattan, Mary Hughes, Eilish McAvera. Front: Bronagh McGrattan, Marie Denvir, Nuala McKenna, Rita Braniff, Christina Morgan, Geraldine McKenna and Jean Kelly.
189-26-3

Owing to poor tidal and weather conditions a challenge swim to the Copeland Islands was cancelled in August 1968. However, participants entered the water at Donaghadee Harbour and took part in a two-and-a-half mile swim within the harbour itself. The eventual winner was Billy Hanna in a time of approx. 1 hour and 10 minutes. The swim was organised by the Beaver Amateur Swimming Club in conjunction with the Town Council.
190-66-2

The Newton Olympic team with the Dan Ward Cup which they won in August 1968 after defeating Tower United 4-1 in Donaghadee. Back (from left): R. Houston, K. Neill, D. Rose, M. Brown, J. Foy, J. Vance. Front: B. Smyth, J. Davidson, J. Niblock, J. Stannex and B. Moffett.
189-70-1

Glenford Rangers FC, winners of the Newtownards Boys' League, met the Celtic Supporters team from Portaferry in a challenge match at the end of September 1968. The result was a 5-5 draw.
192-18-3

The Portaferry Celtic Supporters Schoolboys team from Portaferry with the trophies gained during the 1967-68 season.
192-19-1

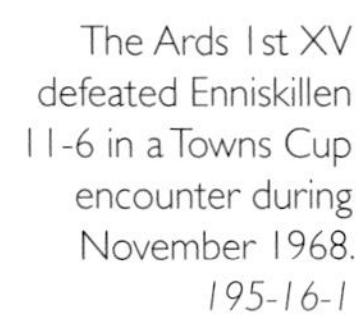

The Ards 1st XV defeated Enniskillen 11-6 in a Towns Cup encounter during November 1968.
195-16-1

Mrs Francis, wife of the Mayor, presents the Junior Qualifying League Section B Cup to Walter Montgomery, captain of the Ards 1st XI cricket team, at the annual dinner and prize distribution, which was held at the end of November 1968 in the West Winds Roadhouse. Included are Mayor Norman G. Francis, club chairman Carl Anderson and secretary Mr E. McAuley.
195-66-2

Dave Crockard in December 1968 with the various cups and trophies he had secured over the previous four years as a motorcycle scrambler.
196-14-3

1969

in the Chronicle

Donaghadee Urban District Council revealed in early January that its ambitious redevelopment plans for Lemon's Wharf, to give that part of the Parade a much-needed facelift, would get under way as quickly as possible. The aim was to create an open-air enclosure suitable for all age groups.

Debts totalling £7.2m were mentioned during an application in the Ulster High Court in mid-January for the winding-up of Cyril Lord Ltd., Cyril Lord Carpets Ltd., and Cyril Lord Carpet Sales. The businesses were "totally insolvent" and a liquidator had been appointed, the court was told.

Jim McCallen, a supervisor at the Glen Laundry in Newtownards, in his spare time wrote plays about life in present-day Ireland, gaining himself something of a reputation in local literary circles. His first play, *The Flight Of The Swallow,* was broadcast nationally on BBC radio in 1968 and in early 1969 he followed this up with *Bottle Up The Wind* on Radio Eireann.

Sittings of Greyabbey Petty Sessions Court moved to the Village Hall in late January, having been held in the Parish Hall for 106 years.

Prime Minister Terence O'Neill was greeted by a jeering crowd of supporters of the

Rev. Ian Paisley when he visited Newtownards on 28 January to address a meeting of the Ards Young Unionist Association. It was his first public speech – and the first ever by a serving Premier to the Ards body – since the resignation of two of his ministers, Brian Faulkner (Commerce) and William Morgan (Health and Social Services).

By the following week O'Neill had called a General Election, with voting taking place on 24 February. Ards MP William Long was returned to Stormont unopposed and was appointed Minister of Development.

Donaghadee Councillor John Scott proposed that the site of the former Baths Hotel at The Parade should be the location for a new town swimming pool, given the existing outdoor pool had been in continuous use for 45 years. The site he suggested was much closer to the centre of the town and therefore would be "most advantageous to townspeople as well as visitors." At the end of October the Council decided to proceed with the purchase of the hotel site and to draw up draft plans for its future use.

A preliminary layout plan to convert the former Ritz Cinema premises at 13A Frances Street into a shopping arcade was approved by the Borough Council at the beginning of March. It opened in late October as Wright's Arcade, billed as 'unique in North Down'.

It was announced that the multiple award-winning Dickson's of Hawlmark – particularly renowned for rose breeding – would be moving its nursery from the 21-acre site it had occupied on the edge of Newtownards for more than 100 years to a new location a mile outside the town. The former site was sold for £90,000 and, in time, became the Ards Shopping Centre.

The company had already moved its plants, seeds and florist business, previously carried out in Belfast, to a 55-acre garden centre at Clandeboye. It was officially opened on 17 March by Franklin Engelmann of the BBC's *Gardeners' Question Time.*

Broadcasting personality Franklin Engelmann talks to Mrs Jean O'Neill, wife of Prime Minister Captain Terence O'Neill, at the official opening of Dickson's new garden centre at Clandeboye in March 1969. Looking on are Alexander Dickson and Mrs Engelmann. *201-19-3*

The golden jubilee of the Donaghadee branch of the Ulster Farmers' Union was marked by a dinner in the New Mount Royal Hotel at the end of March. Special guests included Prime Minister Terence O'Neill, Development Minister William Long and UFU president Mr J. Jordan.

Meeting on 9 April, members of Newtownards Borough Council decided not to introduce fluoride into the local water supply but to keep the matter under consideration. In early October they agreed to delay taking any decision for a further six months.

Pupils of Londonderry Primary School in Newtownards are pictured outside the old building in Regent Street on their last day, in April 1969, before moving to the new school on the Glen Estate. Included are Mr E. Dickson, principal, Mr A. McGilton, vice-principal, and staff members Mrs Duff, Mrs McClements, Miss Scroggie and Mrs Morrow. *202-39-1*

Londonderry Primary School, with almost 160 years of history to its name, moved from Regent Street to a new 15-class building in the Glen Estate on 14 April. The former school building was bought by Scrabo Investments Ltd. for development as a hotel complex.

Rumours that Ballycullen Reservoir outside Newtownards had been targeted by bombers on 25 April were quickly dispelled after it became clear that debris from a meteorite had hit the area. Many people all over Ireland reported seeing a fireball streaking across the night sky and a 16lb fragment was found by a Co. Derry farmer.

New Prime Minister Major James Chichester-Clark appointed Capt. William Long as his new Minister of Education at the beginning of May.

The retiring principal of Glastry Secondary School, Mr T. G. H. Pollock, is pictured with the colour television set presented to him in June 1969 by pupils, staff and friends on the occasion of his retirement. Included are head boy David Wilson, Miss J. McCarthy, who made the presentation, Mrs Pollock, head girl Margaret Watts and incoming principal Mr Eddie Beckett. *207-84-2*

Breadserver Jim Balmer, from Bangor Road, Newtownards, retired in early May after covering a 115-mile route, which included Dundonald, Comber and the Ards Peninsula, for almost 50 years. When he began working for Inglis Bakeries at the age of 14 deliveries were still being made using horse-drawn breadcarts. For Jim the switch to motor vehicles arrived in 1935.

A £32,000 extension to Portavogie Primary School, permitting it to cater for between 130 and 164 pupils, was opened on 16 June by the Education Minister. The scheme also included a kitchen providing 100 school meals a day.

Ards Mayor Norman Francis sent a message of congratulations and good wishes to Prince Charles on the day of his investiture as Prince of Wales on 1 July.

A delegation from Newtownards, including Mayor Norman Francis and Town Clerk Wyndham Scott, visited twin town Kemi in Finland during early July for its centenary celebrations. A tree was planted in Meripuisto Park to commemorate the occasion.

A branch of the New Ulster Movement was formed in the Ards Constituency, with Cecil Hull, of Donaghadee, being elected as chairman.

Plans were approved for a £200,000 hotel with a total of 25 bedrooms and a function room to cater for 250 diners on the site of the former Londonderry School at Regent Street, Newtownards. Demolition work was scheduled for 2 August and it was estimated the hotel would be open for business by June 1970. A second phase envisaged a further 13 bedrooms.

Vigilantes were out on the streets of Millisle in mid-August, purportedly to prevent any damage by the influx of 'refugees' into the village following the loss of many homes in riot-torn Belfast. It was reported that some 200-300 people from Belfast were staying at caravan sites in and around Millisle.

Ards breadserver Tommy Ferris, who was in his mid-50s, retired after almost 27 years with Inglis and Co. to become a ticket collector with the new Strangford car ferry. Although born in Kirkistown, he had lived in Portaferry from the age of 12.

The £110,000 Strangford ferry arrived from Cork on 4 September and after assorted teething troubles went into operation on 15 October, plying the waters between Strangford and Portaferry and thereby saving drivers, and passengers, a road journey of 45 miles. On Sunday 19 October it carried 550 vehicles and 3,600 passengers throughout the day.

Newtownards Chamber of Trade, fearing the new shopping centre (set to open by 1973) would have a major negative impact on town centre businesses, called for the early implementation of the one-way traffic system as it would offer improved parking facilities and a smoother traffic flow.

During the visit by then Prime Minister Terence O'Neill to Newtownards at the beginning of the year several tomatoes were thrown in his direction by hecklers in Conway Square as he entered the Town Hall. One landed in a rose bed where it took root – and by late September it had yielded its first crop, a single tomato, which was left to ripen on a window ledge in the Town Hall.
On that occasion Capt. O'Neill had been attending a meeting of the Newtownards Young Unionists – on 29 September his successor, Major James Chichester-Clark, paid his first visit to the town to address the same group in the Queen's Hall. He told the audience: "The choice, to be absolutely blunt about it, is between absolutely fair and just government in Northern Ireland, or no Government at all. Unionists must recognise that as a reality."

Ballywalter Presbyterian Church held a special celebration evening on 25 September to mark the 25th anniversary of the ordination and installation of the Rev. S. J. McIlveen as their minister.

THE NEWTOWNARDS Chronicle AND COUNTY DOWN OBSERVER

96th Year Thursday, 17th July, 1969 Eightpence

Newtownards represented at centenary celebrations

MAYOR AND TOWN CLERK VISIT 'TWIN-TOWN'

V.I.P. treatment in Finland

A DELEGATION from Newtownards consisting of the Mayor (Councillor N. G. Francis) and the Town Clerk (Mr. Wyndham C. Scott) visited twin-town Kemi in Finland during the centenary celebrations held there from 29th June—6th July, and were the guests of the Kemi City Council.

Conlig luxury housing proposal turned down

The retiring Bishop of Down and Dromore, the Rt. Rev. Dr. Frederick Mitchell, visited Greyabbey on 2 October for a special service to mark the centenary of the Church of St. Saviour. The special speaker was the Rev. Robin Eames, Rector of Gilnahirk.

History was made in Second Newtownards Presbyterian Church on 5 October when a special service was held for the commissioning and appointment of Miss Freda Algie who was leaving to work as a Girls' Auxiliary missionary in Malawi.

A total of 117 members from the Newtownards District of the Ulster Special Constabulary resigned from the force on 13 October, but within a week were back on duty declaring it was "for the benefit of the security of the country." They had been given assurances regarding the future of members of the 'Specials' within the new auxiliary force being established to support the RUC under policing reforms announced in the wake of the Hunt Report.

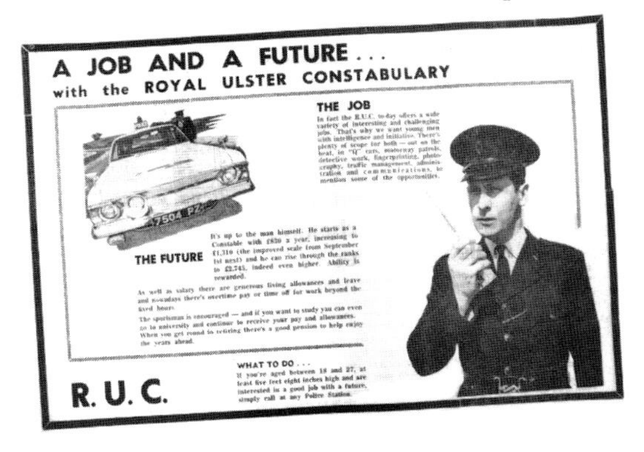

Second Newtownards Presbyterian Church choir member Harry Beale was the guest of honour at a dinner in the Dunallon Hotel in late October to mark his 50 years of unbroken service.

People from the Newtownards area contributed £930 to the Ulster Innocent Victims Appeal Fund, which was set up as a result of the civil unrest in various parts of Northern Ireland. It closed at the end of October, with the organisers expressing the view that it would not need to be extended into the New Year and beyond.

Royal Navy minesweeper *Kellington* was moored two miles off Portavogie in late October to combat the smuggling of guns and ammunition into Northern Ireland by sea.

Singer Ruby Murray, of *Softly Softly* fame, was among the artistes who performed at a concert on 14 November organised by Glastry Women's Guild.

The first phase of a postal delivery modernisation scheme for the Ards Peninsula was implemented on 10 November with the introduction of a central distribution point in Newtownards and, over time, van-only deliveries. The changes spelt an end to the country postman walking or cycling on his daily round. They also meant that country post offices would no longer date-stamp letters and parcels as that would all be done in Newtownards.

The official opening ceremony for the Strangford ferry service was performed on 24 November by Development Minister Brian Faulkner. Before the end of the year Down County Council sought Government approval for a second, bigger ferry, costing £140,000, because of the need to maintain the continuity of the service.

The new courthouse at Regent Street, Newtownards, erected on the site of the old building at a cost of £200,000, was used for the first time on 1 December at a sitting of the County Court, presided over by Judge James Brown QC. The Magistrate's Court had been held in the Town Hall while construction work was under way.

An influenza epidemic over Christmas resulted in both Ards and Bangor Hospitals admitting only emergency cases. One in 10 staff members at Ards Hospital was off sick.

In a Christmas message to the people of the Borough, Mayor Norman Francis stated: "The past year has been a troubled one for the Province as a whole and it is to be hoped the spirit of peace and goodwill, which is always so evident over the Christmas period, will endure after that season is past, bringing an end to strife and bitterness."

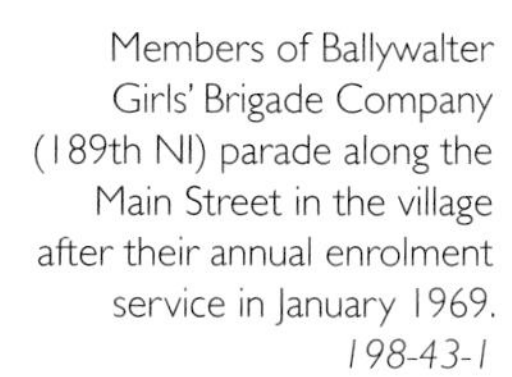

Members of Ballywalter Girls' Brigade Company (189th NI) parade along the Main Street in the village after their annual enrolment service in January 1969.
198-43-1

Members of Sixth Ards Sea Scouts with Irish Wolfhound mascot Shaun and the Admiralty Recognition Pennant which was presented to leader Jack Bell at their parents' night in late January 1969.
199-2-2

Comber Scouts who took part in a cycle rally from St. Mary's Parish Church in February 1969.
198-66-3

Mr Walter Jones (extreme right), president of the Newtownards branch of the Royal Air Forces Association, hands over a painting of two wartime Spitfire aircraft to the Mayor, Cllr Norman Francis, in February 1969, in recognition of the Borough Council's support for the organisation over the years. Included are (from left): Dr A. L. Agnew, Northern Ireland Area chairman, Mr H. D. Marson, branch treasurer, Mr D. M. Algie, branch secretary, Mr William McDonald, branch chairman, the Mayoress and Squadron Leader D. G. Adair (Area secretary). *190-59-1*

Miss Elizabeth Johnston, a missionary to India, shows her sari to members of Second Newtownards Girl Guide Company, who were dressed in Indian national costume for the Company's 'Indian Night' in February 1969. Included are the Rev. R. J. Chisholm (rector), the Rev. C. W. Bell, Mrs Chisholm, Miss Ase Winters Nyheim (visiting Norwegian Guider), the Rev. C. Ruddock and Company leader Mrs J. Dorrian. *200-7-1*

Members of Newtownards Gateway Club look on as Section Leader R. Allen hands over a cheque for £42 10s 0d, the proceeds of a fundraiser held at the local fire station, to treasurer Mrs J. McAlpine in early March 1969. Included are Leading Fireman Robert Bowden and Fireman Michael Dorrian. *200-24-1*

Ards Presbyterian Sunday School Union prizewinners received their awards from the Moderator, the Rev Dr. J. Withers (seated, front), at Shore Street Presbyterian Church, Donaghadee, in March 1969. Back (from left): the Rev. J. E. Glenfield, Lyn Robinson, Judith Farquharson, Margaret Reid, the Rev. D. Bailie, Margaret Wright, John McClean, David Robertson, the Rev. J. C. Buick. Front: June Allen, Janet Wallace, Valerie Thompson and Harold Robinson.
200-63-3

Newtownards sisters Ann and Barbara Murdoch hold the cups they won for character ballet at Bangor Music Festival in March 1969. Ann was awarded the Joan Davies Cup, while Barbara received the Viking Cup.
201-39-1

First Comber Presbyterian Church Robins before their annual inspection at the church hall in March 1969.
201-27-2

The beginners and primary departments of Second Newtownards Sunday School pictured with some of the mothers and teachers at their annual social event in the Palmer Memorial Hall in March 1969.
201-86-1

Carrowreagh Primary School's choir, along with principal Mr W. J. Lemon (right) and music teacher Mr J. Drennan, are pictured after winning the William McKnight Cup at Belfast Music Festival in April 1969, for the third year in a row. All the more remarkable was the fact the school had opened only four years earlier.
202-21-2

Eleven-year-old Maria Murphy, from Comber, holds the cup she won at Bangor Folk Dancing Festival in early April 1969 for being the most promising dancer. She was a pupil at the McCann School of Dancing in Newtownards.
201-96-2

Some of the members of the Scrabo Hall Every Boys Rally before their second annual display in April 1969.
203-15-3

Children and teachers of Donaghadee Parish Sunday School at their annual party in the Admiral Leslie Hall towards the end of April 1969.
203-40-1

Members of First Comber Cub Scout Pack (St Mary's Parish Church) at their parents' night in late April 1969.
203-23-1

Manchester United soccer star George Best signs autographs during a visit by the Northern Ireland team to the Blaxnit factory in Newtownards in May 1969.
204-58-2

Senior Section members of Carrowdore Presbyterian Church Girls' Brigade Company at their annual display in May 1969.
204-84-3

Five-year-old Amanda Reid, from Ballyrogan Road, Newtownards, won three medals at the Adele Sloan Ballet Festival in Belfast at the beginning of June 1969.
206-58-2

Some of the competitors in the Scrabo Secondary School sports day, held in June 1969, take advantage of a break to enjoy a short rest.
206-77-3

Conlig Orange Hall was about to disappear, in June 1969, to make way for a new housing development. Pictured in front of the building were three of the village's oldest residents: Billy Spiers (70), Mary Lightbody (72) and Andy McGimpsey (82). The hall's foundation stone was laid on Easter Monday 1884 by LOL 2008. Over the years it was used by a number of Lodges, including LOLs 695, 862 and 1056, as well as RBP 632.
206-76-2

Some pupils of Victoria Primary School, who left the school at the end of the summer term, in June 1969, relax on the grass during the school sports.
207-65-1

Scouts from the 11th Down (St Mary's Star of the Sea) Troop in Kircubbin, pictured after their investiture in July 1969. Included are Fr Jordan, Donaghadee, Scout leader Joseph Rotherham, and Fr McStravick, who conducted the investiture.
210-81-2

Comber girl Margaret Johnston (17), a student at Regent House School in Newtownards, finally met her Icelandic penpal of two-and-a-half years, Gudrun Ingibjorg (Inga) Snorradottir, in August 1969. During a short stay the latter visited much of Counties Down and Antrim, indicating she was very impressed by Northern Ireland's landscape.
210-95-3

P3 pupils of St. Finian's Primary School, Newtownards, pictured in early September 1969 at the beginning of the new term.
211-41-1

Donaghadee schoolboys Brian Ardis (left), from Killaughey Road, and Harold Moore, from Bennett's Avenue, both aged 15, jumped fully-clothed into the local harbour in late September 1969 to save a seven-year-old Belfast girl after the punt she was in capsized. The child became trapped under the boat in water that was 20ft deep, but she was saved thanks to the prompt action of the boys.
212-73-1

Pictured after their investiture in Donaghadee towards the end of October 1969 are local members of the Third Down (St Finian's) Scout Troop. Included is leader Charles Thomas and leaders from the Newtownards and Comber Troops.
213-91-1

Mrs Emma Acheson retired in November 1969 after serving as postwoman for the Greyabbey district for 19 years, covering a daily route of 27 miles on her bicycle. Local residents showed their appreciation by presenting her with a clock and a cheque. She is pictured with local men Messrs James Brain, J. Brown, W. Harkness and Hugh Brooks. Another community representative, Mr Robert McCutcheon, was unable to attend due to illness.
215-30-1

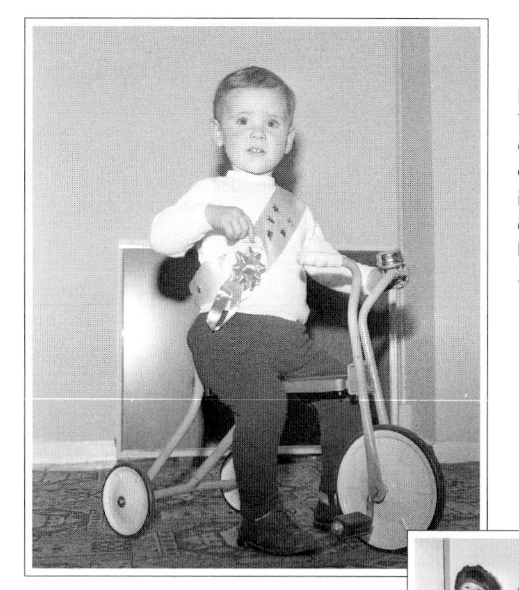

Nineteen-month-old Keith Taylor, son of Mr and Mrs George Taylor, Main Street, Greyabbey, won first prize in a village bonny baby competition held in early November 1969.
214-13-2

Members of Second Comber Brownie Pack, attached to the town's Non-Subscribing Presbyterian Church, raised £24.10s in December 1969 towards the cost of the new National Children's Home in Jamaica. The children hoped their donation would go towards the equipping and furnishing of a large nursery room in the home.
216-15-3

Some of the younger pupils of Londonderry Primary School, Newtownards, who took part in the annual Christmas concert in December 1969.
216-27-3

Sport in 1969

in the Chronicle

British Legion won the Newtownards Vintners' Darts League for the third year in a row, following a 7-3 victory over Castle Gardens at the end of February.

The Ards Rugby Club 1st XV, beaten by rivals Bangor in the Towns Cup final in April 1969. Back (from left): D. Heron, J. McFerran, I. Coffey, N. Edgar, D. Calvert, G. Ferguson, G. McCreavy, B. Jordan, Bert Cromie. Front: G. Kennedy, Roy Cromie, N. Christie, R. Bishop, W. Dickson (captain), W. Montgomery, D. Nash and T. Robinson. *202-76-3*

Ards Rugby Club 1st XV suffered their first defeat in 22 games – stretching back to 4 September 1968 – when they went down 19-6 to Queen's IIA in a Junior Cup fixture on 15 March. Unfortunately, the club went on to lose the Towns Cup to neighbours Bangor at Ravenhill on Easter Monday, 7 April. The margin of victory was 14-12, with all the Ards points being scored through penalties by Derrick Nash.

Newtownards rider Winston Norwood won six events at a scramble organised by the Munster Motorcycle Club at Ovens, Co Cork, at the end of March. Riding 400cc and 500cc Husqvarnas, Norwood took the 250cc, 500cc, experts graded, unlimited and both handicap races.

Ards won the Irish Cup for the third time in the club's history, and the first time in 17 years, defeating Distillery 4-2 at Windsor Park after extra time on Wednesday 23 April. Billy McAvoy was hero of the night, scoring all four goals. The replay followed a 0-0 draw the previous Saturday. McAvoy was subsequently named Ulster Footballer of the Year.
Manager George Eastham's winning team was: Kydd, Johnston, Crothers, Bell, Stewart, Nixon, Shields, McAvoy, Brown, Humphries and Mowat.

Ards RFC IIAs won the Forster Cup at Ravenhill on 22 April, defeating Portadown IIIAs 6-3 after extra time. Sid Elliott scored a penalty in both normal time and extra time to secure the cup for Ards.

When Ards FC travelled to Limerick for a Blaxnit Cup fixture on 28 April they became the first Irish League club to use air services as a means of travel for a match in Ireland. The speedy turnaround was necessary because of the club's packed fixture list. They lost the match 2-1.

Ards Boys FC, winners of the Dunmurry and District Youth League and Francis Cup, as well as runners-up in the Irish Youth Cup and Barry Cup, pictured with club officials in May 1969. *205-55-3*

Ards Boys, with a panel limited to 14 first team players, ended the 1968/69 season playing 10 games in just 12 days. The first nine games all ended in victory for the Boys, with their sole defeat being against Cregagh Swifts in the Barry Cup final, where the winning goal was scored in the final seconds. Nevertheless, Ards Boys were still Dunmurry and District Youth League champions and Francis Cup winners.

Scrabo Golf Club won the Ulster Cup with an 8-6 aggregate victory over holders Lisburn. Ards had won the first leg 6½ to ½ and the overall result seemed a formality; however, a reverse of fortunes for Lisburn saw them winning five straight games with one game tied in the second leg. Scrabo won the final game to secure the cup – just!

The Ards Club drew Roma in the first round of the European Cup Winners' Cup, their reward for winning the Irish Cup. The first leg was set for the Oval in Belfast on 17 September, with the return leg in Rome on 1 October.

Ards beat Stoke City – including England goalkeeper Gordon Banks – 2-1 in a pre-season friendly at Castlereagh Park. The home side's two goals were scored by George Eastham (junior), on temporary 'loan' from Stoke.

Chanteuse, owned by Newtownards builder John Dorrian, won the Pegasus Maiden Stakes at Newmarket on 2 August – at odds of 25-1. However, Mr Dorrian hadn't expected the horse to win and was watching the race on television back in County Down when it romped home.

Donaghadee 1st XI reached the final of the Junior Qualifying Cup after a convincing six-wicket victory over Armagh II on 5 July – including Ronnie Elliott's devastating nine wickets for 11 runs. In the final at Sydenham they defeated BRA Former Pupils by 26 runs to lift the cup for the second time in five years. In mid-September the team also secured the Section C championship with promotion to Section B.

In the first leg of their European Cup Winners' Cup tie against Roma, Ards achieved a commendable 0-0 draw at the Oval. The only downside was the low attendance, with the gate money adding up to £600, around one-sixth of the anticipated figure. Civil unrest in Northern Ireland and recent poor performances by Ards were cited as likely reasons.
In the second leg, a fortnight later, Ards put up a plucky fight but were defeated 3-1, the sole goal for the Co. Down team coming from full-back George Crothers in the 75th minute.

Ards made history in late September by becoming the first Ulster rugby club to win the Oval Trophy, which had been donated by Arklow RFC. In the semi-final they tied 11-11 with Sligo but went through to the final thanks to a 6-3 success in a goal kicking competition. Leinster representatives Edenderry were the other finalists, with Ards coming out on top by 13-3.

After 30 years as a table tennis player Harry O'Prey decided to call it a day in the competitive sphere. His retirement, at the end of October, coincided with an announcement that for the first time in 40 years Newtownards would not be represented in senior league table tennis.

Irish Cup holders Ards FC finished the year undefeated and joint top of the Irish League with Glentoran on 18 points, having won seven and drawn four matches.

Ballygalget senior Camogie team with the cups and trophies they won during the 1968-69 season. They were handed over to the team at a celebration ceili in St. Patrick's Hall, Ballygalget, at the beginning of March 1969.
200-30-1

Members of the Ballygalget minor Camogie team, runners-up in the 1968-69 Minor League, with the trophies they received at the celebration ceili in March 1969.
200-31-2

Members of the St Patrick's billiards team from Newtownards pictured in May 1969 with the various trophies they won during the season. Back (from left): G. Quinn, S. McGuigan, J. Carson, H. Quinn. Second row: L. McGuigan, O. McGuigan, N. Cafolla, J. Campbell. Front seated): T. McBride and W. Delaney (founding members).
205-27-3

Prizewinners, officials and supporters of the White Horse Inn Darts Club in late May 1969 with trophies won during the 1968-69 season.
205-49-1

Home side Millisle Ladies FC beat their Portaferry counterparts 3-1 in a friendly match at the end of May 1969. Back (from left): Jean McCallum, Freda Hackworth, Mary Wilson, Mary Starton, Joy Mulholland, Annette Pollock. Front: Jean Wilson, Martha Wilson, Molly Keenan, Norma Martin and Betty Millar.
204-82-2

Donaghadee 1st XI cricket team pictured after defeating Millpark in a home league game in late May 1969.
205-61-3

David Craig (back, centre), the Newcastle United and Northern Ireland international, who was a former member of First Comber Scout Troop, presented the Ards Group Cub Scout Football Shield to the First Comber team at a celebration party in St Mary's Hall in July 1969. Included are leaders W. Strickland, W. Lewis, C. Hiles and S. Haskins.
208-6-1

Members and officials of the Kircubbin junior football team in September 1969.
211-3-1

Ards 1st XV made history in late September 1969 by becoming the first Ulster club to win the Oval Trophy, which had been donated by Arklow RFC and was contested by the Towns Cup winners from each of the four provinces.
212-51-2

Comber Rec were defeated by Ards Rangers in the second round of the Border Cup in October 1969. *212-91-1*

Members of the Blaxnit Ladies five-a-side soccer team with trainer Billy Nixon (of Ards FC fame) in November 1969, following their success in a tournament at Greyabbey, during which Isobel McBratney scored no fewer than 10 goals. Also included are Margaret Knox, Anne Harvey, Gracie Cairnduff, Susan Sloan and Elizabeth Dickson. *214-71-1*

Ards Rangers II pictured in November 1969. Back (from left): J. Murphy, G. Stannage, C. Johnstone, B. Mills, J. Muir, G. Irvine, A. Kearney, D. Murphy (trainer). Front: N. Plunkett, J. Pinnance, S. Whitla, W. Kearney (manager), D. Brown, R. Murphy and D. Adams. *214-12-2*

Dear Reader,

I hope you have enjoyed this publication from Ballyhay Books, an imprint of Laurel Cottage Ltd. We publish an eclectic mix of books ranging from personal memoirs to authoritative books on local history, from sport to poultry, from photographs to fiction and from music to marine interests – but all with a distinctly local flavour.
To see details of these books, as well as the beautifully illustrated books of our sister imprint Cottage Publications, why not visit our website **www.cottage-publications.com** or contact us on +44 (0)28 9188 8033.

Timothy S Johnston